The
BEGINNER'S
Guide to
REAL ESTATE
INVESTING

The BEGINNER'S *Guide to* REAL ESTATE INVESTING

SECOND EDITION

GARY W. ELDRED, PhD

WILEY

John Wiley & Sons, Inc.

Library of Congress Cataloging-in-Publication Data:

Eldred, Gary W.
    The beginner's guide to real estate investing / Gary W. Eldred.—2nd ed.
        p. cm.
    Includes bibliographical references and index.
    ISBN 978-0-470-18342-7 (pbk.)
        1. Real estate investment.   I. Title.
    HD1375.E353 2008
    332.63′24—dc22

Printed in the United States of America.
10 9 8 7 6 5 4 3 2 1

CONTENTS

ABOUT THIS BOOK

The Beginner's Guide to Real Estate Investing covers all topics that first-time real estate investors need to know—but does so in less depth than I've included in my previous Wiley titles.

Here you'll find discussions about credit scoring, mortgages, seller financing, negotiation, foreclosures, bargain-hunting, appraisal, valuation, creating value, cash flow analysis, property management, and dozens of other topics. In this book, you'll gain a profit-generating introduction to the complete range of knowledge you need to begin building wealth in real estate.

In other words, we might have titled this book *Real Estate Investing in a Nutshell*. I have directed chapters toward those readers who want to sample all investment topics in one easy-to-read volume.

In contrast, for those readers and experienced investors who prefer depth on each of the topics discussed herein, I suggest that you select from some combination of these titles: *Investing in Real Estate*, 5th ed., *Make Money with Flippers, Fixers, and Renovations*, 2nd ed., *Make Money with Affordable Apartment Buildings and Commercial Properties*, 2nd ed., *Make Money with Condominiums and Townhouses, The 106 Mortgage Secrets All Borrowers Must Learn—But Lenders Don't Tell*, 2nd ed., *The 106 Common Mistakes Homebuyers Make—and How to Avoid Them*, 4th ed., and *The Complete Guide to Second Homes for Vacations, Retirement, and Investment*.

Either way, whether you select this abridged volume or some combination of my other titles, you will find that I offer readers the most detailed and practical guides to investing in real estate that are available. Although property offers you your best opportunity to build wealth and financial freedom, I never mislead you into thinking that such wealth will come without applying knowledge, time, and effort. Anyone who believes those gurus who promise an "easy, no cash, no credit, no knowledge" system to build wealth is headed for disappointment.

You *can* still profitably invest in real estate. But you must learn to analyze properties, neighborhoods, risks, and potential rewards. And that's exactly what this book (and my other Wiley books) shows you.

In closing, I would like to acknowledge special people who have contributed to my work and this book. First and foremost, I want to thank His Highness Sheikh Dr. Sultan Bin Mohammed Al Qassimi, Supreme Council Member, UAE, Ruler of Sharjah and Founder and President of the American University of Sharjah (AUS). Due to his generosity, leadership, and vision, in less than a decade, the American University of Sharjah has emerged as the leading university in the Middle East.

My thanks, too, go to Dr. R. Malcolm Richards, Dean of the School of Business and Management, for inviting me to AUS to develop a curriculum in real estate and for providing a first-class working environment in what has become the world's most dynamic and fastest growing property market. In addition, my student assistants at AUS, Mohsen Mofid, Omer Shabbir Ahmed, and Sadaf A. Fasihnia, deserve recognition for their research help, without which I could not have made my publisher's deadlines. For her long-term help (20 manuscripts) and continued assistance, I owe a deep debt of appreciation to Barbara Smerage of Santa Fe, New Mexico.

Gary W. Eldred, PhD

PART ONE

Mindset + Knowledge = Wealth

Start Now

With this book, you will become motivated and educated. You will get started in real estate. From this book, you will see that real estate investing still leads you to a lifetime of wealth and personal fulfillment. No matter what financial goals you set for yourself, no matter how little cash, credit, or income you currently possess, *if you choose to*, you can build your fortune in real estate.

> **You can still build wealth in real estate.**

Just Say No to Excuses

"But hold on," you might say. "You can't be talking to me. In my town, property prices have climbed sky-high. Besides, I don't think I have enough cash, credit, or time to get started. And even if I did, real estate seems too difficult. I don't know how to begin."

As I travel throughout the country and talk with would-be property investors, I repeatedly hear excuses. But it may surprise you to learn that I've heard similar excuses repeated over and over for 30 years.

Naysayers Thrive in All Times and Places

When times are good, people fret over the deals they've missed. When markets slow down, folks claim that real estate no longer makes a good

3

investment. Either way, they always find some way to color the future bleak (see Box 1.1).

Yet, since the early 1970s I have seen all types of booms and busts. I have seen 18 percent mortgage interest rates. I've lived through the multiple turmoils of double-digit rates of inflation, the disastrous 1986 Tax Reform Act (which reduced profitable real estate tax shelter techniques), and the recent market of sky-high prices. Yet I (and nearly all other savvy investors) have figured out how to make money in every one of these markets and all of the other types of markets in between.

> **You can make money in all types of markets.**

For the past several years, the media have headlined the so-called subprime mortgage meltdown, increasing foreclosures, and a growing inventory of listings for sale. Just as occurred during previous decades—and previous housing cycles—financial journalists fail to recognize that we have once again entered a great buyers' market.

Among all the lessons history teaches, none proves more certain than the fact that property prices will go up. Regardless of how high you think prices are today, they will be higher 10 years from now and much, much higher 20 or 30 years into the future. Don't talk yourself into believing that "property prices have reached a peak." Before you accept the "sky is falling" clamor of so-called economic experts, take a quick trip through some of their Chicken Little predictions from years gone by:

- ◆ "The prices of houses seem to have reached a plateau, and there is reasonable expectancy that prices will decline" (*Time*, December 1, 1947).
- ◆ "Houses cost too much for the mass market. Today's average price is around $8,000—out of reach for two-thirds of all buyers" (*Science Digest*, April 1948).
- ◆ "If you have bought your house since the War . . . you have made your deal at the top of the market. . . . The days when you couldn't lose on a house purchase are no longer with us" (*House Beautiful*, November 1948).
- ◆ "The goal of owning a home seems to be getting beyond the reach of more and more Americans. The typical new house today costs about $28,000" (*Business Week*, September 4, 1969).

(continued)

Box 1.1 People Who Believe the Forecasts of Doom and Gloom End Up with a Pile of Regrets

◆ "Be suspicious of the 'common wisdom' that tells you to 'Buy now . . . because continuing inflation will force home prices and rents higher and higher'" (*NEA Journal*, December 1970).

◆ "The median price of a home today is approaching $50,000. . . . Housing experts predict that in the future price rises won't be that great" (*Nation's Business*, June 1977).

◆ "The era of easy profits in real estate may be drawing to a close" (*Money Magazine*, January 1981).

◆ "In California . . . for example, it is not unusual to find families of average means buying $100,000 houses. . . . I'm confident prices have passed their peak" (J. E. English and G. E. Cardiff, *The Coming Real Estate Crash*, Warner Books, 1980).

◆ "The golden age of risk-free run-ups in home prices is gone" (*Money Magazine*, March 1985).

◆ "If you're looking to buy, be careful. Rising home values are not a sure thing anymore" (*Miami Herald*, October 25, 1985).

◆ "Most economists agree . . . [a home] will become little more than a roof and a tax deduction, certainly not the lucrative investment it was through much of the 1980s" (*Money Magazine*, April 1986).

◆ "We're starting to go back to the time when you bought a home not for its potential moneymaking abilities, but rather as a nesting spot" (*Los Angeles Times*, January 31, 1993).

◆ "Financial planners agree that houses will continue to be a poor investment" (*Kiplinger's Personal Financial Magazine*, November 1993).

◆ "A home is where the bad investment is" (*San Francisco Examiner*, November 17, 1996).

◆ "Your house is a roof over your head. It is not an investment" (Karen Ramsey, *Everything You Know About Money Is Wrong*, Reagan Books, 1999).

◆ "The trends that have produced the housing boom . . . have nearly run their course. This virtually guarantees . . . plummeting home prices and mass foreclosures . . ." (John Rubino, *How to Profit from the Coming Real Estate Bust*, Rodale, 2003).

◆ "Ten years from now, property prices will almost certainly be less than they are today . . ." (*Money Magazine*, January 2006).

Box 1.1 *(Continued)*

Property Offers Multiple Possibilities

To make money and build wealth with property, you can always locate opportunities. But first develop an educated, entrepreneurial mindset. The idea of a single real estate market or a one-size-fits-all investment strategy runs opposite to reality. Like a chameleon, the savviest real estate investors change their colors to match the ever-changing mortgage lending and property environments. During recent years, for example, many beginning property investors have pursued one or more of the following possibilities:

- Foreclosures, preforeclosures, REOs (bank-owned foreclosures referred to as real-estate owned).
- Self-storage units.
- Fix and flip.
- Condominiums, townhouses.
- Condominium conversions.
- Office condominiums.
- Office buildings.
- Shopping centers, freestanding retail.
- Mobile home/RV parks.
- Gentrifying (turnaround) neighborhoods.
- Properties located in lower-priced areas of the country (and the world).
- Emerging growth areas such as Charlotte, North Carolina.
- Vacation and retirement areas.
- Two- to four-unit rental apartment buildings.
- Multiunit apartment buildings.

These examples merely touch upon the possibilities you will discover throughout this book, but they illustrate one theme that I have advocated throughout my career:

Q.   When's the best time for you to invest in real estate?

A.   Today.

But don't jump to the wrong conclusion. When I say "Invest today," I do not mean that you can never go wrong. Rather, I mean that there's never a wrong *time* to invest if you execute the right strategy. And that's what you will learn in this book.

You Must *Believe* It to See It

Why do the great majority of people miss the wide-ranging possibilities and oversized rewards that property offers? After talks with hundreds of would-be investors, the evidence clearly reveals that most people won't envision the future and they won't believe in themselves.

> **The time to start really is now.**

As a result, most people don't believe in their ability to actually make big money in real estate. These negative thinkers erect a wall of excuses that blocks their possibilities. This wall prevents them from seeing the profit potential that lies in front of them. So, will you join the ranks of the naysayers? Or will you open your mind to a promising future?

Envision the Future

Place yourself in the future. Imagine that you're browsing property web sites or reading the real estate classified ads 10 years from today. You compare listing prices then to those of today.

Are property prices higher or lower than they are today? Are rent levels higher or lower than they are today? If you believe in the continuing growth of the United States, you must believe that just as with every past decade, today's property prices and rent levels will look cheap relative to where they will stand 10 years from now (see Table 1.1).

Reprogram Your Self-Talk

Ask yourself whether you really want to benefit from those near certain increases in property values. Or would you prefer to merely watch others reap these profits? If you want to succeed—yet feel blocked by excuses—reprogram your self-talk.

Table 1.1   Historical Growth in Median Housing Prices

Year	$Price	Year	Price
1965	$18,000	1990	$95,000
1970	23,000	1995	113,100
1975	35,300	2000	138,400
1980	62,200	2005	182,000
1985	75,500	2007	218,000 (est.)

Statistical Abstract of the United States 2007, p. 723

What Is Self-Talk?   In his mind-opening book, *What To Say When You Talk to Yourself* (Pocket Books, 1986, p. 25), Shad Helmstetter writes,

> You will become what you think about most. Your success or failure in anything, large or small, will depend on your mental programming—what you accept from others, and what you say when you talk to yourself.

After years of study, this nationally renowned psychologist has found that as a matter of habit, most of us drown our optimism in a sea of negative self-talk. Evaluate your own thoughts. Do you accept the negative as "true" or "the way things really are"? Do you focus on risks rather than opportunities? Ponder these familiar excuses that you've either said to yourself or heard others say hundreds of times:

> **You must *believe* it to see it.**

- ◆ I can't remember names.
- ◆ I'm always losing things.
- ◆ No matter what I do, I just can't keep the weight off.
- ◆ I never have enough time.
- ◆ I'm too disorganized.
- ◆ I'm no good at math.
- ◆ I'm always running late.

Now think: When you program yourself with negative self-descriptions, will you initiate productive efforts to change these or other undesirable traits and habits? Of course not! And the same result stands true for those beliefs (self-talk) that block you from starting in real estate. Once again, think about these excuses that I frequently hear:

- Prices are too high.
- Prices are softening.
- I can't afford to invest.
- I missed so many good opportunities. Now it's too late.
- I can't get financing because of credit problems.
- It's impossible to find positive cash flow properties.
- I should have invested more years ago.
- Real estate will take up too much time.
- I don't want to deal with tenants, stopped-up toilets, leaky roofs, or broken furnaces.
- We don't have any extra cash. We're spending more than we make.

> **Use self-talk to discover and develop your potential.**

You may or may not identify with any of these specific excuses. But unless you discipline your self-talk far better than most people, you undoubtedly suffer at least a few areas where false beliefs deter you from taking effective action.

As to real estate investing, I urge you to reprogram any negative self-talk and limiting beliefs with consciousness-raising questions such as:

- What are six ways I can save more and spend less?
- Where are the best areas to find bargain-priced properties?
- How might I persuade the sellers to accept owner financing?
- Who do I know with money that I could partner with?
- How can I boost my credit score?
- How can I improve this property to enhance its value?
- What property prices and cash flows exist in other parts of the country?
- What areas of the country are best poised for appreciation?
- What types of financing might make this deal work?

Ideally, erase your negative self-talk tapes. Then rerecord self-affirming self-talk. Instead of bringing yourself down with talk or beliefs that create undesirable habits, attitudes, and outcomes, reinforce the behavior and belief patterns that lead to where you want to go. Ask questions that accent opportunities and problem-solving.

Why Questions?   To solve problems, ask questions. Questions explore possibilities. People who accept preprogrammed conclusions won't ask questions. They believe they already know the answers. They overlook choices the world offers. So, if the program you listen to doesn't enrich and empower, switch the channel.

Lifelong Job?   After the stock market downturn in the early 2000s, journalists filled the financial press with stories of people who had lost 30, 40, even 75 percent of their savings. In reaction, many of these bruised and battered victims of stock market volatility decided that "lifelong" work now looked like their only chance to avoid the soup kitchen. As to investing, CDs, annuities, and bonds received the most votes among those workers over age 50.

> **Questions point you toward your goals.**

When I first read these kinds of all-too-common articles, two thoughts came to mind:

1. Why didn't more of these now-disappointed workers invest more money in real estate instead of stocks?
2. And more important, why don't they at least start now? Even starting late beats never starting at all.

To know that many of these folks now stick their money into low-yielding certificates of deposit, annuities, and government bonds reinforces my point: They're choosing low yields because they hold false beliefs about investing in real estate. No one could choose lifelong employment and meager returns on so-called safe investments if he really believed (and understood) the possibilities that presently exist in real estate.

> **No one needs to accept low yields.**

Two Other False Beliefs   In his popular book, *The Four Pillars of Investing* (McGraw-Hill, 2003), William Bernstein repeats two other widely held, yet false, beliefs about investing. You've probably heard them.

1. *"No guts, no glory."* Bernstein claims that if you want to increase your potential rewards from investing, you must accept more risk. Bernstein writes, "Whether you invest in stocks, bonds, or for that matter real estate, you are rewarded mainly for your exposure to one thing—risk."
2. *"The market is smarter than you are."* Here, Bernstein merely repeats the "efficient market" theory preached by college finance professors. In an efficient market, all asset prices supposedly reflect their true value. According to Bernstein, you can never find bargain-priced investments.

As they pertain to real estate, these so-called pillars of investing sound quite silly. Here's why.

1. *In real estate, you are not rewarded for taking risk.* You are rewarded for applying your intelligence and market savvy. You are rewarded for providing a target market (tenants or buyers) a property that offers better value than competing properties.
2. *You can beat the market.* When you execute the analysis and strategies explained throughout this book, you will earn above-market returns that the majority of property owners (along with those naysayers who shout from the sidelines) consistently miss.

Fortunately, widely held false beliefs work to your advantage. Because financial planners and economists (who typically have no meaningful experience with real estate investing) give such faulty advice, their advice dampens investor competition for properties.

> **The false beliefs of others boost your opportunities.**

When potential investors believe that to earn big returns in real estate they must take big risks, they will not join the game. They leave more opportunities for you.

Summing Up Self-Talk and False Beliefs   No doubt, today's real estate market will challenge you. But keep your eyes on the prize and your

> **It's possible, and it's worth it!**

mind filled with possibilities. You will discover how to build real estate wealth (see Chapter 2). As the dynamic speaker Les Brown says in his motivation video, *It's Possible*, the road may not be easy, but it's worth it!

Set Goals Now

What's a realistic dream? It's a goal with a deadline. To start now, act now to reset your priorities.

Most of us squander time and money pursuing transient pleasures. A new car, a trip to Europe, $10 lunches, TV football weekends—we waste talents and resources. As a result, we suffer long-lasting regrets. But do today what others won't do. Tomorrow you'll live in an enviable style that most people will never experience.

Set goals now. Precisely what goals depend on where you are today and what you wish to achieve.

If you're like many beginning investors, here's a good place to start:

1. Dramatically cut your spending and increase your cash savings.
2. Shape up your credit profile.
3. Closely read the real estate classifieds in your local paper.
4. Diligently telephone sellers, and go out and look at properties.
5. Join a real estate investment club.
6. Read at least five more books on real estate within the next three months. Also read at least three books by "personal coaches" such as Tony Robbins, Wayne Dyer, Les Brown, Shad Helmstetter, and Maxwell Maltz.
7. Commit to your first real estate investment within the next three months.

Spend Less, Save More

When Jack Holden was asked how his family got started investing in real estate, here's how he responded. "We scraped, borrowed, and leveraged from every resource we had to muster the funds we needed. . . . For seed money we cashed in saving bonds and borrowed from our insurance policies. . . . The entire family went on an austerity plan to cut back our food, travel, and entertainment expenses. Today we're thankful we made those early sacrifices."

Thankful, yes, and also wealthy. Because of their disciplined spending, saving, and investing, the Holdens (an otherwise average family) built a real estate net worth of $4.7 million that includes not only their home equity of $600,000, but also a variety of rental houses and small apartment buildings.

Like most people who make big money in property, the Holdens didn't start with cash. As Jack Holden says, his family scrimped, saved, leveraged, and borrowed every way they could.

> **Commit to build wealth before you get the money to invest.**

So what's the lesson to learn? To build wealth in real estate, don't wait until you get the cash or credit and then decide to invest. No! First, commit to investing, then figure out how to come up with the money. You can keep "wishing and a-hoping" to invest *someday*. Or you can decide to own property and immediately begin to shape up your finances and create a plan to invest.

To start your austerity plan, raise cash, and strengthen your credit. Adopt these suggestions.

> **Set priorities today according to what you want to achieve within five years.**

Never Say Budget No one likes to budget. It sounds like work. Instead, think priorities. Think reward. The quality of your life improves as you allocate your money according to your highest values. To own investment real estate, put your money where it yields the smartest returns. For example . . .

Stop Paying Rent If you don't yet own your own home, rent is probably your biggest money waster. Can you figure out how to eliminate or reduce your rent payments? Can you switch to a lower-cost apartment? Can you house-share? Can you find a house-sitting job for the next 3 to 12 months? Can you move back with your parents or stay rent-free with relatives or friends? Bank your rent money for 6 to 12 months, and for the rest of your life you need never pay rent again.

Cut Your Food Bills in Half   Eliminate eating out. Brown-bag your lunches. Buy unbranded foods in bulk. Prepare your food in large quantities and freeze portions in meal-sized servings. Forget those $3 to $4 microwave lunches and dinners. Locate a remainder and closeout grocery like Save-a-Lot, Big Lots, or Drug Emporium. Or maybe you can shop the food warehouses that have opened in most cities. Food prices in discount stores sometimes run 20 to 50 percent less than big-name supermarkets. When you find bargain-priced items you regularly use, buy them by the case.

Cut Your Credit Cards in Half   Credit card spending is just too easy. Put yourself on a strict diet of cash. Nothing holds back spending more than counting out real cash. Besides, credit card bills zap strength from your borrowing power. Even worse, by the time you've finished paying off credit card balances at 18 percent interest, you will pay back $2 for every dollar you originally charged—and that's in after-tax, take-home dollars. When you consider that you only take home 60 to 80 percent of the amount you earn, you'll see that you may have to earn $3 to pay back each dollar you charge to your credit cards. To pay for that $150 pair of shoes you charged will require more than $300 of earnings.

> **Credit card spending kills wealth building.**

Don't Put the Car Before the Investment Property   I recently saw an article in the personal finance section of the *Charlotte Observer*. A 22-year-old young man, fresh out of college, had just bought a new car and saddled himself with car payments of $522 a month for 60 months. Did the article criticize such a foolhardy expenditure? No. It talked about what a smart shopper he was—because he had purchased a Prius. "I'm going to save $1,000 a year on gas," this proud purchaser boasted.

Interestingly, just above this article was a story of another proud purchaser. Only this young woman had just moved into her first home—a newly constructed three-bedroom, two-bath single-family house. Her monthly mortgage payment (before any allowable tax deduction for mortgage interest) equaled just $896—and she had placed just 3 percent down.

Dear readers, to build wealth, don't put the car before the house. Own assets that appreciate, not depreciate. Even a Prius will prove itself a lousy investment when compared to property.

Buy Your Clothes in Thrift Shops   In her newspaper column, *Dress for Less*, Candy Barrie writes, "I'm a big fan of these [consignment and thrift] shops for the fashion bargains you can find there. . . . Get on down and you'll discover we're not just talking about 20, 30, or 40 percent discounts. Sometimes you can get your clothes for 90 to 95 percent off retail."

Save thousands on clothing. Follow Candy's advice: Check the recycled, discount, and closeout clothing stores in your area (or in a nearby big city). Whatever your tastes and price range, you'll find that you can slash clothing costs by 50 percent or more. I regularly shop at a small, local store where the owner provides excellent service and advice along with well-known name brands such as L.L. Bean, Eddie Bauer, and Lands' End, at 40 to 70 percent off their catalog prices.

Don't Buy New Furniture or Appliances   As with their cars and clothing, most would-be investors spend too much, too soon for furniture and appliances. Even worse, instead of paying cash, they charge it. They chain themselves to several years of payments at high interest rates. Increasingly, they are hooked into those "no payments, no interest for six months" types of promotions that make credit purchases almost too easy to pass up. Do yourself a favor: Resist this temptation to spend and borrow.

When you buy cars, furniture, or appliances, let someone else suffer the depreciation. Pay for the usefulness of the product. The less money you waste on depreciating assets, the quicker you can build wealth through real estate investments.

Shape Up Your Credit Profile

Go to www.myfico.com and print copies of your credit reports and credit scores. Examine your reports for errors. If you find errors, start the paperwork now. Correcting credit errors can require weeks—and sometimes months.

If your debt load is too high or your payment record too slow, commit now to change. Reduce your balances. Pay accounts before their due date. Fortunately, when the myfico computer program calculates your credit score, the credit scorers will give your recent and righteous credit experience more weight than your past undisciplined credit habits. (You'll find many more tips on credit scoring in Chapter 3.)

Browse Property Web Sites and the Real Estate Classified Ads

Read the real estate listings closely. You'll learn the relative prices and rent levels that prevail among and within the various neighborhoods and communities in your area. For prices in other areas, go to realtor. com and loopnet.com. Also, stay alert for easy buying techniques such as lease option, owner finance, and contract-for-deed. Notice, too, the prices, rent levels, and potential cash flows of various types of properties.

A few months back, I spotted a six-unit, renovated apartment building for sale in the San Francisco Bay Area (Oakland) at a price of $550,000. Even better, the seller was willing to carry the financing. What a great way to crack the affordability problem. Can't afford to buy a $500,000 median-priced house? No worries. Buy this apartment building, move into one of the units, and let your tenants pay most of your mortgage. Seek and ye shall find.

Telephone Sellers (Agents) and Look at Properties

To begin, do not necessarily look to buy—you look to learn the market. Randomly select and view properties. Detail desirable and undesirable features. Drive through and explore neighborhoods and communities that are new to you. Discover how much "for sale" and "for rent" inventory sits on the market. Watch trends in property selling prices, apartment vacancy rates, and rent concessions.

Call agents, FSBOs (for sale by owner), leasing agents, and property managers. Engage them in conversations about properties and markets. Take notes.

Join a Real Estate Investment Club

Join a local apartment owners' association or real estate investment club. In addition, in most midsized and large cities, real estate and lending pros often offer free (or low-cost) seminars on investing and financing.

Attend investment group meetings. Talk with others who have learned investing through years of experience. Ponder the lessons they've learned and the trends they're noticing. Then, verify what you hear with facts. Some realty pros observe carefully and possess sharp insights. Others bluster with ill-formed opinions—especially to an eager listener. Perfect your ability to distinguish the sage from the braggart.

Read More

The bookshelves in my offices are loaded from top to bottom with hundreds of books on real estate. Yet I still buy and read nearly every new book in the field. Likewise your search for knowledge, your search to improve your investing techniques and profitability, should never cease. Knowledge not only guides you toward building wealth, it conquers fear.

Read Local Papers Besides reading books on real estate, read the real estate and community sections of your local newspapers and business journals (or from newspapers/web sites that pertain to areas where you're developing knowledge. From these articles learn about emerging neighborhoods, new property developments, zoning and regulatory issues, price and vacancy trends, business growth, and foreclosure filings. Savvy investors stay on top of property-related events and adapt their investment strategy to profit from ever-present change.

Read Self-Improvement Books, Improve Persistently As said earlier, read books in the self-help/motivational field. I like the work of Tony Robbins, Wayne Dyer, Les Brown, and Shad Helmstetter. But within the broad field of self-help I include books on health, fitness, time management, and dealing with people. If you prefer, *listen* to books. You can find nearly all self-enhancement topics on cassette tapes and CDs. Rather than waste time when you're driving, put those hours to productive use.

And browse the collection of books, CDs, and tapes at your public library. To change your life—financially and personally—let books and CDs help you improve your habits, thinking, self-talk, and performance. Your greatest power remains the power to choose the life you want.

Commit to Invest Within Three Months

How many times have you heard people lament? "You know, we've been thinking about getting started in real estate investing for years. But I don't know. We just never seemed to get around to it. Gosh, would we be set now if we had only done what we were thinking."

Over the years, I've heard laments like this thousands of times. For some reason, people love to lament and regret—yet they still fail to act. When you find yourself regretting or procrastinating, escape from these traps. Act now! (See Box 1.2.)

> **Action cures fear and regret.**

Action cures regret. Action prevents future regret. Action creates the wealth you want. Regret mires you in a past that cannot change. Set your most important goals now. Commit to your first real estate investment within the next 90 days. Mark it on your calendar. You will find that once you get started, your progress accelerates. Not only does experience teach you, but experience makes your reading pay much larger dividends.

Now, let's start. You are about to learn how to profit from real estate in multiple ways.

Someday I should list all the
deals that I have missed;
Bonanzas that were in my grip—
I watched them through my fingers slip;
The windfalls which I should have bought
Were lost because I overthought
I thought of this, I thought of that,
I could have sworn I smelled a rat,
And while I thought things over twice,
Another grabbed them at the price.
It seems I always hesitate,
Then make up my mind much too late.
A very cautious man am I
And that is why I wait to buy.
When tracks rose high on Sixth and Third,
The price asked was, I felt absurd;
Those apartment blocks—black with soot—
Were priced a thirty bucks a-foot!
I wouldn't even make a bid,
But others did—yes, others did!
When Tucson was cheap desert land,
I could have had a heap of sand;
When Phoenix was the place to buy,
I thought the climate was too dry;
"Invest in Dallas—that's the spot!"
My sixth sense warned me I should not.
A very prudent man am I
And that is why I wait to buy.

How Nassau and how Suffolk grew!
North Jersey! Staten Island, too!
When others culled those sprawling farms
And welcomed deals with open arms . . .
A corner here, ten acres there,
Compounding values year by year,
I chose to think and as I thought,
They bought the deals I should have bought.
The golden chances I had then
Are lost and will not come again.
Today I cannot be enticed
For everything's so overpriced.
The deals of yesteryear are dead;
The market's soft—and so's my head.
Last night I had a fearful dream,
I know I wakened with a scream:
Some Indians approached my bed—
For trinkets on the barrelhead
(In dollar bills worth twenty-four
And nothing less and nothing more)
They'd sell Manhattan Isle to me.
The most I'd go was twenty-three.
The redmen scowled: "Not on a bet!"
And sold to Peter Minuit.
At times a teardrop drowns my eye
For deals I had, but did not buy;
And now life's saddest words I pen—
"IF ONLY I'D INVESTED THEN!"

—Anonymous

Box 1.2   The Investor's Lament

CHAPTER 2

Multiple Paths to Building Wealth

You're now going to see why real estate offers you better opportunities to build wealth than any other type of investment. With real estate, you can make money in dozens of different ways. For starters, here are 16 potential paths to profit:

- Appreciation in market values
- Inflation
- Cash flows
- Mortgage payoff
- Buy at a bargain price
- Create property value
- Create site value
- Create neighborhood value
- Condominium conversions
- Improved management
- More-profitable market strategy
- Tax shelter
- Discounted notes and tax deeds
- Real estate stocks (REITs, home builders, mortgage lenders)
- Emerging markets

Appreciation in Market Values

Over periods of 5 to 10 years, nearly all properties gain in real value because population, jobs, incomes, and wealth (buying power) grow faster than the amount of new construction. Over the long term, more people with more money consistently push real estate prices up.

"Okay," you say, "but that was then and this is now. Surely prices can't continue to increase as they have in the past?" Experience says,

"They can and they will." To see the future, just weigh together these price-increasing trends:

1. *Population growth.* During the next 20 years, the population of the United States will increase by 40 million people.
2. *Incomes.* During the next 20 years, employees, entrepreneurs, professionals, and business owners will see their incomes rise by over 50 percent.
3. *Vacation homes.* During the next 20 years, at least 10 million more Americans (and foreign nationals) will choose to buy vacation homes within the United States.
4. *Echo boomers.* During the next 20 years, more than 60 million echo boomers (children and grandchildren of the baby boomers) will enter the housing market to buy homes and rent apartments.
5. *Restrictions on development.* During the next 20 years, zoning, environmental laws, building regulations, and land shortages will continue to restrict development in those areas where most people want to live.
6. *Construction costs.* During the next 20 years, the costs to construct houses (and other types of buildings) will trend upward.
7. *Immigrants and minorities.* Currently only 40 percent of our fastest growing immigrant and minority groups (Hispanics, blacks, Asians) own their own homes. In contrast, more than 75 percent of whites live in homes they own. With government programs and lender outreach efforts, during the next 20 years people in these minority and immigrant groups will continue to buy homes in record numbers. Federal, state, and local governments in cooperation with private lenders will work hard to close the home ownership gap.
8. *Investors.* During the next 20 years, more than 60 million baby boomers will need a retirement income. They will increasingly turn to investment real estate to meet this need. Demand for property as a source of investment income will continue to grow.
9. *Foreign investment.* Relative to most other countries, U.S investment real estate offers more safety, lower prices, and higher yields. As world wealth increases (Middle East, India,

China, etc.), much of that money has and will continue to be used to purchase U.S. properties.

10. *Exchange rates:* With U.S. deficits increasing, the value of the dollar has fallen dramatically against the euro, C\$, A\$, Asian currencies (excepting Japan, for now anyway), and the British pound. Cheap dollars means cheap U.S. prices become even cheaper when measured in other leading and foreign currencies.

You don't need advanced knowledge of economics and demographics to recognize the fact that many economic and social trends will combine to push real real estate prices upward.

Inflation

Each year and every year the Federal Reserve system increases the money supply. As more money chases after a slowly increasing supply of properties, property prices go up—even *without* an overall favorable change in the underlying forces of supply and demand (market appreciation). The Federal Reserve specifically designs its monetary policies to create an (1.5 to 3.0 percent) annual gain in the Consumer Price Index (CPI).

> **Even without market appreciation, inflation will push real estate prices up.**

Sometimes, though, the Fed loses control of inflationary price increases (late 1940s, the entire 1970s, early to mid 1980s). During those superheated, inflationary times, real estate prices experience inflationary gains of 6 to 12 percent a year. Buy now with fixed-rate financing. Then cheer for inflation.

Interest Rates and Inflation

Journalists spread the myth that "*historically low* mortgage interest rates" caused the large 2000–2005 run-ups in property values.

In reality, 30-year mortgage interest rates of 6 to 7 percent seem low relative to the mortgage rates of 8 to 16 percent that the U.S. experienced

> **Today's mortgage interest rates sit above their long-term average—not below.**

throughout much of the 1970s, 1980s, and early 1990s. During most of our country's 225-plus years of history, mortgage interest rates typically have fluctuated between 3 and 6 percent. So, 6 to 7 percent rates actually stand toward the high-average end of history—not the "historically low." But, still, you might ask, "What happens to real estate prices if interest rates climb substantially from the levels of today?"

Higher Interest Rates Reflect Higher Expected Inflation

Long-term interest rates climbed dramatically during the 1970s and 1980s because the Consumer Price Index (inflation) jumped from 2.5 to 4.0 percent in the early to mid 1960s to 13 percent in 1982. During those 16 years of increasing inflation and skyrocketing interest rates (from 1970's 6.0 percent to 1981's 16 percent), most property values nearly tripled.

Although inflation drives up interest rates, inflation also drives up incomes, rent levels, and construction costs. Even better for investors who own real estate, when inflation heats up, the smart money flees financial assets (stocks and bonds) in favor of hard assets (real estate, gold, collectibles). As a result, property prices are pushed even higher as stock and bond prices stagnate or decline.

> **During periods of high interest rates, real estate strongly outperforms stocks and bonds.**

Indeed, in 1979 *Business Week* ran what has become one of its most famous cover stories, "The Death of Equities." This article detailed how (throughout the 1970s) stocks and bonds had lost value as real estate investors had prospered.

In 1964, the stock market's Dow Jones Industrial Average peaked at close to 1,000. In 1981, it sat at less than 800—20 percent below its high mark of 17 years earlier. During this same 17-year period of higher interest rates and inflation, the nationwide median house price zoomed from $25,000 to nearly $75,000.

History proves—contrary to journalistic bombast—that over lengthy periods, higher interest rates *do not* hurt property values. Quite the opposite, higher interest rates (which reflect high inflation) propel property prices upwards.

Higher Interest Rates? Lower Interest Rates? Either Way, You Gain

Say you buy today and obtain a 30-year, fixed interest rate of 6.5 percent. If interest rates go down, refinance and take advantage of lower payments (more on this topic later).

If inflation goes wild and interest rates climb to 8, 10, 12 percent or higher, you gain as inflation pushes the price of your property up and reduces the real dollar (inflation-adjusted) amount of your mortgage debt. You borrow dollars when their purchasing power is strong. You pay them back when their buying power has fallen. You gain. Your lender loses. Unlike mortgage lenders in many countries, lenders in the United States typically carry the risks created by both higher interest rates *and* lower interest rates. When rates go down, you can refinance. (However, some loan agreements mitigate the lender's refinance risk by including a prepayment penalty.) When rates go up due to inflation, you collect higher rents and pay your loan off in cheaper dollars. Regardless of which direction interest rates move, real estate investors (mortgage borrowers) reap gains for themselves.

> **You profit regardless of whether interest rates head up or down.**

Cycling through Property Markets

Nothing I've written denies the fact of real estate cycles. Every smart real estate investor knows that rent levels and property prices seldom move upward at an even, steady pace. In some years, prices bolt ahead. In others, they crawl. And every now and then, short-term events (excessive job loss, a jump in forclosures, temporary overbuilding) can pull down property prices. But rather than seeing doom, savvy investors work the down cycle to enhance their profits.

> **Use a market slowdown to buy properties at depressed prices.**

I prefer slow markets because it's easier to find and create great buys. Throughout this book, I will show you how to profit in any type of real estate market. You adapt your strategy and techniques to whatever market conditions emerge. As a savvy investor, ignore the media chatter about bubbles, peaks, hard times, and depressed markets. Instead, look for opportunities—no matter what type of market you face.

Just as important, realize that all types of properties, all market niches, and all geographic areas of the country (and the world) do not cycle together. You can locate a boom, bust, or stable market somewhere at almost any time. Moreover, with worldwide information readily available from the Internet, market knowledge of distant cities is available to anyone who searches for it.

Cash Flows

Most real estate produces cash flows from rent collections. Even though today's cash flows currently throw off *unleveraged* annual net incomes of 4 to 8 percent a year, cash flow amounts are sure to increase over time. Inflation and market demand will likely push rents up an average of 3 to 5 percent a year. Within 15 years, a rent level of $1,000 per unit, per month can increase to $1,500 to $1,800 per unit, per month (or possibly more).

You also will boost your cash flows during years when interest rates decline. Say that, due to a refinance at a lower interest rate, the mortgage payment on your investment property falls from $6,000 per month to $5,300 per month. That refinance just put another $700 a month ($8,400 a year) of cash flow into your pocket.

Mortgage Payoff (Amortization)

Imagine that inflation ends and also market demand (property appreciation) stalls. You collect only enough rents from your property to pay your operating expenses and mortgage payments. With stable rent collections and property values, has your investment produced lousy returns? Not at all.

As you pay off your mortgage balance, your equity in the property continues to grow—even without an increase in your property's value.

> **You earn good returns in real estate—even without increases in rents or property prices.**

Your Equity Grows Tenfold

Assume, for example, you buy a $100,000 property with a $10,000 down payment. After 30 years, you own that property (still valued at $100,000) free and clear. Even without positive cash flows or price increases, you've multiplied your original investment of $10,000 ten times over. Your gain from amortization (paying off the mortgage with rent collections) alone equals an annual rate of return of 8 percent.

Amortization Alone Often Beats Other Investments

You might not think 8 percent sounds like much of a return. But it certainly beats bonds, annuities, certificates of deposit, and even stocks (during most decades of our economic history). Indeed, the famous stock market bull, Wharton professor Jeremy Siegel, forecasts total stock market returns over the next 10 to 20 years of just 6 to 8 percent a year. Why? Because stocks today remain richly priced relative to historical norms.

> **Earn 8 to 12 percent a year just by paying off your mortgage with rent collections.**

Remember, too, assume that your 8 percent property returns result only from mortgage payoff, whereas the returns from the other investments cited refer to *total* returns (dividends or interest *and* asset appreciation).

As an aside, note that had your rent collections permitted you to pay off your mortgage loan in 20 years instead of 30 years, your return from amortization would climb to an annual rate of 12 percent.

Buy at a Bargain Price

Property investment permits you to increase your wealth at the moment you buy a property. Unlike other investments, you can buy real estate for less than its market value. Distressed owners, owners who want to sell fast and hassle-free, lenders who own foreclosures (called REOs), and poorly informed sellers frequently part with their properties at prices (or terms) that immediately add dollars to your net worth.

> **Bargain prices help you build wealth fast.**

Some investors flip properties that they buy at a bargain price to generate quick cash. Others hold for the long term and use the bargain price (or terms) to boost their long-term rates of return. Either way, bargain prices offer a great benefit to property investors.

Create Value with Property Improvements

Most investors (and homeowners) fail to maximize the values of their properties. As a result, entrepreneurial investors—an investor like you who can spot multiple opportunities for improvements—can dramatically and quickly boost the values of the properties you buy. Plus, when you choose to operate entrepreneurially, you also gain because you strategically manage your properties to bring in higher rents.

Multiple Ways to Improve

Most property owners look only for profit-making cosmetic changes: Lay some new carpet, paint the walls, clean up the yard, and put new tile floors in the kitchen and bathrooms.

As you will see in Chapters 13 and 14, you can (and should) go beyond cosmetics. As an entrepreneurial investor, you'll design a total fix-up and renovation plan that might include remodeling kitchens and baths, reconfiguring a floor plan, adding skylights or ceiling height, and attic or basement conversions.

As an entrepreneurial investor, you survey competing properties,

> **Create value with *wow factors.***

look for unmet tenant (buyer) wants, and then strategically design a plan of improvement to create the *wow* factor. With *wow* factors in place, you not only add to the value of your building, you attract topflight tenants and collect higher rents.

Don't Overlook Site Enhancement

As part of your total property improvement plan, you will also focus on potential improvements that you create with the site. Maybe design a view to a newly beautified backyard, add parking spaces, eliminate a drainage problem, or even slice off part of the lot to construct another residence.

In high-priced areas of the country, site value can account for more than 50 percent of a property's value. When you find better ways to use the property's site, you immediately boost the property's value. Walkways, fencing, landscaping, driveways, storage, and redevelopment may all offer promise for profit. As an alert, entrepreneurial owner, you will think through a dozen or more potential ways to enhance site value.

Improve the Neighborhood *and* the Neighbors

"Buy in the best neighborhood you can afford. The best neighborhoods always appreciate the fastest." So says one of the oldest clichés in real estate. But, in fact, it's the turnaround neighborhoods that often shoot up in value the most. Throughout the United States, many once downtrodden and shunned neighborhoods have experienced gentrification.

> **Look for up-and-coming neighborhoods.**

Although some investors wait for these neighborhoods to show strong signs of renewal, other investors jump in early while prices are still rock-bottom cheap. They find neighborhoods that show potential. Then they work with other property owners, neighborhood residents, local government, and not-for-profits to revitalize an area.

Either way, you profit big. Even during those periods when average property prices and rent levels merely edge up (level off or turn down), some neighborhoods remain prime candidates for rapid price escalation. Turnaround neighborhoods give you the chance to realize every investor's dream, "Buy low, sell high."

Convert the Use

From time to time some real estate markets get overbuilt with apartments, office buildings, shopping centers, gas stations, or other types of property. When such overbuilding occurs, alert investors go bargain hunting. Although some bargain hunters hold for the long term, others go for the quick profits by converting properties from one use to another.

For example, New York City recently suffered from a glut of office space. In contrast, housing prices and apartment rents climbed in response to New York's perpetual shortage of homes and apartments. So, what route to profits did some New York real estate investors take? They bought office buildings on the cheap and converted these properties into apartments and condominiums.

Dynamic Markets Precipitate Change

When I-70 came through my hometown, slow-to-adapt motel owners along the previously heavily traveled route U.S. 40 went broke. Alert real estate investors spotted opportunity. They bought the defunct motels at rock-bottom prices and then profitably converted them into efficiency apartments for the growing number of single persons within the city's population.

> **Stay alert for the chance to profit from conversions.**

In a dynamic economy, demand for property grows. But the need for specific property uses ebbs and flows. When oversupply or tough times hit some property uses, that spells profit for investors who figure how to find new uses for now obsolete (or unprofitable) buildings.

Neighborhood Changes

For the past two decades, many close-in neighborhoods with obsolete factories and warehouses have experienced a renaissance as real estate investors have bought cheap, old industrial buildings and converted them to loft apartment buildings. New York City's Soho District,

Watch for neighborhoods where uses are changing.

San Francisco's South of Market (SOMA) area, and Chicago's near north neighborhood represent this trend.

Likewise, as commercial areas sometimes encroach into residential neighborhoods, smart property investors have rezoned the area, then converted large houses into professional offices aimed at those ever-expanding legions of lawyers, accountants, dentists, real estate brokers, and insurance agents.

Condos into Apartments

In the early 1990s, I worked with an investment group that bought controlling interest in defunct condominium projects. After the Texas bust of the late 1980s, large blocks of condo units were selling for as little as $15,000 per unit.

As rentals, these condo units would bring $350 to $425 a month. Given sinking condo prices and relatively high rent levels, more than a few condo projects were converted into apartment buildings. Then, when condo prices revived in the late 1990s, our investment group was able to reconvert and sell off individual apartments at $40,000 to $60,000 per unit. (May be we should have held longer. Today the units fetch nearly $80,000 each.)

Apartments into Condos

In the early 2000s, rapidly escalating condo prices, rising vacancy rates in apartment projects, and softening rents encouraged investors to buy apartment buildings and convert them into condominiums. Similarly, facing soft office markets, some investors are converting office buildings into *commercial* condominiums. Large numbers of doctors, lawyers, and accountants (or investors) have bought such units.

Ride the condo cycle to earn big profits.

Always remember that as relative property prices and rent levels change, the opportunity to convert from one use to another can yield solid profits. (More on this topic in Chapter 14.)

Manage and Market Your Properties More Profitably

Most small-time investors mismanage their rental properties. They go to sleep. They fail to keep up with changes in the market. They fail to make desirable improvements to their properties. They fail to develop a planned strategy of niche marketing.

> **Effective management yields easy profits.**

All in all, such neglect by other investors means that you can boost profits from any property by managing and marketing it more effectively. As a bonus, managing more effectively requires you to put in *less* time and effort. Effective management reduces vacancies, increases lease renewals, and attracts more desirable tenants.

Protect Your Profits from the IRS (Tax Shelter)

To build wealth, protect your earnings from the grasping hand of government. Fortunately, the income tax laws permit owners of property to escape taxation in at least five important ways:

- ◆ Serial home selling
- ◆ Section 1031 exchanges
- ◆ Cash out refinance
- ◆ Depreciation
- ◆ Retirement planning

Serial Home Sellers

Growing numbers of Americans profit by investing in their homes *tax free*. Here's how it works.

Generally, when you own an investment property, you pay a capital gains tax on your resale profits at the time you sell. However, when you sell a personal residence, your gains come to you tax free up to $250,000 ($500,000 for couples). As long as you have lived in the property for two of the previous five years, you need not report this profit to the IRS.

Even better, repeat this purchase and sale every two years. Ideally, find a property with strong fix-up and renovation potential. Buy it. Create value. Resell and reinvest your tax free profits in additional properties. Continue this process until you achieve your desired level of wealth (or until you tire of moving).

> **Serial renovators earn big tax free profits.**

For singles or couples without children, serial "home" ownership can prove to generate quick, tax free profits. Or if you do have kids, get them involved. Put them to work. They'll learn some valuable lessons about real estate renovating and investing.

Section 1031 Exchanges

In addition to buying and selling a series of personal residences tax-free, you can also sell your investment properties tax-free. All you need to do is follow the rules as set forth in Section 1031 of the Internal Revenue Code. Specialist realty pros can easily set up the necessary paperwork to pull off these tax free "exchanges." I put *exchange* in quotations because the tax law does not require you to trade properties with another owner. Instead, you sell one property and buy another one within a period of several months.

Cash Out Refinance

You reach your goal. You own $2 million of real estate free and clear. Although you enjoy the cash flow, you would really like to tap into some of that equity you've accumulated—yet you don't want to sell the property and pay taxes on your large gain. No problem.

Just as you can withdraw tax free cash from your home equity through a HELOC (home equity line of credit), so, too, can you withdraw tax free cash from your investment properties. Through either a line of credit or a cash out refi, you can have your cake and eat it. Your tenants, bless them, will once again pay off your borrowings.

Although you can also borrow against the value of stocks (bonds) you hold, to do so provides big risks and no advantage. If your stocks (bonds) fall in value, you'll get a margin call and the bank (or brokerage firm) will require you to provide more collateral. Moreover, unlike the rents from property, the stock dividends (or bond interest) that you earn on your portfolio of financial assets falls woefully short of the amounts you will need to pay back your borrowings.

Property—should you choose to—permits you to spend (or reinvest) your gains tax-free. Stocks and bonds do not provide a similar benefit.

Depreciation

In most businesses, the IRS taxes your net cash annual income. But when you own rental properties (apartments, houses, condos, offices, retail, mobile homes, self-storage, etc.), you can shelter (protect) much of your cash flow from taxes by using a noncash tax deduction called depreciation.

Say an apartment building (exclusive of land value) is worth $500,000. Your pretax cash income from that property equals $20,000 per year. But you don't pay taxes on that $20,000 of income. You only pay taxes on $1,950 ($20,000 of income less $18,150 for allowable depreciation).

What happens to that $18,150 deduction for depreciation if, say, your rental property yields only $10,000 a year in pretax cash income? In that situation, you may be able to write off (deduct) that $8,150 ($18,150 depreciation less $10,000 property income) of unused "loss" from the taxable amounts you earn from your other taxable income (wages, business profits, interest, dividends). Otherwise, you carry it forward to offset future rental income or capital gains from that property or others that you own.

> **Depreciation gives you tax free income.**

Tax-Deferred Retirement Plans

Do you own an IRA retirement plan? If so, you may be able to invest all or part of it in property.

Most people believe that they can only invest these retirement funds in corporate stocks, bonds, mutual funds, or money market accounts. Wrong! Patrick Rice fully explains these real estate investing techniques in his book, *IRA Wealth: Revolutionary IRA Strategies for Real Estate Investment* (Garden City Park, N.Y., Square One, 2003, p. 3). Here's what Rice says:

> After the sharp decline of the stock market, many of us could only stand by and watch our retirement savings lose their value. Few [investors] knew that an alternative offered both safety and growth. That alternative is real estate. . . . Contrary to what you may have believed, it is possible and perfectly legal to hold real estate in an IRA account. . . .

If you have accumulated funds in a tax-favored retirement fund, I urge you to talk with a financial pro or read Rice's book. Quite likely, you will find it wise to diversify at least a portion of your IRA monies into real estate. IRA funds invested in real estate build tax free within that account just the same as stocks, bonds, and CDs.

Taxes: Summing Up

The tax laws remain too complex to detail in this beginning book on investing in real estate. Nevertheless, appreciate the fact that, to a large degree, far better than any other asset class, you can protect your real estate profits from the IRS.

To learn how to legally avoid taxes on real estate, I recommend these two books:

◆ *Aggressive Tax Avoidance for Real Estate Investors* by John T. Reed (available at www.johntreed.com).
◆ *Real Estate Investors Tax Guide* by Vernon Hoven (Chicago: Dearborn, 2003).

Throughout this book, I will show you how to make money in real estate. Reed and Hoven show you how to pocket these profits without losing a good-sized portion to the government.

Discounted Notes, Tax Liens, Tax Deeds, and Realty Stocks

Want to make money in real estate without managing tenants or lifting a paintbrush? Consider the high-return business of buying (and perhaps selling) discounted notes and mortgages.

The Basics of Discounted Notes

Often, sellers of houses, condos, and investment properties carry back (owner finance) some or all of their buyer's purchase price. A buyer then makes monthly payments directly to the sellers.

After some period of time passes, a seller may decide that he or she wants cash instead of those monthly payments. To get this cash, the seller (note holder) sells the note to another investor-usually for an amount somewhat less than the balance on the note owed by the buyer (now debtor) of the original noteholder's property.

> **Buy $100 bills for $80—or less.**

Assume I sell you a property and carry back a mortgage note for $25,000. After a few years of payments, the remaining balance on this note drops to $21,500. I want cash. To entice an investor to buy this note from me, I agree to sell it for $17,500.

You might wonder, "Why sell a $21,500 mortgage for just $17,500?" Because that's the way this market works. In most cases, noteholders who wish to sell must accept a discount.

How much discount? It depends on a number of factors such as the value and condition of the collateral property, the borrower's credit score and payment record, and the current level of interest rates.

Just realize that tens of thousands of investors throughout the United States make outstanding returns in this field. If you choose to, you can too. (For a description of this technique, see *The Stefanchik Method*, Morrow, 1994.)

Tax Liens and Tax Deeds

When owners fail to pay their property taxes, local governments place a tax lien against their properties. If the taxes remain unpaid, the government eventually sells the property via a tax deed. The "free and clear" infomercials of Ed Beck promise to show investors how they can make money buying these tax liens and tax deeds.

Although not so easy and risk-free as Beck's infomercial makes it sound, once you learn your area's rules and procedures, you can compete to earn tens of thousands of dollars a year by buying these government-issued certificates. I say "compete" because in recent years the supply of potential investors has exceeded the supply of profitable properties. To succeed, you need property research and expert knowledge of market value.

Stocks of REITs and Homebuilders

Most investors directly own and manage their real estate. When you participate directly in the real estate market, you will outearn passive investors. Nevertheless, as one more real estate alternative, you can buy the stocks issued by real estate investment trusts (REITs) and corporate homebuilders such as Toll Brothers, K&B, Lennar, and WPP. REITs are companies that own and manage multi-million-dollar office buildings, shopping centers, warehouses, and apartment complexes.

Long after the stock market downturn of early 2000, the stocks of REITs and homebuilders continued to register returns of 10 to 25 percent a year. Also, unlike the stocks of most companies, REIT stocks have historically paid cash dividends of 6 to 8 percent a year. More recently, REIT cash dividends of 3 to 5 percent have proved more typical.

Any investor who wants to build wealth in stocks should definitely own shares in at least several REITs and homebuilders. These companies not only offer good returns, they reduce the overall risk of your investment portfolio. Real estate stocks diversify your holdings of stocks and bonds. Just as property values experience up and down cycles, so do the stocks of REITs and homebuilders. Time the cycle correctly, and you can buy low and sell high.

> **Real estate stocks add both diversity and yield to your stock portfolio.**

How to Raise Money

CHAPTER 3

Strengthen Your Credit Power

To convince a lender, seller, or investment partner to help finance your property investments, think about your credit profile according to these three attributes:

- ◆ Consistency.
- ◆ Character.
- ◆ Credit score and payment record.

The most important of these three Cs is Credit. With strong credit—even without much cash or income—you will find it easy to buy investment real estate. Yet credit's not the only attribute that counts. If you lack a platinum-power credit score, if your "pay as agreed" has fallen short, you can still dress yourself up for success. Emphasize your consistent ability to perform and your sterling character.

Consistency: Fast Track or Flake

Have you job-hopped or job-flopped? Have you lived in more places than you can remember? Did you jump through six majors before you finished community college? Do you suffer bouts of binge spending and borrowing? Does your background look more like tossed salad that's been thrown against a wall than the impeccable dinner presentation of an expensive French restaurant? If so, you've got some explaining to do.

Loan representatives, loan underwriters, potential partners, and sellers who offer financing want to make sense of your life as it's displayed on your mortgage application, business plan, or investment proposal.* They want to evaluate where you've been and where you're headed.

To satisfy their penchant for consistency, figure a theme or angle that ties your loose ends together. Instill confidence that six months after you've closed your loan, you won't abandon the property to join a Hare Krishna colony or move to Soho to write romance novels. Lenders (and others who provide you money) want to envision your job promotions and career advancement. In borderline cases, a good story can make the difference.

> **Tell the lender
> a life story that
> makes sense.**

All in all, you want to persuade the lender, seller, and partners that the path you're traveling is leading you toward success. Before I judge a potential deal, I judge the person who presents it. So do most others I know and do business with.

Character Counts

The famous banker, J. P. Morgan, declared, "I wouldn't loan money to a man I did not trust on all the bonds of Christendom." Don't you feel the same way? Well, so does your lender (seller). You've got to convince the lender (seller) that you'll honor your obligations and commitments. Your credit score provides one indicator. But, when desirable or necessary, bolster the impression this score creates with other types of written information:

1. *Employer.* If your lender requires a completed VOE form (verification of employment), ask your supervisor to enclose a letter that commends your dependability, integrity, and responsibility at work.
2. *Credit blemishes.* Explain how misplaced bills, your vacation, a move of residence, or other non-character-indicting reasons account for these lapses that you deeply regret. Even better,

---

*Throughout much of this chapter's discussion, I will use the term "lender" to include sellers who offer their buyers owner financing (called OWC).

discuss the new bill-paying systems that you have now put in place to prevent future lapses.

3. *Credit wreck.* Explain a serious problem as a once-in-a-lifetime, beyond-your-control event that you coped with as honorably as possible. If your lapses really were due to irresponsibility, emphasize that "you've learned your lesson the hard way" and now live well within your means. Put together objective evidence to support your "new you" claims.

4. *Personal references.* In the old days of lending, younger borrowers were awarded loans merely on the basis of family character and reputation.* "Why I've known Luke Jr.'s family for 30 years," the loan rep says. "They're great people. Loan approved." Now, in our big-city, automated world, personal references seldom count as much. Still, if you've established good rapport with people who could prove influential, it wouldn't hurt to enlist their help.

    Remember, too, your behavior today, the way you treat people, the diligence you show as you honor (or dishonor) your commitments will determine the quality of your future references. As your real estate career advances, your character and track record will open doors—or shut them.

> **If your credit score is low, document your good character.**

If desirable, accent the fact that you're a good risk by showing alternative documentation. Otherwise, the lender will infer personal worth from the shading provided by your formal record of credit and consistency. When adverse facts color too bleak a picture, add brighter hues to the mix. Think. What evidence highlights your better qualities?

What loans or merchant accounts have you repaid on time that don't show up in your credit file? Will your current and past landlords vouch for you? Have you consistently paid your utilities and phone bills promptly? Often, lenders accept such alternative evidence to discern your reliability and good character. What do people say who have previously worked or invested with you?

---

*In fact, many loan applications used to include spaces for personal references similar to those found on job applications.

Credit Scores Count Most

With a high credit score (say above 720, but above 760 really draws favorable attention), lenders may lay aside their magnifying glass. With strong credit you will worry less about high qualifying ratios, low down payments, self-employment (difficult to determine income), piles of verifications, inconsistent life patterns, or character flaws. As a strong credit borrower you win the lowest interest rate, the best terms, and the fastest approval. You need not suffer the claw marks of subprime or hard money lenders.

> **Learn how to raise your credit score.**

But, if you do need to boost your credit score, here are pointers that will help you gain platinum-power borrowing status.

What Is Credit Scoring?

Through credit scoring, lenders try to minimize individual human judgment in the mortgage lending decision. Credit scoring data with auto loans, department store accounts, and credit cards proves that computer statistical programs can distinguish among platinum, gold, copper, lead, and plastic borrowers far better than back-office loan clerks or front-office loan reps.

To create these credit scoring programs, math whizzes study the credit profiles, borrowing habits, and payback records of hundreds of thousands of people. Then they search for statistically significant correlations that tend to rate borrowers along a continuum from "walks on water" (say, 800 or higher) to "even a life jacket won't help" (say, 500 or lower). Credit scores range from 350 to 850. More than 75 percent of Americans fall within the range of 600 to 800.

Credit Scoring Spreads Its Influence

If you've received a preapproved credit card in the mail, or obtained instant credit at Sears, Home Depot, or Best Buy, you've been run through a credit scoring program. That's why the store could make the credit decision so quickly with only minimal information from you (Social

> **Employers and insurers also judge you by your credit score.**

Security number, name, address). Even insurance companies (especially auto and homeowners) turn to credit scores to decide whether to insure you, and if so, at what price. Employers, too, run credit scores on job applicants and, in some cases, current employees.

Your Credit Score Doesn't Necessarily Represent Your Credit Strength

Contrary to what many loan reps (and others) believe, your credit score doesn't necessarily represent your credit strength. You may never have paid a bill late in your life and still earn a credit score of less than 660.

Credit Scores Do Not Rate You Personally   The credit scorers select certain characteristics that you share with others who have (or have not) paid their bills as scheduled. Then, based on these selected characteristics, the scorer's mathematical formula assigns you a number. Supposedly, this assessment accurately gauges the risks you present. But it doesn't. Why? Because you are a unique individual. Although you share some similarities with this computer sample of borrowers, you also differ in many ways of which the credit scoring programs have no knowledge. These unaccounted-for differences may give you more (or less) borrowing credibility than your credit score indicates.

You can easily see the parallel here with SAT scores and other college admission tests. If you fail to register a top score, you can kiss Stanford goodbye—unless, that is, you write a superlative admissions essay and beef up your application with science fair awards and club presidencies.

> **Your perfect payment record doesn't mean you'll receive a top-level credit score.**

You're Not Just a Number   Remember Bob Seger's classic hit, "Feel Like a Number"? When you seek OPM (other people's money), persuade the funds provider that you're more than a number. Do all that you can to boost your credit score. But never let a lender (or seller) confuse the total *you* with your credit score.* By the same token, never assume that your astute loan

---

*Unless, perhaps, your credit score makes you look better than you deserve.

rep and underwriter will intuitively recognize your worthwhile qualities. Just as the aspiring Stanford applicant must document why she deserves admission, you, too, must persuasively document why the lender (seller, investor) can count on you to pay back that $250,000 you're trying to raise.

Discover Your Credit Scores

To discover your credit scores, go to www.myfico.com. There you can see (for a fee) all of your credit reports (Trans Union, Experian, Equifax). Each report includes an associated credit score.

These three scores may not vary much from each other. But sometimes they do. That's because Equifax, Experian, and TU maintain independent data bases. Different credit data yield different credit scores. Big differences in credit bureau data may cause big differences in each of the credit scores you receive.

Want to Save Money?

If you don't want to spend the money to obtain credit information, you've got several other choices:

1. *Mortgage loan sites.* Some mortgage web sites provide a free, no obligation credit score that simulates, but doesn't mirror, the Equifax-FICO score (trade-named Beacon). However, I have found that these free simulated scores do not provide consistent results, nor do their scores replicate your FICO scores. Because most mortgage lenders use FICO scores, simulated FICO figures provide information of limited use.

2. *Consumerinfo.com.* This web site operated by Experian will give you a free credit report, but it also will automatically enroll you in a $79.95 credit-monitoring service. Cancel this service within 30 days and you owe nothing.

3. *Free reports.* Various states require credit bureaus to provide reports for free (or at nominal cost). Also, under federal law you may receive free reports from each of the credit repositories if (1) you're unemployed and looking for work, (2) you're on welfare, or (3) you've been turned down for credit during the past 30 days.

4. *Commentary.* For the latest (usually critical) commentary about credit scoring and credit reporting, go to www.creditscoring .com and www.creditaccuracy.com. Also, the Federal Trade Commission maintains consumer information on all types of credit issues at www.ftc.gov.

How to Improve Your Credit Score

Credit scorers place your credit data into their computer programs and out pops a number. But they won't reveal how they calculate that figure. However, after you've paid your fee at myfico.com, the web site info will give you some pointers on how to improve your Beacon-FICO score. To learn how much your score actually does improve (if any) over the next 12 months, you will need to pay another fee. For that cost, you get four more periodic Beacon®-FICO reports.

Piecing together clues from myfico.com and loan reps, you can use these tips to raise your credit scores:

1. *Number of open credit accounts.* You can have too few or too many. The optimum number probably ranges between four and ten. One highly paid, credit perfect (no lates) executive I know scored 640. After closing 6 of her 12 credit card accounts, her score went to 780. (But it took six months before her score climbed up to that level.) Note, closing an account does not remove the previous payment record from the scoring process. However, its effect will fade—for better or worse—as the years pass by.
2. *Balances.* Open accounts with balances reduce your score more than open accounts per se.
3. *Balances/limits.* Numerous accounts with balances sitting close to the limit will bring down your score. Do not close accounts if these closures significantly increase your percentage of credit utilization.
4. *Credit inquiries.* Whenever someone checks your credit file, it counts against your score. However, multiple checks within, say, two weeks do not hurt if it appears that you're merely shopping different lenders for one loan. Your personal inquiries don't affect your score.

5. *Payment record.* Obviously, late payments hurt your score. But, supposedly FICO doesn't distinguish between late mortgage payments and late payments on your Visa or student loan. (Mortgage lenders, though, most certainly do care. Always pay your mortgage or rent first.)

6. *Recency counts.* Late payments two years ago don't hurt as much as two months ago.

7. *Black marks.* Multiple lates on multiple accounts, collections, unpaid judgments, and tax liens devastate your score.

8. *Kiss of death.* Go straight to credit scoring purgatory if you're within two years of a past bankruptcy discharge or a foreclosure sale. Chapter 13 bankruptcy plans and credit counseling debt management plans also count heavily and negatively. Nevertheless, FHA will approve mortgages for homebuyers who have not only experienced a bankruptcy discharge, but also those currently enrolled in a Chapter 13 payment plan.

Myfico.com also shows that some categories weigh more than others:

- Age of credit (15 percent).
- Mix of credit (10 percent).
- Amount of balances (30 percent).
- Payment history (35 percent).
- Recent credit inquiries (10 percent).

These clues shed light on credit scoring. Most importantly, they show why "perfect credit" in the sense of "no lates" does not necessarily generate the highest FICO score. To improve your score, pay your bills on time, but also manage your credit according to the likes and dislikes of the FICO (or other) credit-scoring programs.

Garbage In, Garbage Out   Computer data researchers everywhere know of GIGO (garbage in, garbage out). Clearly, this saying also applies to credit reporting. Credit scoring computer programs pull in raw data from the files of Equifax, Trans Union, or Experian. If your credit files include errors (as most files do), your credit scores will err.

> **Don't wait until you need credit. Check for errors now.**

Examine Your Reports Now   Seventy-five percent (or more) of mortgage loan applications require tri-merged credit reports and correspondingly three credit scores per borrower. Because each credit repository holds more than 200 million files and registers billions of computer-generated entries every year, you are unlikely to find three flawless, perfectly matched reports. Thus inconsistencies and mistakes can slow down or derail your mortgage approval.

What to Look For   Look for errors, but what kinds of errors? More than you might think:

1. *Inconsistency.* Evaluate whether your three reports differ significantly from each other. Does each report accurately show your credit accounts along with an appropriate "open" or "closed"?
2. *Late payments.* Make sure that all late payments shown were in fact lates. Also, check the category of lates 30, 60, and 90 days or over. Sometimes creditors overstate the number of days a payment has been late. Watch for rolling lates; you miss a payment, then get back on schedule. Every subsequent payment may show up as late.
3. *Balances.* Verify that the outstanding balances and credit limits don't misstate your true credit position. Remember, when balances push against limits, your credit score goes down.
4. *Disputed claims.* Have you justifiably refused to pay any creditor's bills? Health clubs (and other service contract providers) often continue to bill (and report unpaid) fees for membership that customers canceled long ago.
5. *Credit experience counts.* Do the reports accurately indicate the length of time each account has been opened? Accounts opened for many years add to your scores.
6. *Omissions.* Have you established excellent credit with a credit card, landlord, or retail merchant that does not show up in your credit files? Some creditors withhold excellent payment records and balance information. Why? If your credit score goes up, that lender's competitors will start mailing you offers to switch to their better terms or higher limits.

7. *Tax liens.* This type of claim nearly always must be paid before your mortgage loan closes.

8. *Judgments.* Ditto for judgments unless the statute of limitations has passed—or they total an inconsequential amount.

9. *Collections/write-offs.* For collections and write-offs, lenders may require that you settle them. Or the lender might calculate your qualifying total debt ratio as if you were paying 5 percent of these delinquent balances each month. If you combine a high current credit score with write-offs more than five years old, the lender may simply ignore them.

10. *Time limits.* See if any derogatory information shows up in violation of these legal time limits: credit inquiries (2 years); foreclosure (7 years); lates, collections, write-offs (7 years); judgments and tax liens (usually until statute of limitations runs out). To calculate time limits, work back from the "date of last activity" on the debt. Also, creditors often sell their bad debts to credit vultures. These outfits may report debts beyond their lawful date of removal. Beware: You can trigger a new time limit by partial payment or settlement. Bankruptcy starts the clock on the date of discharge, not filing. Also, for larger loans, longer time limits may not apply.

11. *Other information.* Verify all other information such as names, addresses, employment, date of birth, and so on.

12. *Consistency with application.* Remember, your loan underwriter verifies the data in your credit files with the liabilities and other information you list on your mortgage application. Do they match up?

What to Do Next

If you discover errors, omissions, or inconsistencies that push down on your credit score, act immediately to correct them. If you wait until a loan rep inquires about these derogatory entries, you could lose your loan and the property you have agreed to buy. Some problems can disappear in a matter of days, but others may take months to clear up.

Contact the Credit Source and the Credit Repository Simultaneously Most credit advisors tell you to notify the credit repository, point out the change you deserve, and formally (in writing) seek compliance with your request. Good advice except for one critical fact. Credit repositories report public records data and the information your creditors give them. Unless the repository has botched the data it's been given (which does happen), the repository must contact the misreporting creditor. If the creditor does not respond within 30 days, the repository must remove the disputed item.

However, if the creditor says, "Sorry, no mistake on our part," the record remains as is. The problem's back in your lap—but now 30 days may have passed by. To head off this potential delay, contact the original source of the information simultaneously and ask to have new, corrected info sent to the repository. Upon request some friendly creditors will even eliminate derogatory remarks if you're a customer the creditor values.

> **Credit bureaus only report the data creditors provide them.**

On the other hand, if you deal with a hostile or indifferent creditor, you could face a prolonged battle. In that case, the loan underwriter will either waive the "derog" upon suitable explanation from you; offer you a higher-cost, less-desirable loan; or suspend commitment until you obtain the creditor's correction or release.

To close a mortgage on schedule, many borrowers have had to pay disputed claims. Acting early prevents forced settlements on eat-crow terms. Carefully review your credit reports now. Avoid a borrowing dilemma where you most offer last-minute pleas under deadline conditions.

> **Your spouse or partner's low credit score can squelch loan approval.**

Multiple Borrowers, Multiple Scores   When you and your spouse (or other coborrower) want to buy and finance an investment property, all borrowers will need credit scores (or explanations) that equal or exceed lender minimums. Without meeting this requirement, the low-score borrower must withdraw as a coborrower. The lender will then limit the loan amount to the qualifying capacity of the high-score borrower.

When you buy an income property, you can work around this problem. Bring in another person with strong credit (parent, partner, sibling, friend) to serve as cosignor or coborrower. Be cautious, though. If you don't make the loan payments on time, the lender will report these late payments to the credit repositories (Experian, Equifax, Trans-Union). The derogs will show up in your file. But they will also count against the credit record and credit score of your coborrower or cosignor.

One Borrower, Multiple Credit Scores   When your credit records show different credit scores, which score will the lender choose to use if one of your scores falls below the lender's cutoff point? To a certain extent, it will depend on the persuasive story you tell about yourself and the reported discrepancies. In other instances, the lender may average the scores or select the middle score. This method discounts your highest score, again underlining the importance of getting all low-scoring files updated and corrected before you apply for your financing. Then verify the weighting (or exclusionary) practice of the lender(s) you're talking with.

> **When they differ, the lender may average out your credit scores.**

Your Ex-Spouse Can Ruin Your Credit (and Other Tales of Double-Counting)

Are you divorced, married, or planning to wed? Might you buy a property with a partner or significant other? Then you're going to face the multiple-score, multiple-person problem of credit scoring and mortgage approval.

The Ex-Spouse Dilemma   If a competent lawyer handled your divorce, you should have cut up all joint credit cards and closed all joint accounts. If you and your ex-spouse owned a home with a joint mortgage, one spouse should have bought the other spouse out and refinanced solely in his or her own name. Without these precautions, you're still on the hook for these debts, and they will count against you when you apply for property financing. If you haven't yet eliminated this potential debt overload, work out something now.

> **Get your ex-spouse's name off all of your accounts.**

Your Ex-Spouse Can Ruin *Your* Credit   Even worse than debt overload (for purposes of mortgage approval), your ex-spouse's poor repayment habits on joint debts will show up to bruise your credit. These same types of problems also confront married couples who are separated (either legally or by informal agreement). When ending your lives together, abolish all joint credit accounts. Sometimes a lender will permit you to explain away poor credit where the full responsibility actually falls on your ex, but the lender will not overlook joint credit obligations that remain open. When the law imposes legal liability on you for the debt, then as far as the lender's concerned, it's your debt. Or it's your credit line for as long as it remains open or unpaid. The lesson: Get rid of all joint accounts that do not result from a current, trusting, continuing relationship.

Summing Up

For the top 20 to 30 percent of U.S. investors, credit scoring and automated underwriting greatly ease the pain of financing a home or investment property. On the other hand, if you're a borrower without platinum-power credit (say a FICO score below 720), to improve your credit score you must do something more than "pay your bills on time." You must align your credit behavior with FICO (or other credit scoring systems). You (and your coborrowers) will achieve the lowest interest rates, highest loan amounts, best terms, and least hassle when you play the credit game according to the rules laid down by these new sultans of mortgage credit. The higher you lift your credit score, the greater your borrowing power.

CHAPTER 4

How to Invest Using Little (or None) of Your Own Cash

You can profit in real estate without much cash—especially if you've strengthened your credit score. But even when you lack platinum-power credit, you can draw on a variety of little-or-no-cash-down techniques to get you started as a real estate investor.

Why Low-Cash Deals Magnify Your Returns

Before we go into little-or-no-cash-down techniques, you need to see why deals with small down payments can magnify your returns. Even if you're hoarding a pile of cash, you may still choose to hang onto your money as you benefit from the power of leverage.

The Power of Leverage

Leverage (other people's money, commonly referred to as OPM) means that you buy (or otherwise control) a property that's worth perhaps 10 times as much as your original cash investment. To illustrate, simply suppose you invest $10,000 in a $100,000 rental property. You finance this investment with a 30-year, $90,000 mortgage at 7.75 percent. After eight years you will have paid down your mortgage balance to $81,585.

> **Four percent appreciation can give you 20 percent returns.**

> **Investors call leverage the eighth wonder of the world.**

With 4 percent a year appreciation for eight years, your property's value will have grown to $136,860. When you subtract the balance of $81,585 from the property's appreciated value of $136,860, you find that your original $10,000 investment has increased more than fivefold to $55,275 of equity. That result gives you an annual growth in equity of around 24 percent (see Table 4.1). Through the power of leverage, you gained a return six times larger than the 4 percent rate of appreciation. Now you see why real estate investors call leverage the eighth wonder of the world.

At times, leverage even yields higher returns. And used foolishly—as you will soon see—leverage can magnify your losses. But, over the long run, the great majority of homebuyers and investors gain

Table 4.1 With Leverage, Even Modest Rates of Appreciation Create Substantial Wealth

Today	
Property purchase price	$100,000
Original mortgage	90,000
Cash invested	10,000
Eight Years Later	
Market value at 4% appreciation	$136,860
Mortgage balance	81,585
Your equity	55,275

Growth In Your Equity

$10,000 $55,275

|___|___|___|___|___|___|___|___|___|
0   1   2   3   4   5   6   7   8 years

Annual growth rate of equity = 24%. Of course, proportionately increasing the rental income, the down payment, and the purchase price of this property would still yield a 24 percent rate of return. These figures assume that you financed this property with a 7.75 percent mortgage amortized over 30 years. The interest rate you pay (discussed later) depends on the current mortgage market; your skills of presentation and negotiation; LTV (down payment); cash reserves; loan documentation (full or sparse); property type, condition, and location; credit score; and other factors.

tremendously from leverage. That's why real estate moguls such as Donald Trump rely on OPM to acquire and finance property investments.

Leverage Can Also Magnify Your Annual Cash Returns

Although leverage accelerates your wealth building from appreciation, it also magnifies your returns from cash flows. Say you pay $100,000 for a rental property. It yields a net operating income (called NOI) of $10,000 a year. If you paid all cash for this property, you would receive a return of 10 percent:

Example 1: $100,000 all-cash purchase

$$\text{ROI (cash on cash return)} = \frac{\text{Income (NOI)}}{\text{Cash Investment}}$$
$$= \frac{\$10,000}{\$100,000}$$
$$= 10\%$$

Say you either want to compare this all-cash (no OPM) return to the return would receive using either 75 percent or 90 percent financing, respectively. Assume that you can borrow money at 6.5 percent and pay it back over a term of 30 years. Here's how leverage (OPM) boosts your yearly returns from cash flow.

Example 2: $25,000 down payment; $75,000 financed. Yearly mortgage payments equal $6,607 (75 × $7.34 × 12). Net cash flow after mortgage payments (called before-tax cash flow) equals $3,394 ($10,000 NOI less $6,606).

$$\text{ROI} = \frac{\$3,394 \ (\text{BTCF})}{\$25,000 \ (\text{Cash investment})}$$
$$= 13.6\%$$

Example 3: $10,000 down payment; $90,000 financed. Yearly mortgage payments equal $7,927 (90 × $7.34 × 12). Net cash flow after mortgage payments (before-tax cash flow) equals $2,073 ($10,000 NOI less $7,927).

$$ROI = \frac{\$2,073 \text{ (BTCF)}}{\$10,000 \text{ (Cash investment)}}$$
$$= 20.7\%$$

Using the figures in these examples, the highly leveraged financing (90 percent LTV, 10 percent down payment) yields a cash-on-cash rate of return more than double that of a cash purchase. Ideally, the more you borrow and the less cash you invest in a property, the greater your cash returns. Of course, these examples merely illustrate the principle of leverage. The examples show how leverage *may* boost your returns. In practice, the properties you find may produce numbers that look better or worse than the returns you see here. Still, the fact that nearly all *wealthy investors* finance their properties with large mortgages proves that leverage works.

> **Even wealthy investors use low-down-payment techniques to increase their leverage.**

In other words, you might borrow because you lack the funds to pay 100 percent cash. But even if you could pay cash, you would generally choose to borrow. OPM used wisely accelerates you ability to build wealth.

Leverage Can Increase Risk

> **Never combine high leverage with financial recklessness.**

Wise investors reap the rewards of leverage. Foolish investors can lose their shirts. What makes the difference? Financial discipline and cash reserves.

Financial Discipline If you can't responsibly handle money, borrowing to the hilt can swamp you in debt. Never substitute "nothing down" for financial discipline. It doesn't work that way. As I emphasize in Chapter 1, before you invest in real estate, make sure you're living *below* your means. Learn to carefully manage your everyday spending and borrowing.

Don't let the real estate gurus lure you into believing that high leverage alone can make you rich. No! High leverage can help you get started. High leverage can boost your returns. But without financial discipline, high leverage can push you into foreclosure or bankruptcy.

Cash Reserves   Foolish investors only view the future through rose-colored glasses. These investors never anticipate an unexpected streak of vacancies, a roof that needs to be replaced, or a spiked increase in property taxes, maintenance expenses, or insurance.

Over the long term, rent collections and appreciation will put hundreds of thousands of dollars into your bank accounts. Over the short term, rent shortfalls and unbudgeted expenses can cause unprepared investors to miss their mortgage payments and suffer foreclosure, or perhaps force them into a quick sale at a loss (to an opportunistic investor such as you?). To benefit over the long run, you must navigate through storms along the way. When high seas are trying to drown you, cash reserves will prove to be your life jacket.

> **Always keep a reserve of cash and credit.**

With words of caution in view, we turn to the lowest-cost, easiest qualifying, high-leverage financing available.

Minimize Your Down Payment with Owner-Occupant Financing

By far, the easiest, safest, surest, and lowest cost way to borrow all (or nearly all) of the money you need to invest in real estate centers upon owner-occupied mortgage financing. In other words, lenders give their most favored interest rates and terms to investors or homebuyers who intend to live in their property (for a minimum of 12 months). Numerous high LTV (loan-to-value) owner-occupied loan programs are readily available for single-family homes, condominiums, townhouses, and two-to four-unit apartment buildings.

Owner-Occupants Get the Lowest Down Payments

Many owner-occupied loan programs offer 3 percent, 5 percent, or even 0 percent down payment loans. With strong credit, some lenders will even loan you 125 percent of a property's purchase price (if you agree to live in the property). In contrast, if you do not plan to live in the property, many mortgage lenders (banks, mortgage bankers, savings institutions) often require investors to put 20 or 30 percent down. However, during the late, great property boom, some lenders financed rental properties with just 5 or 10 percent down. As property markets have softened, many previously liberal lenders have shut their easy credit windows and have asked investors to put more cash into their deals and to provide stricter verifications.

Besides offering owner-occupant low-down-payment financing, lenders also qualify these investors with less exacting standards. Plus, interest rates for owner-occupant loans fall below the rate charged for investor loans. If lenders charge, say, 6.5 percent for loans to owner-occupants with strong credit, the rate on creditworthy investor loans will probably range between 6.75 and 7.5 percent. As a beginning real estate investor, explore owner-occupied mortgage loans.

Owner-Occupied Buying Strategies

If you don't currently own a home, you can easily begin building wealth in income properties. Select a low-down-payment loan program that appeals to you (the most popular ones are described later in this chapter). Buy a one- to four-family property, live in it for (at least) one year, then rent out your living unit and repeat the process. Once you get your owner-occupied financing, that loan can remain on a property even after you move out and move a tenant in. The second, third, and even fourth properties you buy and move into will still qualify for high-LTV financing. You can quickly accumulate several rental properties as well as your own residence-all without large cash investments.

Although you will be able to go through this process two, three, maybe four times, you can't execute it indefinitely. At some point, lenders will shut you off from owner-occupied financing because they will catch on to your game plan. Nevertheless, buying houses (or 2- to 4-unit apartment buildings) and holding on to them as you successively move in, move out, and move up makes a great way to accumulate investment properties.

> **To build wealth fast, use multiple owner-occupant loans.**

Current Homeowners, Too, Can Use This Method

> **You may already own an investment property— your home.**

Even if you own a home, weigh the advantages of using owner-occupied financing to acquire your next several properties. Here's how: Locate a property (condominium, house, two- to four-unit apartment building) that you can buy and move into. Find a good tenant for your current home. Complete the owner-occupied financing on your new property and move into it. If you really like the home where you currently live, at the end of one year, rent out your recently acquired investment property and move back into your former residence. Or alternatively, find another "home" to buy and again finance this property with an owner-occupied mortgage.

Why One Year?

To qualify for owner-occupied financing you must tell the lender that you *intend* to live in the property for at least a year. Intent, though, does not mean *guarantee*. You can (for good reason, or no reason) change your mind.

Nevertheless, to succeed in real estate over the short and long term, you must establish, maintain, and nurture your credibility with lenders—and everyone else. Always build your deal making on a foundation of trust. When you sidestep agreements, slip through loopholes, make false promises, or connive in similar slights, you dilute credibility. Unless you encounter an unexpected turn of events, honor a lender's occupancy requirement. When you establish and nurture your credit and credibility, you will attract money as a horseshoe attracts a magnet.

> **Never fib to a lender about owner-occupancy.**

Where Can You Find Low-Down-Payment, High-LTV, Owner-Occupied Mortgages?

Everywhere! Look through the business directory of your telephone book under "Mortgages." Call banks, savings institutions, mortgage bankers, mortgage brokers, and credit unions. Also, many mortgage lenders

> **You can find dozens of low- or no-down-payment mortgages.**

advertise in local daily newspapers.* Check, too, with your state, county, or city departments of housing finance. Homebuilders and Realtors also will know various types of low- or nothing-down home finance programs. An hour or two on the telephone or surfing the internet will turn up dozens of possibilities.

Although space here doesn't permit a full discussion of all low- or no-down-payment possibilities, here are a variety of widely available programs.

Don't Overlook FHA

The Federal Housing Administration (FHA) offers the most well-known low-down-payment home finance plans. Many homebuyers believe that

> **FHA does not restrict its loans to low- or moderate-income individuals.**

FHA limits its loans to people who earn low or moderate incomes. For instance, one of Florida's largest newspapers continues to describe FHA as a program for "low-income homebuyers." Not true. No matter how much you earn, FHA may provide the key to your property financing. (At present, FHA does not offer investment financing [i.e., non-owner-occupied] except for larger, affordable-housing, apartment buildings.)

FHA 203(b)

When Realtors and mortgage lenders talk about an FHA loan, they are typically referring to the FHA 203(b) mortgage. Historically, this program has served as the largest low-down-payment loan throughout the United States.

---

*For more extensive tips and insights on mortgage lending see my book, *The 106 Mortgage Secrets All Borrowers Must Learn—But Lenders Don't Tell*, 2nd ed. (Hoboken, NJ: John Wiley & Sons, 2008).

You can get into this type of FHA mortgage for just 3 or 5 percent out-of-pocket cash—sometimes a little more, sometimes less. On a $250,000 property you would pay less than $10,000 out-of-pocket. To finance a $125,000 property you'd pay approximately $6,000. I recently sold a $74,000 house to a 21-year-old college student. He financed 100 percent of the purchase price using an FHA loan program.

How Much Will FHA Finance?

FHA sets loan limits for each locale around the country. In high-priced cities such as Los Angeles, San Diego, Washington, D.C., and Boston, the FHA maximum loan currently tops out (for *single-family* houses, condos, and townhomes) at $362,790. In the lowest priced areas of the country, the maximum FHA home loan comes in at $200,160. Because FHA limits vary, go to hud.gov and check the current FHA insurance limits for the area and type of property you have in mind. (Currently, HUD/FHA is lobbying hard to significantly increase FHA loan limits.)

Buy Rental Properties

As another choice, buy a duplex, triplex, or fourplex. As long as you live in one of the units, you still get a low down payment. Here is a sampling of FHA loan figures for two- to four-unit properties:

	Lower Cost Areas	*Highest Cost Areas*
Two units	$256,248	$464,449
Three units	309,744	561,411
Four units	384,936	697,696

> **To get on the fast track to investing, buy a two- to four-unit building.**

If you buy a two- to four-unit property, you won't have to qualify for the loan using just your monthly earnings. The rents that you collect from the property also will count. Because my first investment property was a five-unit apartment house, I am partial to this approach.

Other FHA Advantages

Besides low (or no) down payments, FHA offers borrowers other advantages:

1. You can roll many of your closing expenses and mortgage insurance premiums into your loan. This cuts the out-of-pocket cash you'll need at closing.
2. You may choose from either fixed-rate or adjustable-rate FHA plans. (FHA adjustable-rate mortgages give you lower annual caps and lower lifetime caps than nongovernment ARM programs.)
3. FHA authorizes banks and other lenders to use higher qualifying ratios and easier underwriting guidelines (see Chapter 5). After you shape up your finances, FHA will do all it can to approve your loan.
4. If interest rates drop (and as long as you've paid on time for the previous 12 months), you can "streamline" refinance your FHA loan at the current lower interest rates without a property appraisal and without having to requalify.
5. If you can persuade parents or other close relatives to gift you the down payment, you won't need to come up with any closing-table cash from your own pocket. (Undoubtedly, many gifted down payments are really loans in disguise.)
6. Unlike most nongovernment loans, FHA mortgages are assumable. Someone who later agrees to buy your property need not apply for a new mortgage. When mortgage interest rates are high, an assumable low-rate FHA mortgage will give your property a great sales advantage.

> **Don't choose your financing until you've talked with an FHA loan specialist.**

The Verdict on FHA 203(b)

If you're a cash-short investor who wants to begin acquiring properties, definitely consider the FHA 203(b) finance plan. The U.S. Department of Housing and Urban Development or HUD (the parent of FHA) is pushing for favorable changes in the 203(b) program. Lower costs, higher limits, and faster closings are three important goals.

Discover FHA's Best Kept Secret: The 203(k) Program

Like many renters, Quentlin Henderson of Orlando, Florida, hoped to invest in real estate some day. Yet, with little savings, Quentlin thought he wouldn't realize his hopes for at least three to four years. He never dreamed that within six months he would own a completely renovated, three-bedroom, two-bath house of 2,288 square feet—more than two and a half times as large as his previous 900-square-foot apartment.

How did Quentlin achieve his goal? He discovered the little known FHA 203(k) mortgage loan program. FHA 203(k) allows owner-occupant investors to acquire and improve a rundown property with a low- or no-down-payment loan. "The property needed a new roof, new paint, new carpeting; and a bad pet odor needed to be removed," says Quentlin. "There was no way I could have paid for the house plus the repairs at the same time. And there was no way I could have otherwise afforded a house this size."

Locate an FHA 203(k) Specialist

To use a 203(k) plan, first locate a mortgage loan advisor who understands the current FHA 203(k) purchase and improvement process. In the past, FHA often stuck borrowers in red tape for months without end. But now with recent FHA streamlining and special software, Robert Arrowwood of California Financial Corporation reports that up-to-date, direct endorsement (DE) firms like his can "close 203(k) loans in four to six weeks instead of four to six months." (HUD lists 203(k) specialists on its web site at hud.gov.)

Search for Good Value

> **The 203(k) program helps you build instant equity.**

After you've located 203(k) advisors, search for a property that offers good value. In Quentlin Henderson's case, his Realtor found him a bargain-priced, six-year-old house that was in a sorry state because its former owners had abandoned it as a result of foreclosure. "The good news for people who buy such houses," says Bob Osterman of FHA's Orlando, Florida, office, "is that purchase prices are relatively low so that after repairs are made, the new value often produces instant equity."

Inspect, Design, Appraise

Once you locate a property that you can buy and rehab profitably, you next come to terms with the owners on price and other terms of sale. With agreement in hand, the house (or condo or two- to four-unit apartment) is then inspected, a formal plan of repair and renovation is designed, and the home is appraised according to its value *after* you complete the improvements. Your loan can equal your purchase price plus rehab expenses approximating 100 percent of the property's renovated market price.

Eligible Properties and Improvements

As long as you plan to pay more than *$5,000 in rehab expenses*, you can use a 203(k) mortgage to acquire and improve nearly any one- to four-unit property. In terms of specific repairs and renovations, the 203(k) mortgage permits a long list of possibilities. Here are some examples:

- Install skylights, fireplaces, energy-efficient items, or new appliances (stove, refrigerator, washer, dryer, trash compactor, dishwasher).
- Finish off an attic or basement.
- Eliminate pollution or safety hazards (lead paint, asbestos, underground storage tanks).
- Add living units such as an accessory apartment or two.
- Recondition or replace plumbing, roof, or HVAC systems.
- Improve aesthetic appeal (paint, carpet, tile, exterior siding).
- Install or replace a well or septic system.
- Landscape and fence the yard.

As you can see, the FHA 203(k) program can really help increase the value of a property—using little or none of your own cash.

Too Many Vets Pass Up VA Loans

If you're a veteran with eligible active military service, or if you have served at least six years in the reserves, the Department of Veterans

Affairs holds your ticket to nothing-down investing. The VA mortgage is truly one of the best benefits offered to those who have worn our country's uniform. Millions of veterans have benefitted from this loan program. Here are several advantages a VA mortgage offers.

- ◆ *No down payment.* With a VA loan vets can finance up to $417,000 without putting any money down. If you want to buy a higher-priced property, you need only come up with 25 percent of the amount over $417,000. For instance, if the property you want to buy is priced at $517,000, you'll need a down payment of $25,000 (0.25 × $100,000)—or about 5 percent of the purchase price.
- ◆ *Liberal qualifying.* Similar to FHA, VA loans offer liberal qualifying guidelines. Many (but not all) VA lenders will forgive properly explained credit blemishes. The VA loan also permits higher qualifying ratios. I've seen veterans with good compensating factors close loans with a 0.48 total debt ratio. (See Chapter 8.)
- ◆ *Closing costs paid.* Often homebuilders and cooperative sellers will pay all of the veteran's settlement expenses. In fact, builders sometimes advertise that veterans can buy homes in their developments for just $1 total move-in costs.
- ◆ *Two- to four-unit properties.* As with FHA loans, VA will finance a single-family house or an owner-occupied two- to four-unit property. However, unlike FHA, VA does not raise its loan guarantees for duplexes, triplexes, and quads.
- ◆ *Assumable.* As with the FHA, a buyer who is not a veteran may assume a VA mortgage when you sell the property. Also like FHA, if interest rates fall you can streamline a no-appraisal, no-qualifying refinance. (Also, as we discuss in the next chapter, you can seek out an FHA or VA assumption as part of your buying strategy.
- ◆ *No mortgage insurance.* But unlike FHA, when you use a VA loan, you won't have to buy mortgage insurance. You will have to pay a one-time "funding fee" ranging between 1.5 to 2.75 percent of the amount you borrow. If you don't want to pay this fee in cash at closing, you add it to your mortgage loan balance.

> **Choose an FHA/ VA loan rep who specializes in these types of loans.**

As with some other types of mortgages, VA loans may require piles of paperwork. You will need to comply with rules that look into job history, property condition, property value (called a CRV), and seller prepaids. Work only with a mortgage loan advisor who is skilled and experienced in the day-to-day job of getting VA loans approved—a professional who knows the ins and outs of the VA application and approval process.

> **Conventional lenders (non-governmental loans) now offer multiple types of low-down-payment loans.**

Even Fannie and Freddie Accept Little- or Nothing-Down Loans

Since the mid 1990s, both Freddie Mac (see www. homesteps.com) and Fannie Mae (www.fanniemae. com) have committed to making more little- or nothing-down loans. In addition to their standard 5 percent down loan, Fannie and Freddie pioneered community homebuyer programs, 3 percent down loans, and even 103 percent LTV loans—meaning qualified borrowers can go through closing with almost no cash out of their own pocket. For a full view of Fannie/Freddie programs, visit these companies' web sites.

Tougher Credit Standards and Lower-Cost Private Mortgage Insurers

Fannie Mae and Freddie Mac low-down-payment loans do apply tighter credit standards than either FHA or VA, but their loan limits reach much higher. Also, borrowers whose credit scores top 620 will pay less for private mortgage insurance with these loan programs than they would with FHA.

Borrowers with FICO scores of less than 620 may find that FHA's mortgage insurance premiums (MIP) now fall below the premiums of the private insurers who guarantee Fannie Mae and Freddie Mac's low-down-payment mortgages (LTVs greater than 80 percent). That's because the private mortgage insurers kicked up their costs to give marginal borrowers a real wallop—an increase of nearly $200 per month on a $200,000 mortgage.

Fannie Mae/Freddie Mac Loan Limits

Unlike FHA loans, the maximum amount you can borrow under Freddie Mac and Fannie Mae programs does not vary by area of the country—except for Alaska, Hawaii, Guam, and the Virgin Islands, where loan limits are 50 percent higher than in the continental United States. Generally, Freddie and Fannie loan limits are high enough to finance good properties in decent neighborhoods. Freddie Mac and Fannie Mae programs will lend up to the following amounts (adjusted upward each year):

Maximum Loan Limits (Continental United States)	
Type of Residence	Loan Limits
One-family	$417,000
Two-family	533,850
Three-family	645,300
Four-family	801,950

A Fannie or Freddie low-down-payment loan can get you a property valued in excess of $800,000. All you need to do is move into the property for a minimum of 12 months. What a great way to buy a fourplex—yet still benefit with high leverage and the lowest investment property mortgage interest rates available (except for some sellers, assumptions, and subject to financing—see following chapter).

Summing Up

Whether you currently rent or own, if you're cash-short, consider financing your next investment property with a low- or no-down-payment owner-occupied loan. In fact, even if the amount of your bank balance climbs up to six figures, remember the great (potential) benefits of high leverage. Whatever your financial situation, carefully weigh the advantages of owner-occupied financing.

If you can't (or don't want to) go for this type of easy financing, you've still got other low- or no-cash possibilities. For those techniques, turn to Chapter 5.

Avoid Banks, Seek Seller Financing

When the late Robert Bruss (nationally syndicated real estate columnist, attorney, and investor) was asked, "Where's the best place to get a mortgage? At a bank, savings and loan, or credit union?" He answered, "None of these is the best. The best source of financing is the seller." If you can persuade the sellers to help with your financing, you might negotiate following benefits:

1. *Little (or nothing) down.* Although some sellers insist on a 20 or 30 percent down payment, many owners who offer OWC (owner-will-carry) financing accept 10 percent down (or less).
2. *Lower credit standards.* Although toaday's banks offer more flexible underwriting than in decades past, they're still tougher than many sellers.
3. *No qualifying income.* As we discuss in Chapter 8, many sellers expect you to pay their monthly payments from the income the property produces rather than use their own earnings. As long as your rent collections look as though they're enough to cover all of your expenses, the seller won't usually ask for your W-2s or income tax returns. (As discussed elsewhere, some lenders offer low-doc, no-doc loans—but such loans are made at higher interest rates than full doc.)
4. *Flexibility.* Price, interest rate, monthly payments, and other terms are set by mutual agreement. You and the sellers can put together a financing package in any way that works. Bank

regulators don't set underwriting rules and guidelines for sellers as they do for financial institutions.

5. *Lower closing costs.* Sellers seldom require points, origination fees, and loan application costs. Unlike lending institutions, sellers cover office overhead.

6. . *Less paperwork.* Although sellers may ask for a credit score, they generally won't require an appraisal, inspections, a stack of documents, or asset.

7. *Quicker sale.* Seller financing reduces time on market. For properties that require extensive repairs or renovations, seller financing can make the difference between a sale and no sale.

> **Even sellers who do not advertise OWC will often accept it.**

The types of seller-assisted financing cover a wide territory. But not all owners who accept OWC financing advertise that fact. Indeed, Robert Bruss says, "I've bought many properties with seller financing. But I can't recall a single one that was advertised 'seller financing.' Until they saw my offer, none of the sellers had informed their agent that they would help finance the sale."

Although many sellers do advertise, Bruss is right. Regardless of whether sellers state their intention to carry back financing, you won't know until you write an offer.

For examples of seller-assisted financing ads from the pages of recent newspapers, see Box 5.1. Look through your newspaper ads and other listing websites. More than likely you'll find similar types of ads. And even if you don't, never fear to make seller financing a part of your offer.

How to Persuade the Sellers

If you suddenly pop the question out of the blue and ask the sellers to carry back financing, many will answer with a quick no. So, always write your proposal into your purchase offer. Don't expect oral concessions. However, prior to writing an offer, I frequently pose feeler questions such as, "Have you given any thought to financing the property?" Most importantly, before you write an offer, explore the seller's needs and motives:

> **Use OWC feeler questions.**

Lease With Option to Buy $1,450/mo. 1 year-rent toward down payment on purchase price of $156,000.

315 DOVER—MUST SEE. Completely Remodeled Brick bungalow, foyer, 21 BR, large kitchen and living room, oak cabinets, dishwasher, range, recessed lighting, gas frplc, part. Fin. LL, big yard w/privacy fence. CALL 555-5555 Broker

$25,000 DOWN on this 3 Bdrm ranch with ceiling fans, fncd yrd. Just redone in pale grays with new carpet, paint, etc. Paid off in full in 25 yrs! $1,500 per mo. OWNER CONTRACT! $225,000. Low interest rate. NO BALLOON! 555-5555. R.E. Lic./owner.

NO QUALIFY 51 Bdrm, 4 Ba. $295K. Owner Financing, only 48K dn. 4118 Catalina Pl. Call 555-5555.

$5000 DOWN, $1695 mo. Poway, 2yr new, 4br. 3ba, pool, 3car gar, $249,500. 1 or 2 year lse. 555-5555

1Level Beauty $173,500 Contract Terms/Lease Option Wonderful 1 level 2 bdrm plus den/ 3rd BR, 2BA, A/C, island kitchen, masonry frplc, security, 2 car garage,

fncd. More! Westside Realty Co. 555-5555

OWNER MAY CARRY 2ND!! Near schools, best area, 3 BR. Make Offer! Only $340,000 Century 21 555-5555

LEASE/PURCHASE. You can own your home & move now through a flexible lease/purchase w/little down. Lovely 3 BR, 2 BA Cape Cod w/bsmt on a beautiful, prvt, wooded ac lot. Convenient location. Hurry! Low $200s. Buddy Boone 555-5555. Remax 555-5555

OWNER FINANCE 21 acre estate. Large brick home with full bsmt, pool, workshop, and more—$564,900. Low down payment. V. Purser 555-5555 METRO BROKERS 555-5555

DOUGLASVILLE NEW HOMES LEASE PURCHASE No credit check! $160s. $1300/ mo. 5% down moves you in. 555-5555 C21 GM

DOUGLASVILLE OWNER FINANCE 3BR 2BA, large lot, 2 car garage, hardwood flrs, new carpet, fireplace, screened porch. $122K. $4000 down. $950 mo. ReMax West, 555-5555

TOWN LAKE Lease Purchase/Owner Finance

4BR/2BA on basement, brick front, nice neighborhood, fenced yard. $199,900. 555-5555 www.easyhousebuy. com A1A R.E. Solutions

TOWN LAKE Nearly new. LR, DR, fam rm, 2-stry brick trad. 0 down pay as low as $800 Pl. Poss. Trade. All credit considered. R. Stone. Re/Max Realty Group 555-5555.

OCOEE AREA— OWNER FINANCE! NO BANK QUALIFY! ONLY $8K/dn. Huge 4/4.5/3, plus Library, big POOL/ SPA. 3,700 htd sq ft. $2850/mo. Across from big lake. Call 555-5555

NORTH MIAMI Four-plex all 1/1, $339K 25% down. Owner finance. No brkrs. 555-5555 after 4 p.m.

POWDER SPRINGS No Credit Check RENT TO OWN 4 homes avail. Immediately. $1100- $1500/mo. Down payment neg. $140's. 555-5555 C-21 GM

TOWN CENTER Mall area. Owner financing. 3000 s.f. traditional. $399,900. By Owner. www.ownerfinancing.tk

OWNER FINANCING 2 BR, Sun Rm, corner lot, renovated. Greenleaf. $6,500 down $770 mo. 555-5555

SOUTHWEST ORANGE—No money down for deposit or closing costs. Below appraisal 555-5555

SoBch 17 Apts Ocean Dr. Owner Finance— 10% down. Rudy, The Singing Rltr. BestInv. RE 555-5555

JONESBORO—Open hours Sat & Sun. 2-5 Lease Option. 1-3 yr. Lse. 3BR/2BA ranch. Owner Fin. $149K. 555-5555

JONESBORO Owner Finance/Lease Purchase. Lovely 3BR brick condo, $94,900. $795/mo. Owner. 555-5555 anytime

JONESBORO SALE OR LEASE/PURCH. Reno. Brk. Ranch, 3BR, 2BA, LR, DR, carport. $118,900 $985. 555-5555. By Owner

2 BR, 1 BA—All Brick! 1100sqft. $109,900. Motivated owner will finance, make offer. 555-5555

Gainesville Mobile Home Park 100 Pad w/6 extra acres. Owner finance. 1.2 Million. 555-5555.

WINTER PARK—RENT TO OWN. 4/2/2 car gar, new & loaded! $4495 moves you in, $1250/mo. Free 24hr msg 555-5555

Box 5.1   A Sample of Actual Ads That Feature Seller-Assisted Financing

1. Do they want or need a quick sale?
2. Do they seriously need cash?
3. Would a safe 6 to 8 percent return seem attractive to them?
4. If the property is currently owned by investors, what kind of capital gains tax liability will these sellers incur from an all-cash sale? Would an IRS-approved installment sale save the sellers taxes?
5. What do the sellers plan to do with the proceeds of sale?
6. What pressures of time, money, family, or work bear on the sale?

These questions suggest lines of inquiry. Tactfully learn as much about the sellers as you can. Then draft your offer to play into their most pressing needs.

Explain point-by-point how your offer alleviates their concerns without giving rise to new ones. Are you a credible buyer? Does the proposal create too much risk? A skilled Realtor may be able to help you achieve a good result. A confused mind often says no. Eliminate seller doubts with clear and compelling reasons.

What Type of Seller Financing?

"Seller financing" doesn't refer to a single technique. As you gain experience, you'll find that the wide flexibility of seller-finance techniques gives OWC considerable advantage over bank financing. Here are several of the most popular ways that sellers can cooperate and participate in the financing arrangement:

- ◆ Mortgage or trust deed
- ◆ Contract-for-deed
- ◆ Lease option
- ◆ Master lease
- ◆ Lease purchase
- ◆ Mortgage assumption
- ◆ "Subject to" purchase
- ◆ Wraparound

Generally, when you finance your property with a bank, the bank loans you money (which is immediately turned over to the sellers), and you sign a mortgage (or depending on the state where you are buying property, the lender may use a deed of trust). By signing a promissory note and mortgage, you assume personal liability and pledge the property as security for the loan. If you fail to make payments, the lender can follow a legal procedure to auction the property at a public foreclosure (trustee) sale and/or levy against your income or other assets.

Seller Mortgages (Trust Deeds)

Seller mortgages work about the same as bank mortgages—except that no money (aside from your down payment, if any) changes hands. Instead, the sellers deed you their property in exchange for your pledge to pay the sellers installments (usually monthly payments).

But like a bank, if you fail to pay as agreed, the sellers can file a foreclosure lawsuit against you. If the sellers win, the property will be sold to the highest bidder at a public auction. You (and quite likely the sellers) will lose money. Foreclosure sales seldom bring in enough money to make everyone whole. You might also suffer a deficiency judgment just as is possible with lender financing.

> **Persuade the sellers with credibility and benefits.**

Because OWC sellers can lose money if you default, most owners prefer to cash out at the time of sale. They don't want the risk. Therefore—especially in low-down (or nothing-down) deals—emphasize two points to persuade the sellers:

Your Credibility and Reliability   Even though few sellers will put your credit and finances under a magnifying glass, they still want to believe that you will pay on time, every time. You must persuade sellers of your credibility and reliability.

To achieve this goal, marshal as much convincing evidence as you can. Emphasize your consistency, character, and when favorable, credit scores (see Chapter 3). In addition, if you've built a significant net worth, accumulated cash reserves, or maybe you earn a good income from a secure job, accent any or all of these positives.

Seller Benefits   Also explain the benefits the sellers will receive. Many sellers fear to carry back financing because they prefer the peace of mind provided by a cash sale. But after I persuade them of my credibility *and* the advantages they can reap, as often as not, they are willing to negotiate the issue.

What do the sellers get out of the deal? Sellers carry back financing for some combination of these six reasons:

1. *No bank financing available.* A property may not qualify for bank financing. The property might suffer poor condition; be located in a less-desirable neighborhood; or stand functionally out-of-date (rooming house, apartment units with shared bathrooms, irregular floor plan). Also, many lending institutions won't write mortgages on condominiums where more than 30 or 40 percent of the units in the complex are occupied by renters instead of owners.

2. *Quick sale.* To sell quickly, take back financing. Do the sellers want to move on with their lives? Then follow the adage, "a buyer at hand is worth two 'maybes' six months into the future." Emphasize the here and now.

3. *Higher price.* Property owners who accept financing can often sell at a higher price than they otherwise could expect to receive.

4. *High interest on savings.* Sellers who plan to deposit the cash they receive from a sale in certificates of deposit or money market accounts can get a higher return on their money by financing a buyer's purchase of their property. A 6 to 8 percent return from an installment sale beats a 4 or 5 percent return from a bank certificate of deposit.

5. *Low closing costs.* With OWC financing, sellers (and buyers) pay less in closing costs. You both avoid much of the expense that a mortgage lender would charge.

6. *Tax savings.* For investors, an installment sale produces a smaller income tax bite than does a cash sale. Installment sales permit sellers to spread their taxes on depreciation recapture and capital gains over the entire term of the mortgage.

As we look to the future, the aging of the U.S. population will bring about more seller-financed transactions. Savings accounts offer too little interest. Stocks offer too much risk. As a result, more seniors will prefer the larger returns of seller financing.

Who Handles the Legal Work?

In a some states, chiefly in the northeast, lawyers get themselves involved in most property purchases—with or without seller financing. In the majority of states, sellers and buyers set up an escrow account with a title insurance company. Experienced personnel at the title company then take care of the paperwork. I have used this approach many times and have never run into any difficulties.

> **Typically, a title company can handle the OWC paperwork.**

Nevertheless, as a beginning investor, you may want to discuss the details of your deal with a knowledgeable and trustworthy real estate attorney. True, lawyers often create more problems and expenses than they're worth. And many real estate investors feel this way. Still, when necessary, we do use them.*

Try a Contract-for-Deed

Among the most famous lines in American silent film history (in *The Perils of Pauline*) is Oil Can Harry's repeated warnings to Pauline, "If you don't give me the deed to your ranch, I'm going to tie you to the railroad tracks." Oil Can Harry knew that if Pauline signed over the deed to her ranch, that deed would transfer the property's title to Harry. Although Oil Can Harry's no-money-down approach to property ownership was somewhat unorthodox (not to mention illegal), typically, whenever people buy real estate, they receive a deed at the time of purchase. With the deed comes ownership (albeit often subject to a mortgage).

> **Some types of OWC delay the transfer of deed.**

In some purchases, though, buyers don't receive a deed at the time of sale. Instead, they contract for a deed via an installment plan. In this type

---

*For more on taking advice from lawyers, real estate agents, friends, and family, see my book, *The 106 Common Mistakes Homebuyers Make—And How to Avoid Them*, 4th ed. (Hoboken, NJ: John Wiley & Sons, 2006), pp. 222-226.

of purchase, buyers usually pay the sellers a small down payment and promise to pay monthly installments. In return, the sellers give the buyers possession. But unlike a mortgage, the sellers don't deliver the deed at closing. Rather, they agree to deliver a deed to the buyers only after the buyers have completed their scheduled payments (or perhaps after, say, five years of timely payments—after which a mortgage is issued to secure the remaining installments.

This type of OWC agreement is known by various names such as *contract-for-deed, installment sale*, or *land contract*. For beginning investors, a land contract can provide a good way to buy property. I know from experience.

Why Sellers Are Willing

When I turned age 21, I wanted to acquire real estate as quickly as possible. At the time I was an undergraduate college student. I had little cash, no full-time job, and no credit record. In those days, banks would not write mortgages for unemployed college students. But this fact didn't deter me. I searched for owners who would sell their properties on an installment contract. By the time I completed my Ph.D., I had bought more than 30 houses and small apartment units. The cash flow from these properties paid my college expenses.

My sellers accepted this type of OWC financing for most (or all) of the reasons I listed. But the contract-for-deed then offered sellers one more important advantage. If I failed to make payments, the sellers could repossess the financed property—almost as easily as a bank can repossess a car.

Today, though, many states have made it tougher for sellers to repossess properties. Now, courts sometimes force contract-for-deed sellers to file a foreclosure lawsuit. Buyers gain more protection, but sellers want to avoid such a burden. So (in the tough states), the land contract has lost much of its popularity to the lease option (discussed later).

Follow These Guidelines

When you and the property you buy meet the qualifying standards of a lending institution, great. You can weigh the relative costs and benefits of each type of financing. But, if bank financing is not available, negotiate a contract-for-deed (or seller-held mortgage). Buying from a seller on the installment plan beats not investing at all. If you're a cash-short buyer, you can gain in the following way: Buy a rundown property with an installment contract. Create value through improvements. Refinance based on the now higher value of the property. Pay off the sellers and put title in your own name.

Nevertheless, stay alert for potential pitfalls. When you finance a property with a contract-for-deed (or other type of OWC), follow these guidelines:

1. *Buy the property, not the financing.* Don't use easy credit to purchase an overpriced property. When the numbers make sense, you might in good judgment pay a price slightly higher than market value. But you would not pay $8,000 for a 1998 Taurus from Easy Ed's "buy here, pay here" used car lot just because Easy Ed will sell it to you with nothing down and low monthly payments. This same principle applies to investment properties. Beware of the real estate gurus who urge you to entice the seller with the proposition, "You name the price; I'll name the terms." Verify value through an appraisal or other professional opinion. Pay only the amount the property is worth.

2. *Watch for hidden defects.* A property that seems priced right might suffer hidden defects. Take care to obtain experienced and knowledgeable estimates for repairs or renovations. Never "ballpark" or casually figure the costs necessary to bring a property up to the standards you want. Obtain professional property inspections and cost estimates before you invest.

3. *Law governs contract terms.* State law and court decisions as well as the language of the installment sale contract set your rights and responsibilities. Under such a contract, your relationship with the sellers differs from the relationship you acquire when you finance a property with a mortgage or trust deed.

Before you sign an installment-sale agreement, consult a real estate attorney who can explain the applicable land contract law. Many lawyers warn against buying a property on the installment plan because these contracts pose more risk to buyers than a mortgage agreement. These

> **Don't let a lawyer derail you without detailing benefits as well as risks.**

lawyers look at risks without considering benefits and opportunities. (Using similar logic, such lawyers would advise against marriage because you might suffer the pain of divorce.)

Get a lawyer who understands rewards and risks. Then negotiate a contract-for-deed that can work for you and the sellers. Over the years, millions of people have successfully bought houses and rental properties on the land contract installment plan. I am one of them.

Assume a Low-Interest-Rate Mortgage

Although technically not a form of seller financing some sellers do permit you to take over their current mortgage. This process is called "assuming the sellers' financing." Seller assumables may offer distinct advantages over new financing:

- ◆ Lower interest rate
- ◆ Easier qualifying
- ◆ Low closing costs
- ◆ Little or nothing down

Return to the Past with an Assumable Loan

When market interest rates climb up, you need not pay those higher rates. Instead, shop for a property with a low-interest-rate assumable loan. Say it's three years into the future and you want to buy a property. But market interest rates are again hovering around 9 percent. You recall those bygone days when 30-year fixed rate loans were available at 6 percent. If only you could climb into a time machine. You can. Here's how.

When you assume a mortgage, you roll back the clock and take over the mortgage of the seller at the rate the seller is paying—even if that rate sits well below current market rates. Years ago, nearly all sellers

> **Many assumable mortgages still exist.**

could transfer their low-rate mortgages to their buyers. By the early 1980s, however, most lenders had changed their mortgage contracts to include the "due on sale" clause. This clause prohibits routine assumptions and upon sale (or long-term lease) requires sellers to pay off their mortgage balance.

To their detriment, most people today erroneously believe that *all* assumption possibilities have died. To compound this mistake, loan reps seldom tell borrowers about assumptions because assumptions take place directly between sellers and buyers. You cannot walk into a lender's office and say, "I'd like one of those low-rate, assumable mortgages that's going to save me tens of thousands of dollars." Before you can assume a real estate loan, you must locate a seller who has one.

Which Sellers Can Offer Assumable Financing?

Generally, sellers who have financed their properties with FHA, VA, or many types of adjustable-rate mortgages can offer an assumption to their buyers.

For example, over a period of 5 years on a $100,000 loan, as compared to a 9 percent new mortgage, a 7 percent assumable will

> **Loan assumptions can save you big dollars.**

save you $8,400 in interest. Over 10 years, the savings are nearly $17,000; and over 25 years, you'll keep an extra $42,000. And those numbers don't include the $2,000 to $4,000 that an assumable might save you in points, origination fees, appraisal, and closing costs. Now, you can see why a good low-interest assumable is worth a pile of $1,000 bills.

Short-Term Strategies

In some instances, you can even gain when you assume a mortgage that carries a higher-than-market interest rate. Say current rates are at 6.5

percent and you negotiate with a seller whose assumable mortgage carries an interest rate of 7.5 percent. Not worth assuming? Don't jump to that conclusion. Assumptions usually cost less in terms of time, effort, and cash-to-close than new mortgage originations. So, this 7.5 percent loan assumption could prove profitable if

1. You plan to sell the property within two or three years.
2. Inflation has dropped to almost zero, and interest rates are likely to fall. You want to wait to originate your new mortgage to coincide with the lower rates that you foresee.
3. You plan to improve the property to increase its value. Then, take out a new loan based on the higher property value that you have created.
4. Your borrower profile displays some warts. New financing at the lowest rates available could prove iffy. In contrast, qualifying for the assumption probably will not require the same exacting standards. One year or two years of perfect payments could set you up to then qualify for a new loan as an "A" borrower.

How to Find Assumables   Right now, millions of outstanding FHA and VA loans (fixed-rate and adjustable) permit assumptions. Plus, most conventional (Fannie Mae/Freddie Mac) and portfolio lenders will allow sellers to transfer their adjustable-rate mortgage (ARM) loans to buyers. To find these loans requires you to ask sellers and investigate. Sellers or their realty agents either don't know or don't publicize mortgage assumptions. But, when interest rates shoot up, the search for assumables becomes intense. Savvy sellers and agents then tout their assumables to favorably differentiate their properties from others that require buyers to obtain costly new financing.

> **You can assume (as an owner-occupant) any FHA/VA mortgage.**

> **ARMs also offer assumable possibilities.**

Lower-Rate Assumable ARMs   Nearly all adjustable-rate mortgages include lifetime rate caps. No matter how high market interest rates climb, ARM borrowers know that their loan rate will max out at 8, 9, 10, or 12 percent (or possibly higher). Therefore, in periods of very high mortgage rates, you may find ARMs that are maxed out (or close to maxed out), yet still sit below the going rates for new ARMs or new 30-year, fixed-rate mortgages. In that case, you're sitting pretty. Your (assumable) ARM rate can't go up (much), but it can go down as rates again cycle to lower levels.

Search for Sellers with Low-Equity Assumables

You've seen that in periods of higher interest rates, you can slash thousands from your interest costs by assuming a mortgage that carries a below current-market interest rate. In addition, assumables can help you buy with little or nothing down. Locate a seller who has bought (or refinanced) recently with a low-down, high-LTV assumable mortgage. Within the past three or four years, FHA and VA have originated more than a million low- and nothing-down loans.

> **Assumables give you another low-down-payment possibility.**

Because original loan balances often add in closing costs and fees, most of these recent buyers (now sellers) have built little equity in their properties. In many instances, you can assume for less than 10 percent cash out-of-pocket. In cases where sellers do own substantial equity, ask for a seller carryback or arrange a second mortgage through a mortgage lender.

"Assume" a Nonassumable Mortgage

Most (but not all) *non*-FHA/VA long-term fixed-rate mortgages include a clause that reads (in part) as follows:

> ¶ 18. If all or any part of the [mortgaged] property or an interest therein is sold or transferred by the Borrower *without Lender's prior written consent. . . . Lender may, at Lender's option, declare* all the sums secured by this Mortgage to be immediately *due and payable.*

Few people understand this clause, but understanding holds meaning for you.

What This Clause Does and Does Not Say

Notice that nothing in this paragraph prevents owners from selling you their property *without* first paying off their mortgage. This clause only gives lenders the right to call the mortgage due and payable if such a transfer occurs without "Lender's prior written consent."

You Can Assume a "Nonassumable" Mortgage

Nothing prevents you and a seller from asking a lender to give its written consent. Why would the lender agree to accept your request? Here are several reasons:

1. The sellers have fallen behind in their payments, and you agree to bring the mortgage current.
2. The interest rate on the mortgage equals or exceeds the current market rate. Lenders hate "portfolio runoff" of their market or above-market rate loans.
3. You, the sellers, or both parties give the lender substantial amounts of other business (loans, CDs, savings and checking accounts).
4. You (or the sellers) promise to move much of your banking business to the lender.

Will these or other reasons persuade the lender to consent? Sometimes yes, sometimes no. But it pays to ask. When the situation warrants, lenders oblige.

Take care, though. Most people ask the wrong question and therefore get the wrong answer. When looking at a property, they query the seller or agent, "Is the financing assumable?" If the mortgage includes a due-on-sale clause, the sellers or real estate agent will routinely answer, "No, the mortgage is not assumable." Wrong answer. The correct answer is, "Yes, it's assumable with the lender's consent. If you would like to try to assume it, we can make the lender an offer."

Buying Subject to: "Assuming" without Consent

Again I emphasize that the "due on sale" clause does not stop owners from selling a mortgaged property to anyone they choose to. Nor in such sales does the clause *require* the sellers or the buyers to pay off the loan. This clause merely gives the lender the right (or option) to call the loan due.

> **Sellers willing, you can buy any property with "subject to" financing.**

Sometimes when buyers and sellers believe that a lender won't grant an assumption, they complete the sale anyway and never inform the lender that the property has passed to a new owner. The new buyer then continues to make the payments to the lender on the same terms and interest rate that applied to the sellers. Contrary to what some people say, this "subject to" technique is neither illegal, immoral, or fattening. It does not even violate the mortgage contract.

How I Have Used a "Subject To"   I have used "subject to" financing with a number of property purchases. Some years back, for example, market mortgage rates were at 16 percent. I bought a property "subject to" that carried a mortgage rate of 10 percent. Because this property was a "flipper," I only owned it 18 months. But even during that short period, the "subject to" mortgage arrangement saved me $17,000 in interest, points, and closing costs.

> **Never use "subject to" financing without weighing risks.**

Beginners Beware   Several current authors and real estate get-rich-quick gurus are now peddling the "subject to" technique to the uninformed and inexperienced. Only instead of advising it for saving money on interest, they're pushing it to the credit-impaired as a means to buy a property without lying prostrate before a lender. Here's my advice: Beginners beware! Although this technique can prove appealing in some situations—short-term holding periods, high interest mortgage environment, credit impaired—don't blindly fall for the sweet talk of the gurus. "Subject to" financing holds risks for sellers and buyers. If you don't pay the lender on time, the lender chalks up late payments in the seller's credit record. If the lender calls the loan due, someone must either pay up or refinance the property.

Will Lenders Really Call the Loan?   Some real estate gurus say, "Don't worry. Here's a bag of tricks. Use these tricks, and the lender won't find out about the property transfer. Surely what the lender can't see won't hurt you. No problem. Just keep the lender in the dark."

Do these tricks work? Maybe, maybe not. After suffering through the tumultuous 1980s and early 1990s, lenders have become more savvy. Within a year or two after a sale, the lender will probably learn that the previous owner (and original borrower) has sold you the mortgaged property.

"No worry," the gurus say. "Even if the lender discovers the transfer, chances are the lender won't call the loan due. Most lenders follow a 'don't ask, don't tell' policy. But they're not going to advertise their forbearance. As long as your mortgage payments keep flowing in on time and the property taxes and insurance get paid, your risks are small."

On this point (for now at least) the gurus may be right. That's because today interest rates on most "subject to" mortgages do not differ much from market rates. If rates spike up, though, lenders may send out the enforcers. Stay prepared.

Use "subject to" financing to solve a *short-term* need. But, over the longer term, you'll probably need to come up with another source of financing—especially if the spread between the "subject to" interest rate and the market rate hits 3 percent or more (e.g., 6 percent old rate and 9 percent current market rate).

CHAPTER 6

Five More Techniques to Finance Your Investments

You find a property that you would like to buy, but instead of a mortgage assumption or "subject to" purchase, the seller proposes a wraparound mortgage. Especially in times of higher interest rates, a *wraparound* mortgage can provide a win-win solution for buyers and sellers.

Wraparounds Benefit Buyers and Sellers

Wraparound financing yields big savings for buyers at the same time that it puts profits into the pocket of sellers. Only the lender gets short-changed. Here's how a wraparound could work to overcome higher market interest rates:

Financial Facts

Asking price	$200,000
Mortgage balance	$100,000
Interest rate	6%
Term remaining (years)	20
Monthly payment	$716
Market interest rate	9%

You offer to buy the property for $200,000. If the seller agrees to finance $180,000 at 7.5 percent fully amortized over 20 years, your payment (P&I) equals $1,450 per month.* The underlying $100,000 mortgage remains in place, and its monthly payments will be paid by the seller. To complete the purchase, you sign a land contract, mortgage, or trust deed with the seller.

Each month the seller collects $1,450 from you and pays the bank a mortgage payment of $716 for a monthly net in the seller's pocket of $734 ($1,450 less $716). Because the seller has actually financed only $80,000 ($180,000 less the 100,000 still owed to the bank), he achieves an attractive rate of return of 11.1 percent.

$$Seller \text{ ROI } = \frac{\$8,808 \ (12 \times \$734)}{11.1\%}$$
$$= 11.1\%$$

Yet, you, too, gain. Had you financed $180,000 with a bank at the market rate of 9 percent amortized over 20 years, your payment would to-

> **You gain a lower interest rate. The seller gains a high return.**

tal $1,619 per month instead of the $1,450 that you'll pay the seller. The actual spread between the current market interest rate, the seller's old bank rate, and the interest rate you pay the seller will depend on the motives and negotiating power of you and the seller. But this example shows how a wraparound can benefit both parties—true win-win financing.†

Lease Option

Would you like to own a property? Yet, for reasons of blemished credit, self-employment (especially those with off-the-books income or tax-minimized income), unstable income (commissions, tips), or lack of cash, do you believe that you can't currently qualify for a mortgage (at a reasonable cost) from a lending institution? Then the lease option (a lease with an option to purchase) may solve your dilemma. The lease option permits you to acquire ownership rights in a property and gives you time to improve your financial profile.

---

*You also pay for the property insurance, property taxes, maintenance, and upkeep.

†If the lender can enforce a due-on-sale clause, this technique does bring about that risk. In that situation a wraparound works better as a short-term financing strategy. If the lender calls, there may be no long term.

How It Works

As the name implies, the lease option combines two contracts into one: a lease and an option to buy. Under the lease, you sign a rental agreement that covers the usual rental terms and conditions (see Chapter 17), such as:

- Monthly rental rate.
- Term of lease.
- Responsibilities for repair, maintenance, and upkeep.
- Sublet and assignment.
- Pets, smoking, cleanliness.
- Permissible property uses.
- House rules (noise, parking, number of occupants).

The option part of the contract gives you the right to buy the property at some future date. As a minimum, the option should include (1) the amount of your option payment, (2) your purchase price for the property, (3) the date on which the purchase option expires, (4) right of assignment, and (5) the amount of the rent credits that will count toward the purchase price of the house.

Benefits to Tenant-Buyers (an Eager Market)

Since the mid-1990s, the benefits of lease options to tenant-buyers have been extolled by the respected, nationally syndicated real estate columnist Robert Bruss as well as by most books written for investors and first-time homebuyers. For example, in my book, *Yes! You Can Own the Home You Want* (New York: John Wiley & Sons, 1995, p. 59), I write,

> There's simply no question that lease options can bring property ownership closer to reality for many people in at least six ways:
>
> 1. *Easier qualifying.* Qualifying for a lease option may be no more difficult than qualifying for a lease (sometimes easier). Generally, your credit and employment record need meet only minimum standards. Most property owners will not place your

financial life under a magnifying glass as would a mortgage lender.

2. *Low initial investment.* Your initial investment to get into a lease option agreement can be as little as one month's rent and a security deposit of a similar amount. At the outside, move-in cash rarely exceeds $5,000 to $10,000, although I did see a property lease optioned at a price of $1.5 million which asked for $50,000 up front.

3. *Forced savings.* The lease option contract typically forces you to save for the down payment required when you exercise the option to buy. Often, lease options charge above-market rental rates and then credit perhaps 50 percent of your rent toward the down payment. The exact amount is negotiable. And once you commit to buying, you should find it easier to cut other spending and place more money toward your "house account."

4. *Firm selling price.* Your option should set a firm selling price for the home, or it should include a formula (perhaps a slight inflation-adjustment factor) that can be used to calculate a firm price. Shop carefully, negotiate wisely, and when you exercise your option in one to three years (or whenever), your property's market value could exceed its option price. If your property has appreciated (or you've created value through improvements—see below), you may be able to borrow nearly all the money you need to close the sale.

5. *100 percent financing possible.* You also can reduce the amount of cash investment you will need to close your purchase in another way: Lease-option a property that you can profitably improve through repairs, renovation, or cosmetics. After increasing the property's value, you may be able to borrow nearly all the money you need to exercise your option to buy the property.

Assume that your lease option purchase price is $75,000. Say by the end of one year, your rent credits equal $2,500. You now owe the sellers $72,500. Through repairs, fix-up work, and redecorating, you have increased the property's value by $10,000. The property should now be worth around $85,000. If you have paid your bills on time during the previous year, you can easily locate a lender who will finance your purchase with the full $72,500 you need to pay off the sellers. Or, as another possibility, you could sell the property, pay the sellers $72,500 and use your remaining $12,500 in cash proceeds from the sale to buy another property.

6. *Reestablish credit.* A lease option also can help you buy when you need time to build or reestablish a solid credit record. Judy and Paul Davis wanted to buy a home before prices or interest rates in their area rose above their reach. But the Davises needed time to clear up credit problems created by too much borrowing and Judy's layoff. The lease option proved to be the possibility that helped the Davises achieve their goal of home ownership.

Experience shows that when prospective tenants and homebuyers think through this list of benefits, they become a ready market for lease options.

Benefits to Investors

Although the lease option might help you buy a property, it can also prove to be a profitable way for you to rent out your investment property. You can structure lease options in many ways. This type of agreement can typically benefit you as an investor in three ways: (1) lower risk, (2) higher rents, and (3) guaranteed profits.

> **Lease-option tenants take better care of properties.**

Lower Risk As a rule, tenants who shop for a lease option will take better care of your property than would average renters. Because your lease-option tenants intend one day to own the property, they will treat it more like homeowners than tenants. Also, they know that to qualify for a mortgage they will need a near-perfect record of rent payments. (If your tenant-buyers don't know that fact, make sure you impress it into their consciousness.) Typically, lease-option tenants pay first and last month's rent, a security deposit, and, more than likely, an option fee of $1,000 to $5,000 (possibly more). Taken together, these factors spell lower risk for you the investor.

Higher Rents Lease-option tenants will agree to pay higher than market rents because they know you will apply a part of that monthly rent to the property's purchase price. The tenants view these "rent credits"—actually they should be called purchase price credits—as forced savings that will contribute toward a lender's required down payment.

> **Lease-option tenants typically pay higher rents.**

From your view, the higher rent payments increase your monthly cash flow and boost your cash-on-cash return. In high-priced areas where newly bought rental properties awaken a hungry alligator (negative cash flows), the increased rent from a lease-option rental may turn a negative cash flow into a positive.

Guaranteed Profits Experienced investors know that (on average) fewer than 50 percent of lease-option tenants take advantage of their right to buy their leased home. Sometimes they change their mind. Sometimes their finances fail to improve as much as they hoped. Sometimes their personal circumstances shift (separation, divorce, job relocation, additional children).

> **Lease-option tenants often forfeit their option payments and rent credits.**

Whatever the reason, the tenants forfeit (at least in part) their rent credits, option fee, and any fix-up work they have performed around the property. As a caring person, you may feel for the tenants. But as an investor, their loss means your gain. Because your tenants did not follow through with their purchase, you end up with more profit than you would have earned under a traditional rental agreement.

Even if the tenants do buy, you win, because in setting your option price, you added a profit margin to the price you originally paid for the property. The lease-option technique works well in transactions where you have bought at a bargain price. You net more than you would have gained from a straight sale of the property because you didn't have to pay high marketing costs or agent commissions.

For investors, the lease option means win-win. You win when your tenants buy; you win when the tenants don't buy and they forfeit their option payment.

How to Find Lease-Option Buyers and Sellers

To drive the best bargain on a lease option as a buyer/lessee, don't limit your search to sellers who advertise lease options. These sellers are trying to retail their properties. It will be tougher for you to find a bargain here. Instead, look for motivated for-sale-by-owner (FSBO) sellers in the "Homes for Sale" classified ads. Or you might also try property owners who are running "House for Rent" ads. Often, the best lease-option sellers will not have considered the idea until you suggest it.

When you search for tenant-buyers, generally you will choose from three different classified newspaper ad categories: (1) homes for sale, (2) homes for rent, and (3) the specific category "lease option" that some newspapers include. Unfortunately, no one can say which ad category will work best in your market. Experiment with each of these choices. To learn which one is pulling the best responses, ask your callers to tell you in which category they saw the ad. Don't simply assume that any single category listing will draw the largest number of eager callers.

A Creative Beginning with Lease Options (for Investors)

To start building wealth fast without investing much money up front, try the lease-option approach of Suzanne Brangham. Although Suzanne stumbled into her investment career, you can follow her path more purposely. From her book, *Housewise* (New York: HarperCollins, 1987, p. 39), here's Suzanne's story:

> While searching for the ideal career, I was also looking for a place to live. I located a lovely but dilapidated apartment house. The building was making a painful transition from rentals to condominiums. Units were for sale or rent. But sales were practically nonexistent.
>
> With my head held high, preliminary plans and a budget tucked under my arm, I decided to make the manager an offer he couldn't refuse.
>
> I told him that in lieu of paying the $800-a-month rent that was being asked for a 2-bedroom, 2-bath unit, I would renovate the entire apartment. I would agree to spend $9,600 for labor and materials, the equivalent of a full year of rent

payments. Along with a 12-month lease, I also requested an option to buy the unit at its $45,000 asking price.

Three months later, Suzanne was on her way. She then bought her renovated condo unit at her lease-option price of $40,000. Then, simultaneously, sold the unit to a buyer for $85,000. After accounting for renovation expenses, closing costs, and Realtor's commission, she netted $23,000. Suzanne no longer had a home, but she had found a career.

Twenty years, 23 homes, and 71 properties later, Suzanne had become not just independently wealthy, but a nationally recognized author, speaker, and entrepreneur. In her excellent book, *Housewise*, she tells about her renovation experiences and the career she found by chance. As I've said, it's a great book for anyone who would like to learn hundreds of profit-making ideas that can be applied to buying and renovating fixers.*

> **A $50,000 condo lease option led to a multimillion-dollar net worth.**

Lease-Purchase Agreements

As a practical matter, the lease-*purchase* agreement works about the same as a lease option. However, instead of gaining the right to either accept or reject a property, the lease-purchaser *commits to buying* it. As an investor, you can often persuade reluctant sellers to accept your lease-purchase offer, even though they may shy away from a lease option. The lease-purchase offer seems much more definite because you are saying that you will buy the property—you would just like to defer closing until some future date (say, six months to five years more or less) that works for you and the sellers.

"Seems" More Definite

I say "seems" more definite because there's a loophole. You can (and should) write an escape clause into your purchase offer called "liquidated

---

*See also my own book on this topic: *Make Money with Flippers, Fixer-Uppers, and Renovations*, 2nd ed. (Hoboken, NJ: John Wiley & Sons, 2008).

> **Use a liquidated damage clause in your purchase offers.**

damages." With a liquidated damages clause, the sellers could not sue you to go through with your purchase (specific performance) if you chose to back out. Nor could they sue you for money damages that they may have suffered due to your failure to buy. Instead, the liquidated damage clause permits your sellers to pocket your earnest money deposit.

In effect, your earnest money acts like an option payment. No matter what the purchase contract appears to say, you have not legally committed to buy.

Amount of the Earnest Money Deposit

The real firmness of either a lease-option or a lease-purchase contract lies in the amount of the up-front money the seller receives—regardless of whether it's called an "option" fee or an "earnest money" deposit. If you want to show a seller that you intend to complete a lease-option or a lease-purchase transaction, place a larger amount of upfront cash into the deal. If you do want to "keep your options open," negotiate the smallest walkaway fee that you can, even if it means conceding elsewhere in the agreement.

Contingency Clauses

To provide another escape from your obligation to buy a property, use contingency clauses. If the contingency (property condition, ability to obtain financing, lawyer approval, sale of another property, etc.) isn't met, you can walk away from a purchase and at the same time require a return of your earnest money or option fee. (Contingencies, option fees, and earnest money deposits are further discussed in Chapter 16.)

Master-Lease an Apartment Building

To make money in real estate, you need to control a property. Ownership offers ultimate control. Some investors, though, don't buy their investment properties—at least not right away. Instead, they master-lease them. As we just discussed, buyers and sellers typically use a lease-option agreement to convey condominiums and single-family homes. But to acquire (without purchase) apartment buildings, you would use a master lease.

A Turnaround Property

Say you locate a 12-unit apartment building that is poorly managed and needs upgrading. You might offer to buy the property. But you lack the credit to arrange new financing. The owner doesn't want to use a land contract or purchase-money mortgage to finance the sale.

> **You control the property without much cash.**

The property barely produces enough cash flow to pay expenses, property taxes, and mortgage payments. The owner would like to turn this money pit into a money-maker, but lacks the will to invest time, effort, money, and talent.

The solution: master-lease the entire building and guarantee the owner a steady no-hassle monthly income. In return, you obtain the right to upgrade the building and manage the property to increase its net operating income (NOI).

Generally, a master lease gives you possession of the property for a period of 3 to 15 years and an option to buy at a prearranged price. During the period of your lease, you would pocket the difference between what you pay to operate the property, including lease payments to the owner, and the amounts you collect from the individual tenants who live in each of the apartments. Here's how the before-and-after numbers might look:

Before (Owner Management)

Gross potential income at $500 per unit	$72,000
Vacancy losses at 15%	$10,800
Effective gross income	$61,200
Expenses	
Utilities	$14,400
Maintenance	$8,360
Advertising	$2,770

Insurance	$3,110
Property taxes	$6,888
Miscellaneous (evictions, attorney fees, bad debts, vandalism, pest control, bookkeeping, etc.)	$5,000
Total expenses	$40,528
Net operating income	$20,672
Mortgage payments	$19,791
Before-tax cash flow (cash throw-off)	$881

After (i.e., Under Your Management)

Gross potential income at $575 per unit	$82,800
Vacancy losses at 4%	3,312
Effective gross income	$79,488
Expenses	
Utilities	$2,230
Maintenance and upkeep	13,200
Advertising	670
Insurance	2,630
Property taxes	7,300
Miscellaneous (evictions, attorney fees, bad debts, vandalism, pest control, bookkeeping, etc.)	2,500
Total expenses	28,530
Net operating income	$50,958
Leasehold payments to owner (master lessor)	25,000
Before-tax cash flow (master lessee)	$25,958

How to Achieve Your Turnaround

How can you achieve such a large income-boosting turnaround? (1) Upgrade the property and implement a thorough maintenance program; (2) your more attractive property and more attentive management will attract and retain high-quality tenants; (3) meter (or submeter) the apartment units individually to reduce utilities; (4) raise rents to reflect

> **Property turnarounds increase cash flows and boost the property's value.**

the more appealing condition of the property and the more pleasant ambiance created by the new higher-quality, neighbor-considerate, rule-abiding tenants; (5) shop for lower-cost property and liability insurance coverage; and (6) reduce turnover and encourage word-of-mouth tenant referrals to eliminate advertising expenses.

Not only did this turnaround increase the property's net income (NOI), but, correspondingly, the higher NOI, lower risk, and more attractive apartments lifted the value of the building. This means that when you exercise your option to buy, you can arrange 100 percent financing to pay off the owner, yet still give the lender a 70 to 80 percent loan-to-value ratio as measured against the property's new higher market value.

Sell Your Lease-Option Rights

Instead of buying your master-leased property, you might sell your leasehold and option rights to another investor. Given the much higher NOI that you've created, you can assign your rights at a good price markup. In effect, an investor would pay for the right to earn $25,958 per year (plus future rent increases) for the remaining term of the master lease. He would also gain the right to buy the property at your (now below market) option price.

A master lease with option to buy can create great profit opportunities for investor-entrepreneurs who turn a poorly managed, run-down apartment building into an attractive, effectively operated residence for high-quality tenants.

CHAPTER 7

How to Come Up with the Cash to Close

You now know several dozen ways to acquire investment properties with little- or nothing-down financing. Yet, even 100 percent loans may require some cash to close.

Plus, you may find a great mortgage assumption or "subject to" deal where the seller needs to cash out the substantial equity that he has accumulated in his property. So, for most of your investments, you will need to bring some cash to the closing table.

Here are 18 ways to come up with all or part of this money.

Cash Out Some of Your Current Home's Equity

> A low-cost home equity loan makes an excellent source of cash to expand your real estate wealth.

If you've owned a home for a number of years, you've no doubt built up tens (perhaps hundreds) of thousands of dollars in equity. Through either a home equity loan or a cash-out refinance, you can raise money at favorable rates. Some high-equity homeowners refinance their homes with large mortgages and then use the proceeds for cash bids on fix-up properties at discount prices.

If your home has proved to be a good investment, now's the time to leverage up. Put some of that equity into buying and renovating properties. You might downsize. Move (at least temporarily) into a smaller less expensive home. To raise more cash and credit power for investing in real estate, you could even rent for a while.

Don't tie up large chunks of capital in your house when you could use that money to accelerate your wealth building. During the early- to mid-2000s, tens of thousands of California homeowners pulled cash out of their properties to invest in higher cash flow areas such as Nevada, Arizona, Texas, and North Carolina.

> **Millions of people with money and credit would like to invest in real estate.**

Bring in Partners

Think. Who do you know that would like to earn the profits that real estate can provide, but lacks the time or inclination to take an active role? Partners can provide cash to the deal and also enhance your credibility and borrowing power.

> **Partners can provide the money. You provide the talent, time, and business plan.**

Attract Money with a Business Plan

As you gain experience and credibility, you will raise money based on your reputation and achievements. When you start, though, I recommend that you write out a business plan for two reasons:

1. *Think it through.* When you write a business plan, you think through your investment project and goals from start to finish. As you write, you clarify. You see glitches (and perhaps opportunities) that casual analysis misses.
2. *Credibility.* Think from an investor's perspective. Which approach would persuade you to invest in a property? Someone asks, "Hey, how would you like to invest $20,000 in a real estate

deal I'm putting together?" Or she says, "Here's a copy of my business plan for a real estate investment that I'm acquiring. As you can see from this market and financial analysis, a $20,000 secured investment will pay back $30,000 within six months."

To write this plan, highlight the market and property data (discussed later). To boost your credibility, pinpoint risk factors and how you're prepared to deal with them. For example,

- ◆ What if interest rates go up?
- ◆ What if your repair and improvement costs exceed the estimate?
- ◆ What if the rent raises or value-enhancing improvements take longer than planned?
- ◆ What if rental or sales prices begin to soften?

> **Don't overpromise. Anticipate risks.**

All smart investors realize that no one can perfectly predict the future. You can, though, anticipate problems. Then take steps beforehand to alleviate, reduce, or eliminate them. "What if" questions help you build safeguards into your plans and prepare alternative exit strategies.

Seek Favored Partners

Because even the most promising partnerships (that is, marriages) can turn sour, choose your real estate partners carefully. Deal only with someone who's reasonable, easy to get along with, and lives by a personal code of integrity and fairness. If plans go awry as they sometimes do, you want a partner who will sit down and look at reasonable and fair ways to resolve the cause of the detour and cooperatively steer the investment back on track.

> **Choose a person with character first, money second.**

You do not want a partner who insists that you sign a 10-page, fine-print partnership agreement that has been drafted by his or her lawyer. The more you let the lawyers control your agreement, the more likely you and your partner will come to discord. Of course, here I'm talking about small deals—not multimillion-dollar agreements, when like it or not, the lawyers will help draft and negotiate the prospectus and documentation (especially if the deal raises SEC issues).

Lawyers would like you to believe that a good partnership requires an airtight partnership agreement that nails down precisely each partner's rights and responsibilities. Wrong! A good partnership requires good people as partners. If, for small deals, you (or your partner) think that you need a 10-page, fine-print document of legal jargon to set the terms of your agreement, that partnership is doomed from the beginning.

> **No fine-print contract can substitute for your partner's character.**

In your eagerness to do a deal, never jump for the money until you're perfectly confident that you and your investor(s) will work well together. No contract can substitute for the character and disposition of the people involved.

Second Mortgages

Say that you've found a great property, a motivated seller, and a low-interest-rate assumable (or "subject to") mortgage. You face just one problem. The existing mortgage has a balance of $190,000, the owner wants a price of $225,000. You can only come up with $20,000 in cash. How can you cover the $15,000 gap? Use a second mortgage.

> **Seller seconds reduce the amount of cash you need to close.**

A second mortgage stands in back of the lien of a first mortgage. Upon foreclosure, the sales proceeds go first to pay the highest priority lien. Then, if any money is left, lower-priority claims like a second mortgage, a third mortgage, or mechanic liens are paid. On any given property, lower priority liens mean larger risks. That's why second (third) mortgages typically carry higher interest rates than first mortgages.

> **All types of lenders grant second mortgages.**

To arrange second-mortgage financing, ask the seller to carry back a loan for $15,000 of your purchase price. If the seller won't or can't agree, turn

to a bank or private mortgage company. In the world of investment real
estate (and increasingly, too, in the world of home buying), cash-short
buyers use second mortgages to help close the gap between the amount
of the first mortgage financing and the purchase price of the property.

Personal Savings

How much cash can you raise from your personal savings and investments? If your answer comes in at anything under five figures (not
counting decimals!), work through some fiscal fitness exercises. For a
philosophy that leads to sensible spending and wealth building, see *The
Millionaire Next Door* by Thomas Stanley and William Danko (Atlanta:
Longstreet, 1996). Their PWAs (prodigious wealth accumulators) rarely
flaunt their wealth. Virtually every financial expert agrees that before
you can invest profitably, you must learn to spend *well below* your
means. Save, save, save.

Sell Unnecessary Assets

Besides your house, can you sell, trade, or downsize any assets? Do you
own cars, boats, jet skis, or expensive furniture? What about that no-
longer-pursued stamp or coin collection? I recently talked with one of
my readers who wanted to invest in properties but said she lacked cash.
"What would you recommend?" she asked. When I
queried her about assets that she could draw on, she
admitted that she and her husband owned a vacation
property at Lake Tahoe with $150,000 of equity.

> **Nearly everyone owns assets that could be sold to raise investment cash.**

Do you see the problem here? All of us love
our possessions. We don't want to give them up. But
ask yourself whether those assets are truly worth
the price you pay to own them. Several years back,
I owned a Porsche 911. Obviously, a car that I loved
to drive. But when I calculated my out-of-pocket

costs of ownership plus the money I could earn by investing the cash that I had tied up in the car, the decision to sell became a no-brainer.

Your decision to sell wasteful assets becomes even more important when you're shelling out money for monthly payments. Possessions you finance eat up your cash and pull down your borrowing power. Get rid of those unnecessary assets now. The returns you earn over time will permit you to later replace them many times over. (Also, as I have noted, cutting back on costly toys and material possessions leads to a simpler, higher quality of life.)

> **Learn to live with less so you can eventually enjoy far more.**

> **Build wealth to achieve financial freedom—not costly possessions.**

> **Be careful. "Easy-money" lenders play rough if you don't pay on time.**

Easy Money—Hard Terms

On those occasions when you exhaust other sources of cash and financing, you've got a possibility that I hesitate to mention, but will do so anyway. In some limited situations, you may want to turn to an easy-money lender. Within the real estate industry, such lenders actually work under the label of "private money" or "hard money." I call them easy-money lenders because they will loan you money to buy, improve, or refinance almost any type of property as long as you can fog a mirror.

Predatory Lending

In fact, some easy-money (or perhaps I should call them expensive money) lenders intentionally loan money to people who stand little chance of paying it back. Why? Because these lenders *want to foreclose* the property. Such lenders profit from this tactic for three reasons:

1. *Low loan-to-value ratio (LTV)*. Easy-money lenders only make loans where the property value greatly exceeds the amount borrowed.

2. *Immediate collection.* Unlike reputable mortgage lenders, these easy-money folks don't know the concept of forbearance. Miss a payment and they will sic the lawyers on you as soon as legally possible.

3. *High late fees and penalties.* Not only do these predatory lenders go after the delinquent amount owed on the mortgage, they punish you severely for your failure to make your payments as scheduled.

> **Be wary of hard money lenders.**

Both the state and federal governments have initiated an enforcement campaign against predatory lending practices. Two such lenders (Citigroup and Household Lending) recently paid a total of $700 million to settle charges of bilking tens of thousands of their mortgage customers. Although easy-money lenders make borrowing easier for the credit-impaired, such lenders also expect to receive a huge (and perhaps illegal or unconscionable) profit from these hard-money loans.

Why Would You Want to Deal with This Type of "Easy Money" Lender?

Lenders who specialize in easy money (i.e., expensive money) with hard terms appeal to three types of borrowers: (1) the poorly educated who don't really understand the terms and costs of the loan, (2) those who

> **Hard money might serve a short-term profit opportunity.**

need money so desperately that they'll sign away their future for immediate relief from some financial difficulty, and (3) optimistic real estate investors who care nothing about the hard, costly terms of the easy money because they imagine high profits from their venture. Assuming that you're not a type 1 or 2 borrower, I will focus on a type 3, the optimistic entrepreneur.

The Optimistic Entrepreneur   Say you find a desperate (that is, motivated) property owner who will sell you his $300,000 "as-is" property for $220,000 if you can come up with the cash within 10 days. You know that after putting in $25,000 for repairs and sweat equity, you could sell the property for $335,000. You want to grab this deal before someone else beats you to it. But how can you raise $220,000 on such short notice?

The answer: An easy-money-hard-terms lender. What will this loan cost you? Can't say for sure because the private mortgage industry includes thousands of small players as well as some of the major mortgage lenders (who often run their hard-money operations through off-brand subsidiaries). Each player sets its own costs, terms, and loan-to-value ratios. The structure of the deals also varies over time. Sometimes too much money is chasing too few borrowers. At other times, too many borrowers are chasing too little money.

> **Hard-terms lenders specialize in fast-cash deals.**

With all of these caveats in view, Table 7.1 shows how hard money can (in some cases) turn out a profitable deal.

Are these numbers realistic? Yes. Do they reflect a norm? Not necessarily. Expensive easy-money lenders remain idiosyncratic. Each deal is negotiated according to the particulars of the loan, the property, the lender, and the borrower. No Freddie Mac or Fannie Mae dictates rules.

Table 7.1   You *Might* Profit Using Hard Money

Source	Cash Needed	Cash Paid Back
Amount borrowed	$220,000	
Interest at 15% p.a. (6 months)		16,500
Settlement costs		9,000
Mortgage broker fee at 5%		11,000
Mortgage amount		220,000
Total	$220,000	256,500
Net cost of funds for 6 months		36,500
Your Expected Profit		
Sales price of renovated property		$335,000
Marketing costs at 6%		20,100
Cost of funds		36,500
Acquisition cost of property		220,000
Costs of improvements		25,000
Profit (before tax)		$78,500

Plus, this deal showed a great buy on the property, which is possible but not typical.

> **Before you sign up for hard money, take off your rose-colored glasses.**

Nevertheless, this example does show that, on occasion, you can earn a good profit—even after paying the high costs of a hard-terms lender. Before you sign for a loan agreement, though, take off your rose-colored glasses. Sharpen your pencil. Critically work through the numbers. Remember to include a liberal amount for the oops factor. If the profit still outweighs costs and risks, maybe you should go for it.

Where to Find This Easy Money   The classified ad section of most city newspapers includes a category entitled, "Loans," "Financing," or perhaps "Money to Lend." More often than not, these advertisers represent easy-money-hard-terms lenders. Also, look in your telephone book listings under mortgages and mortgage brokers. You're looking for listings that use language such as "credit problems okay," "nonconforming," "secured," "fast closing," "investor loans," "rehab acquisitions," "we buy mortgages and land contracts," or "no income verification." Box 7.1 shows a sampling of "easy-money" ads from the *New York Times* and a local newspaper.

PRIVATE LENDER
BRIDGE LOANS, 1 WEEK CLOSING
$500,000–$300 MILLION
BROKERS WELCOME
555-5555
Loans secured by Real Estate,
(even raw land) or any fixed asset.
No up front fee until agreement signed
http//www.kennedyfunding.com

COMMERCIAL MORTGAGE LOANS LOOK,
LIKE & LEND
NO APPRAISAL. 1 WEEK CLOSING
No adv. Fee. LES 555-5555
NEED MONEY FAST?
3 day closing. $100K—$10 Million

Real estate secured. No credit check.
No advance fee. 555-5555

COMMERCIAL LOANS
Mixed-use, Multi-Unit Busn., Const. No
Fee until agreement. All Type Credit.
$100K + Low Rates 555-5555

A Better Alternative
Good, bad and no credit
Call for 1st & 2nd
Mortgages WE BUY
MORTGAGES Midtown
Mortgage Co., Inc. 555-5555
4200 NW 43 St., # A-1

Box 7.1   Sample Ads for Hard Money Lenders

Use Credit Cards

Although quite risky, some investors take advantage of every credit card offer they receive in the mail. When they need quick cash to close a deal, they raise $10,000, $25,000, or even $100,000 from cash advances. Investors might pay cash for a property with the entire sum raised from credit cards.

> **Remember, though, too many credit cards lower your credit score.**

Naturally, neither you nor anyone else should use cash advances for long-term financing. On occasion, you might find plastic a good source to cover short-term needs. You might, for example, find a "steal" that you can renovate and immediately flip (resell) at a great profit. For example, buy the property "subject to" and cover cash-to-close with cash advances.

Personal Loans

Before credit card cash advances (which today are the most popular type of personal loan), personal loans were called signature loans. As you build wealth through real estate equity, you'll find that lenders will grant you signature loans for $10,000, $25,000, or even $100,000. You can use these signature loans to buy even more real estate. (Signature loans typically charge lower fees and interest rates than credit card cash advances.)

Although some mortgage lenders set rules against using personal loans for property down payments, a seller who finances your purchase will seldom investigate the source of your down payment.

Sweat Equity (Create Value Through Improvements)

Say you find a property that should sell (in tip-top condition) for around $300,000. Yet, because of its dilapidated state of repair as well as an eager seller, you can buy it for $160,000 with short-term no-money-down owner financing. You then contribute your labor and buy $10,000 in materials with your credit card (or signature loan).

Once you complete your work and bring the property up to its $300,000 market value, you arrange a 70 percent LTV mortgage with a lender. Then with the loan proceeds of $210,000, you pay off the seller and your credit card account. Voilà—you not only have achieved 100 percent financing for your acquisition price and expenses, you've created $130,000 of instant equity (wealth).

> **Sweat equity builds instant wealth.**

Eliminate Your Down Payment with Pledged Collateral

Want to borrow 100 prcent of your acquisition costs? Here's another possibility—pledged collateral. "We don't care where the collateral comes from," says Elmer Frank of First American Savings, "As long as we feel secure, we'll consider the loan. We've taken stocks, bonds, mortgages, retirement accounts, and once a Mercedes 300 SL Gullwing. We did, though, refuse to accept a racehorse."

Pledged Retirement Accounts

Elmer Frank adds, "Retirement accounts have become one of the most frequent sources of pledged collateral. We don't even require that the account belong to the buyers. We'll accept funds from any close family member. On no-down-payment mortgages, we usually like to see 30 percent, but for good customers, we've gone as low as 20 percent."

"In other words," Elmer continues, "we'll give homebuyers or investors a no-down-payment, 100 percent loan, if those buyers (or close relatives) move enough of their 401(k) funds to our bank to offset 20 or 30 percent of the property's purchase price. Last week, we closed a loan for a couple in their thirties who bought a $265,000 property. Between them, they earn $70,000 a year; but they had little savings

> **The account you pledge need not be your own.**

because they've been rapidly paying off their student loans. We financed their full purchase price without private mortgage insurance and the wife's mother deposited $75,000 of her IRA monies with us as additional collateral."

Other Types of Pledged Collateral

Retirement funds aren't the only source of pledged collateral you can use to offset a down payment. As Elmer Frank points out, his bank (like other lenders) will accept nearly any type of asset (savings account, stocks, bonds, perhaps even a valuable antique automobile). Of course, equity in other real estate also works as pledged collateral.

Student Loans

I bought my first investment properties while still in college. My friends used their college loans to pay for rent, food, clothing, tuition, and books, I used my student loans to acquire real estate. While my friends were stacking up debt, I was building wealth.

Do you have access to any easy money like student loans? If so, there's the cash you need to close your first investment. Student loans work great because you get a low interest rate, and you don't have to start paying them back until after you've been out of school for a year. Remember, too, I sought out seller financing—and the sellers (unlike banks) didn't ask where I was getting my down payment.

Use Creative Finance

To add to your quiver of finance techniques, here are several other possibilities:

◆ *Agree to swap services or products.* Does the seller need some service or expertise that you can render? Inventory your skills (law, medicine, dentistry, writing, advertising, accounting, landscaping, architectural, etc.). Include all talents and expertise of your profession, trade, and avocation. How about products? Say you own a radio station or newspaper. Trade off advertising time or space for a down payment.

Anything you can produce, deliver, or sell wholesale (at cost) might work. In numerous instances, I have provided real estate consulting services in exchange for a percentage of the development or acquisition.

◆ *Borrow (or reduce) the real estate sales commission.* Although most brokers and sales agents dislike this technique, on occasion buyers and sellers ask the agents involved in a transaction to defer payment until some later date. Some agents prefer to leave their commissions in the deal. In doing so, they avoid income taxes on these fees, while at the same time they build wealth through their interest earnings or by receiving a "piece of the action" (future profits from the later sale of the property).

◆ *Simultaneously sell part of the property.* Does the property include an extra lot, a mobile home, timber, oil, gas, or air or mineral rights? If so, find a buyer who will pay you cash for such rights. In turn, this money will help you close the deal.

◆ *Prepaid rents and tenant security deposits.* When you buy an income property, you are entitled to the existing tenants' security deposits and prepaid rents. Say you close on June 2. The seller of a fourplex is holding $4,000 in damage deposits and $3,800 in tenant rent money prepaid for the month of June. Together, the deposits and prepaid rents amount to $7,800. In most transactions, you can use these monies (credits at closing) to reduce your cash-to-close.

◆ *Create paper.* You've asked the seller to accept owner financing with 10 percent down. She balks. She believes the deal puts her at risk. Alleviate her fears and bolster her security. Offer her a lien against your car or a second (or third) mortgage on another property you own. Specify that when amortization and property lift your equity to 20 percent (LTV of 80 percent), she will remove the security lien she holds against your other property.

CHAPTER 8

Here's How to Qualify

Unless you pay cash for a property, you will need to satisfy a lender's (or seller's) approval criteria. Previously, we talked about character and credit, but you also must persuade a lender that you and/or the property will bring in enough money to meet all expenses, your other debt repayments, and the mortgage payment(s) on the property purchase you want to finance.

For most first-time investors who buy rental houses, condos, and small apartment buildings, this approval process pretty much follows the same qualifying process that you go through to finance a home. However, if you plan to finance an office building, shopping center, or mid-to-larger-sized apartment building, the lender will scrutinize the property's income more than your personal earnings. In this chapter we'll emphasize residential underwriting but will conclude with income properties.

Be Wary of Prequalifying (and Preapproval)

Most supposed experts in mortgage finance give this advice: "Before you even begin to shop for a property, meet with a lender to get prequalified for a loan.* With prequalification you'll learn *exactly* how much property you can afford. You won't waste time looking at properties outside your price range."

---

*Some say "preapproved." But that advice, too, fails to address the critical points raised here.

Superficially, this advice makes sense. Why order filet mignon on a hamburger budget? Yet, at a deeper level, this advice to prequalify does not necessarily promote your needs. You may be able to borrow far more than a prequalification (or preapproval) suggests.

Why Prequalifying Sometimes Underqualifies

In theory, prequalifying (preapproval) for a loan seems to make sense. If you look at properties you can't afford (unless you're just curious), you waste your time, and it may psych you up for a big letdown. But here's the rub: No 10-minute computer-qualifying exercise can measure you for a loan program the way a tailor might measure you for a new suit.

> **Preapproval programs are too simplistic.**

No simple qualifying formula can tell you "how much mortgage you can afford," or more important, "how much property you should buy." Plugging your current credit and finances into a prequalification or preapproval computer program pushes aside the real questions you need to answer:

1. What are your goals to build wealth?
2. How do your budget constraints differ (positively or negatively) from those assumptions embedded in the prequalification program?
3. Are your current spending, saving, and investing habits consistent with your life priorities?
4. How long do you plan to own the property?
5. What steps can you take to improve your credit record or credit scores?
6. What steps can you take to improve your qualifying ratios?
7. What percentage of your wealth do you want to hold in real estate investments?
8. What types of real estate financing (other than those loan programs offered by the lender you're talking with) might best promote your goals for cost savings or wealth building?
9. What types of real estate financing (other than those loan programs offered by the lender you're talking with) might best enhance your affordability?

10. What type of property (fixer, foreclosure, duplex, fourplex, multiunit apartment building, single-family house, condo, etc.) might best fit into your financial goals?

Although *some* loan reps will help you address financial and life-planning issues such as those listed above, most will not. The majority of loan reps lack the time, the intellectual acumen, and the practical knowledge necessary to guide you to your best investment and borrowing decisions. Never forget: Loan reps, like car salesmen, want you to buy the products they are selling. Would the sales agent at the Honda dealer advise you that the Chevy Impala offers better value? No? Then why would you expect the loan rep at the Old Faithful Mortgage Company to recommend loan alternatives that he does not offer?

> **Loan reps want you to buy what they are selling.**

Where You Stand versus Where You Want to Go

Most loan reps measure where you stand financially today. You must look into your personal future. Most lenders emphasize your ability and willingness to pay your mortgage as evidenced by their approval formula. You need not accept their view. You must decide for yourself. Should I buy more (or less) property than the standard underwriting formulas suggest? And correspondingly, should I borrow more (or less) than this lender's guidelines recommend?

> **You determine how much property you can afford.**

You Can Make Your Qualifying Ratios Look Better

If you buy anything up to a four-unit property (condo, single-family house, duplex, triplex, quad) and finance it through a mortgage lender, you will probably need to pass through the lender's qualifying standards. In addition to credit, the lender's underwriting program will likely incorporate two qualifying ratios: (1) the housing cost (front) ratio, and (2) the total debt (back) ratio. These ratios often apply regardless of

> **Always search for ways to improve your qualifying ratios.**

whether you apply for owner-occupied financing or investor financing.

Many run-of-the-mill loan reps will merely plug your financial data into their computer automated underwriting (AU) program. Savvy loan reps will do a "first-review" and then, if desirable, suggest ways that you can improve your financial profile.

Calculating the Ratios

With the widespread use of automated underwriting (AU) by computer, many loan reps and loan underwriters no longer calculate qualifying ratios. Nevertheless, qualifying ratios matter a great deal. Only now the math is hidden in the automated underwriting program.

But make no mistake. If you understand and improve your qualifying ratios, you raise the odds for approval and increase the amount the lender will loan you. Strong ratios may also lower your interest rate and mortgage insurance premiums (if any). Both the housing cost ratio and the total debt ratio give lenders a way to measure whether your income looks like it's large and dependable enough to safely cover your mortgage payments, monthly debts, and other living expenses. Of these two ratios, most AU programs weigh the total debt ratio most heavily.

> **Low ratios may decrease your interest rate and down payment.**

Housing Cost (Front) Ratio   You can easily figure your housing cost (front) ratio with this formula:

$$\text{Housing cost ratio} = \frac{(P\&I) + (T\&I) + (MI) + (HOA)}{\text{Monthly gross income}}$$

where: P&I represents principal and interest (the basic monthly mortgage payment).

T&I represents the amount you must pay monthly for property taxes and homeowners insurance.

MI represents the monthly mortgage insurance premium you may have to pay if you put less than 20 percent down.

HOA represents the monthly amount you may have to pay to a condominium or subdivision homeowners association.

To keep the numbers simple, say that your household income (including anticipated rent collections) equals $7,000 a month. To buy the property you want, you need a loan of $235,000. You want a 30-year, fixed-rate loan at 7 percent interest. This loan will cost $1,563 per month (235 × $6.65; see Table 8.1). Property taxes and homeowners insurance on this property will total $400 per month. No mortgage insurance applies, but you must pay the homeowners association $125 per month to maintain the community swimming pool, tennis courts, and club-house. Here's how to calculate the housing cost ratio for this example:

$$\text{Housing cost ratio} = \frac{\$1563 + 400 + 125}{\$7000}$$

$$= \frac{\$2088}{\$7000}$$

$$= 0.2998 \text{ or } 29.8\%$$

Because the lender you're talking with has set a housing cost guideline ratio of 28 percent, your numbers look as though they may work. So we next turn to the total debt ratio.

Table 8.1   Monthly Payment Required per $1,000 of Original Mortgage Balance

Interest (%)	Monthly Payment $	Interest (%)	Monthly Payment
2.5	$3.95	7.5	$6.99
3.0	4.21	8.0	7.34
3.5	4.49	8.5	7.69
4.0	4.77	9.0	8.05
4.5	5.07	9.5	8.41
5.0	5.37	10.0	8.77
5.5	5.67	10.5	9.15
6.0	5.99	11.0	9.52
6.5	6.32	11.5	9.90
7.0	6.63	12.0	10.29

Note: Term = 30 years.

Total Debt Ratio   The total debt ratio begins with your housing costs and then adds in monthly payments for all of your monthly payments (other mortgages, credit cards, student loans, auto loans, etc.). At present, say your BMW hits you for a payment of $650 a month, the Impala another $280. Your credit card and department store account balances total $8,000 and require a minimum payment of 5 percent of the outstanding balance per month ($400). Here are the figures:

$$\text{Total debt ratio} = \frac{\text{Housing cost} + \text{installment debt} + \text{revolving debt}}{\text{Monthly gross income}}$$

$$= \frac{\$2088 + 650 + 250 + 400}{\$7000}$$

$$= \frac{\$3388}{\$7000}$$

$$= 0.484 \text{ or } 48.4\%$$

With this loan program, the lender would like to see a total debt ratio no greater than 40 percent. Whoops. Looks like you've blown through the limits. But does this mean you won't get the loan—or maybe you'll have to settle for a lesser amount? Not necessarily.

If your credit score (see Chapter 3) is high enough, your loan may still get approved. If that doesn't work, maybe you can increase your qualifying income, reduce your monthly debt, or provide compensating factors.

You Can Lift Your Qualifying Income

In the previous example, we *assumed* that your income totaled $7,000 per month. In the real world, figuring your income presents a somewhat greater challenge (and opportunity). For to calculate *qualifying* income—that specific income amount entered into the denominator of your qualifying ratios—lenders evaluate a range of actual and potential income from sources such as:

◆ Salary	◆ Social Security
◆ Hourly wages	◆ Unemployment insurance
◆ Overtime	◆ Self-employment
◆ Bonuses	◆ Moonlighting/part-time job
◆ Commissions	◆ Tips
◆ Scheduled raises	◆ Disability insurance
◆ Alimony	◆ Stock dividends

◆ Welfare/ADC
◆ Pension
◆ Tax-free income
◆ Child support

◆ Interest
◆ Consulting
◆ Annuities
◆ Rent collections

As you look through this list, you can see that for many borrowers, no precise income figure can be calculated. Consider the entries for overtime, bonuses, and commissions. Over a period of months or years, these amounts could vary widely.

Or what about unemployment insurance payments? How could someone who's unemployed (or expects to become unemployed) ever hope to get qualified for a mortgage? Why would income from this source count? Well, I know a savvy loan rep who routinely gets unemployment insurance counted. His borrowers work during summer stock theater for very good wages. Then during the off-season, they collect unemployment. So, their qualifying income includes both their earnings from summer stock acting and their regular checks from the government.

Regularity, Stability, Continuity   Lenders count most any income that you can show as stable, regular, and continuing. Usually, a two-year history with a promising (realistic) future is enough to satisfy the lender. On the other hand, what if during the past five years you've typically earned sales commissions of $4,000 a month, but during the past eight months that income has jumped to $6,000 a month? Here, the loan rep or loan underwriter must make a judgment call—which you can influence. Show the loan rep persuasive evidence why your more recent earnings should weigh more heavily than those lower earnings of years past.

Or think about alimony and child support. A court order may require your ex-spouse to pay you $1,500 per month. But your spouse displays a casual indifference to honoring this legal decree. Sometimes you get paid. Sometimes you don't. So, what amount will the lender count as qualifying income? Again, a judgment call that you can influence according to how well you explain away your ex's past irresponsibility and provide assurances of future compliance.

> **You can increase your qualifying income.**

Anticipated Earnings   Sometimes you can persuade a lender to accept anticipated earnings that may lack a past or a present. Say your spouse has just taken a new job in Topeka. You previously worked as a teacher, but for family reasons, took leave for the past two years. Once your family gets settled in the new community, however, you plan to return to full-time teaching. Will the lender count your future earnings? With a good argument and evidence of intent, you probably can get at least part of this potential income included. In fact, Fannie Mae and Freddie Mac both offer dispensation for "trailing spouses."

> **Sometimes you can count future income.**

Recent college graduates (or recent graduates of professional schools such as nursing, law, medicine, business, or engineering) also can secure mortgages without immediate past or present income or employment. A contract for a new job may work to establish your qualifying income.

When Current Income Doesn't Count   For the past 12 years, you worked as a master mechanic at a Ford dealer. You earned $5,350 a month. Then, six months ago, you got hooked on Amway products. You quit your job at Ford and became an Amway sales distributor. Business was slow at first, but during the past three months you've cleared close to $25,000. Will this income qualify? Sorry, your newfound success would not impress most lenders. They would tell you to reapply after you prove your Amway sales skills for another 18 to 24 months.

Maximize Your Qualifying Income

> **Use your artistic skills. Paint the lender a pleasing picture.**

To gain loan approval and maximize borrowing power, present your income history, current earnings, and future prospects as optimistically as possible. Anticipate and effectively respond to any negative signals that may cause the lender to doubt the amount, stability, or continuing nature of your income.

Overcome the Negatives   If your earnings were lower last year only because you went back to school to get your M.B.A. so you could advance in your job, make sure the loan rep and loan underwriters know it. If last year you earned $60,000, but as of September 1 this year you've only taken in $40,000, show the lender that your big earnings season runs from September to December. Provide evidence that typically you earn 40 percent of your commissions during the last three months of the year. You're on track to outpace last year's record.

If your income is complicated by self-employment earnings, prepare explanations. For truly complex situations involving important amounts of money, enlist the aid of your accountant. Potential problems, for example, include tax losses offset by positive cash flow, or strong business profits, yet small wage or salary draws from the business (to minimize your personal income taxes). Many loan reps can't effectively understand these issues without guidance or persuasive input from you.

> **Self-employment income needs more explanations.**

Put Positives in Writing   Award-winning explanations can only sway hearts and minds when you put them on paper. Lenders follow this rule: "If it's not in writing, it doesn't exist." Mortgage underwriters need CYA paperwork piled higher and deeper, just in case a loan auditor investigates the files.

> **Write out persuasive explanations.**

Nearly all lenders today monitor loan quality and data integrity through internal audits. Without the paperwork to justify their loans, the lender could run into trouble with regulators, Fannie Mae, Freddie Mac, HUD, or bank insurers. So if you want a lender to view your past, present, and future income more favorably than it otherwise would, write out and deliver your evidence—before the lender formally reviews your application. (Even when an AU system approves your loan application, a human underwriter must still sign off on a loan commitment. You will be called upon to deliver documents and explanations such as tax returns, W-2s, 1099s, tenant leases, verification of employment, verifications of bank accounts, and statements to explain credit derogatories. Without adequate support, the underwriter can reject a loan. Also, with good supporting evidence, an underwriter can accept what AU has failed to approve.)

Reduce Your Disqualifying Debt

The flip side of income is debt. High monthly payments can block your loan approval or reduce the amount you can borrow. Total your current monthly payments from the list below.

◆ Car #1	_____	◆ Alimony	_____
◆ Car #2	_____	◆ Child support	_____
◆ Car #3	_____	◆ Merchant account #1	_____
◆ Motorcycle	_____	◆ Merchant account #2	_____
◆ Jet ski	_____	◆ Merchant account #3	_____
◆ Power boat	_____	◆ Judgments/liens	_____
◆ Furniture	_____	◆ Personal loans	_____
◆ Student loan(s)	_____	◆ Mortgage #1	_____
◆ Appliances	_____	◆ Mortgage #2	_____
◆ Credit card #1	_____	◆ Mortgage #3	_____
◆ Credit card #2	_____	◆ Other	_____
◆ Credit card #3	_____	◆ Other	_____
◆ Credit card #4	_____	◆ Other	_____
◆ Medical bills	_____		

Total monthly debt repayments $_____

What to Count, What to Leave Out

To calculate total debt ratio, lenders usually divide your monthly payments into two types: (1) installment debt, which includes loans you're paying off such as mortgages, autos, boats, medical bills, and student loans, and (2) revolving (or open) accounts, which include Visa, Mastercard, Amex Optima, Home Depot, Texaco, and other credit lines that remains open until you or your creditor closes it.

Not All Payments Count   Most lenders ignore payments for *installment* debts that are scheduled to be paid off within 6 to 10 months from the date of your mortgage application. But if the lease on your auto is set to end within a few months, you're out of luck. Those payments still count against you. The lender assumes (unless convinced otherwise) that you will continue to incur this expense when you lease a new car to replace the old one.

You do, though, get a break for qualifying when lenders look at your revolving debt. Even if you regularly pay hundreds of dollars more per month than your minimum payment(s) due, most lenders only count your payment as 5 percent of your outstanding balances. Or if your minimum payment is less than 5 percent, lenders count that lower amount instead.

Prepare Far Ahead of Time Get your debt situation shaped up as soon as you can. Not only will this fiscal fitness program lift your qualifying ratios, it *may* also boost your credit scores. Here are some tips:

1. *Consolidate bills.* One loan consolidation payment of $280 a month will hurt you less than four separate bill payments of $125 each. However, don't close three accounts and run one up close to its credit limit. Credit scoring doesn't like "high" balances relative to credit limits.
2. *Pay down debt.* If your installment debt has only 11 or 12 months to go, prepay two or three payments. That pushes those debts off the table and out of sight—under the rules followed by most lenders.
3. *Pay off debt.* If you can swing it, get rid of as much debt as you can.
4. *Avoid new debt.* No matter how much you are tempted, do not take on new debt prior to applying for a mortgage. Even if you can easily afford it, wait until after you've closed your mortgage. To build wealth, permanently swear off destructive debt—debt you incur to pay for depreciating assets or wants rather than needs.

These tips especially apply if your ratios push against the lender's guideline total debt limits, if your credit score falls below, say, 680, if you're requesting a low-down-payment loan (a loan-to-value ratio of greater than 80 percent), or if you're trying to qualify for a non-owner-occupied investment property.

A pint-sized debt load will help offset any warts in your borrower profile.

> **List the reasons why you will be able to pay your loan on time, every time.**

Use Compensating Factors to Justify Higher Qualifying Ratios

No two borrowers are exactly alike. That's why many lenders will bend their approval guidelines when you give them prudent reasons to do so.

Types of Compensating Factors What types of compensating factors might lenders consider?

Virtually anything positive that reasonably demonstrates you can make your monthly payments responsibly and control your finances. Here are a dozen examples:

- ◆ You've been making rent payments that equal or exceed the after-tax cost of your proposed mortgage payments.
- ◆ You have a good record of savings. You regularly spend less than you earn and you use credit sparingly.
- ◆ You are situated on the fast track in your career or employment. You have a good record of promotions and raises.
- ◆ For your age and occupation, you have a high net worth (cash value life insurance, 401(k) retirement funds, stocks, bonds, savings account, other investment real estate).
- ◆ You have put aside more than adequate cash reserves to handle unexpected financial setbacks.
- ◆ You or your spouse will generate extra income through part-time work, a second job, tips, bonuses, or overtime.
- ◆ You carry little or no monthly installment debt. This can work well when your housing cost ratio exceeds its guideline, but your total debt ratio falls well within the suggested limits.
- ◆ You've been through a homebuying counseling program that helps homebuyers develop a realistic budget. Fannie Mae and Freddie Mac lenders give special deals to first-time buyers who complete these programs. Many only last four hours, and they're worth the time.
- ◆ You're making a down payment of 20 percent or larger.
- ◆ Your employer provides excellent benefits: auto, cash reimbursement for a home office, a superior health and dental insurance plan, large contributions to your retirement account.
- ◆ You earn an above-average income. Budget-conscious people whose earnings exceed $6,000 or $8,000 a month often enjoy the financial flexibility to devote more money to real estate than typical qualifying ratios indicate.
- ◆ Your nonhousing living expenses are lower than average. You can afford higher mortgage payments because: (1) energy efficient property; (2) walk or drive a short commute to work; (3) no costly vices (smoking, drinking); (4) conservative lifestyle: backpack for vacations, drive an unassuming car, and buy clothes at

outlet stores; (5) handy with tools so you can perform your own property maintenance; or (6) food costs are low because you grow your own garden and enjoy all the fresh and home-canned vegetables you can eat.

Some of these compensating factors may seem petty, but you use details to positively impress the underwriter and establish your overall credit-worthiness.

Put Compensating Factors in Writing After you list reasons why you can afford the mortgage you want, put your reasons in writing. Get supporting letters from your employer, minister, former landlords, clients, customers, or anyone else who can vouch for your good character, creditworthiness, job performance, earnings potential, or personal responsibility. You might even write out a household budget. Deliver your evidence to the loan underwriter. With good explanations, you'll break through qualifying guidelines that would deter or delay other ill-prepared investors. (We'll address issues that pertain to the property—such as collateral—in later discussions.) Your plans for the property can also influence loan approval.

The Application Itself Contains Many Clues to Your Integrity

Most loan underwriters carefully review your loan application. Underwriters search for numerical discrepancies, missing information, gaps in dates, inconsistencies, and anything that smells fishy. "Hmm," the lender muses, "You say you've been out of college only three years. But you show no debts for student loans on your application and you report cash savings of $25,000. Would you mind telling me how you managed that feat?"

Experienced underwriters have examined thousands of loan apps. Their eyebrows rise easily. If your life story evokes an air of mystery, don't leave the lender in the dark. Provide firm evidence that you're traveling the straight and narrow. Even innocent lapses or discrepancies in your application can spell trouble—if not satisfactorily explained.

No Preset Qualifying Income Applies to Commercial Properties

When you finance a one- to four-unit residential property through a mortgage lender, the lender reviews your total finances to calculate whether your qualifying income will cover all your monthly expenses—including all mortgage payments (existing and those for which you are applying).

> **You may not need qualifying earned income to finance an apartment building.**

In contrast, most lenders expect commercial/investment properties to pay for themselves. Commercial property includes all office buildings, shopping centers, and apartment properties of five units or more. Ideally, you will use a commercial property's rent collections to pay its operating expenses and mortgage payments.

An Eight-Unit Money Maker

Consider, for example, this actual eight-unit property. This apartment building generates $40,800 a year in rents. The seller was asking $245,000.* Operating expenses (maintenance, property taxes, insurance, management, yard care, etc.) for the property totaled about $18,000 per year. After allowing, say, $3,000 per year for vacancy and collection losses, an investor would still net (before mortgage payments) $19,000 a year.

Even if you paid this seller's full asking price of $245,000 and financed 100 percent (no down payment), your annual mortgage payments would total just $16,700 (based on 30 years at 7 percent). Your property would throw off a positive cash flow of $2,750 a year—net of all expenses and debt repayment. Because this property would pay for itself, many lenders (or sellers) would not particularly care how much (or how little) you earned from your job. As long as you show that you are a credible and creditworthy buyer, the amount of your personal earnings would not play a major role in the lending decision.

---

*These numbers, of course, look absurdly low to Californians and residents of other high-cost areas. That's why I encourage you to invest elsewhere if prices where you live stand way out of reach.

No Cash, No Credit, No Experience

I began buying properties as a college student. I possessed no wealth, no credit record, and my only earnings came from a part-time job. Nevertheless, by the time I completed graduate school, the income from my rental properties exceeded my job income many times over. In fact, I owed $600,000 in real estate-related debt and earned less than $20,000 a year.*

Are Such Deals Possible?

Are positive cash flow deals still available? Absolutely. They're not as easy to find today—especially in high-priced cities—but this principle applies. As a commercial investor, your borrowing power will greatly exceed your personal qualifying power. I know a 43-year-old investor who earns $51,350 *a year* ($4,280 a month) from her job, yet *each month* she pays $26,430 in mortgage payments. This investor finances properties solely on the rental revenues she collects.

"Low" Income, Inexperienced Developers

As another example of borrowing outside the bounds of one's income, consider this project.

> **Financing development doesn't necessarily require your own cash.**

I was working with an inexperienced development team (an architect, lawyer, and building contractor) that was building a $40 million mixed-use residential/retail/office project. Other than sweat equity for personal (professional) services and some upfront incidental expenses for planning the project, none of the team members put any substantial amount of his own money into the development. As to borrowing power to finance construction, the lender (Wachovia Bank) primarily required that the prelease and presale activity for

---

*These figures are presented in current (inflation-adjusted) dollars.

the project provided strong evidence that the center (when completed) would generate enough revenue to pay back the development loan—or enough net income to justify a new long-term permanent loan (with proceeds from that new loan being used to pay off the development loan.

> **Commercial property investors rarely rely on their personal incomes.**

Although this team of developers earned a combined professional income of around $300,000 a year, in the eyes of the lender this job-derived income plays no significant role in its lending decision. When viewed against a $40 million loan, personal earnings of $300,000 a year don't count for much. The potential revenue from the property determined the lender's decision to finance the project.

The Debt Coverage Ratio

A lender uses a debt coverage ratio (DCR) to help figure out whether a shopping center, office building, or apartment complex yields enough net operating income (NOI) to cover the debt mortgage service and still leave some margin of safety.* Lenders want to satisfy themselves that even if rent collections fall or property expenses increase, you will still be able to make your mortgage payments *without* dipping into your personal funds.

You calculate the debt coverage ratio according to this formula:

$$\text{Debt Coverage income (DCR)} = \frac{\text{Net operating income (NOI)}}{\text{Annual debt service}}$$

An illustration: Let's return to that eight-unit property. Plugging in the relevant numbers, the debt coverage ratio equals

$$\text{DCR} = \frac{\$19,000 \ (\text{NOI})}{\$16,700 \ (\text{mortgage payments})}$$

$$\text{DCR} = 1.137, \text{ say } 1.14$$

---

*To investors, the term "debt service" means the same thing as mortgage payments.

> **Lenders want to see enough NOI to create a margin of safety.**

Most mortgage lenders like to see a debt coverage ratio of at least 1.1, and preferably in the range of 1.15 to 1.3. The higher this ratio, the better. The more net income you collect relative to the amount of your mortgage payments, the larger your margin of safety.

Even though you're a beginning investor, I would encourage you to see what types of small income properties are available in your area.* You will find that these properties (typically 5 to 24 units) will usually give you more cash flow and higher debt coverage ratios than single-family rental houses. As a result, you may be able to finance a larger loan on a more costly property. That has certainly been my experience.

---

*You may also profit by reading my book, *Make Money with Affordable Commercial Properties and Apartment Buildings*, 2nd ed. (Hoboken, NJ: John Wiley & Sons, 2008).

PART THREE

How to Invest for Maximum Gain

CHAPTER 9

Twenty-Seven Ways to Find or Create Below-Market Deals

In real estate—unlike the stock market—you not only make money when you sell, you can gain equity when you buy. In contrast, you can never buy a stock for less than its market value. In real estate such transactions occur every day. If the shares of General Motors sell at $47 each, no investor tells Merrill Lynch to find a GM shareholder who will part with 100 shares at $40 each. But if you want to buy a $250,000 house or apartment building for $200,000 to $225,000, you can probably find a seller who will accommodate you.

> **Buy properties for less than they are worth.**

Why Properties Sell for Less (or More) than Their Market Value

To see why properties sell for less than market value, dig into the meaning of the term "market value." Under market value conditions, a property sale must meet these five criteria:

1. Buyers and sellers are typically motivated. Neither acts under duress.
2. Buyers and sellers are well informed and knowledgeable about the property and the market.

3. The marketing period and sales promotion efforts are sufficient to reasonably inform potential buyers of the property's availability (no forced or rushed sales).
4. No unreal terms of financing apply (e.g., very low down payment, bargain price, below-market interest rate).
5. No out-of-the-ordinary sales concessions are made by either the seller or the buyer (for instance, sellers are not permitted to stay in the house rent-free for three to six months until their under-construction new house is completed).

Think through this description of market value. Owners who hurry to sell may accept a price lower than market value. Likewise, an owner-seller (FSBO) who fails to competently market a property will not receive top dollar. Or, say, the sellers live out of town and don't know recent sales prices. Or maybe the sellers don't realize that their property (or the neighborhood) is ripe for profitable improvement.

Owners in Distress

Every day property owners hit hard times. They are laid off from their jobs, file for divorce, suffer accidents or illness, experience setbacks in their business, and run into a freight train of other problems. Any of these calamities create financial distress. Their way out of a jam is to raise cash. If that means selling a property for "less than it's worth," then that's what they do. For such people do not just sell a property, they buy relief.

> **Money problems force sellers to accept less.**

Under these circumstances, as long as the sellers believe they have gained more from a sale than they've lost, it's win-win for both parties. If you help people cope with a predicament—rather than take advantage of them—on occasion, they will give you the bargain price (or favorable terms) you want.

The "Grass-Is-Greener" Sellers

Karla Lopez was sitting in her office and in walked the executive vice president of her firm. "Karla," she said, "Aaron Stein in the Denver

> **Opportunities elsewhere encourage sellers to accept loss.**

branch just quit. If you want his district manager's job you can have it. We will pay you $25,000 more a year plus bonus. But you have to relocate and on the job working within 30 days."

"Do I want it?" Karla burst out. "Of course I want it. Hope for a promotion like this is why I've been working 75-hour weeks for these past four years."

Will Karla Insist on Top Dollar?   Think about it. In this situation, does Karla think, "Well, I must put my house up for sale and go for top dollar"? Hardly. More than likely Karla will strike a deal with the first buyer who gives her any offer she can live with. Karla eyes the greener grass of Denver. Optimistic about her career and facing a deadline, Karla wants to sell her home quickly.

Grass-is-greener sellers stand in contrast to the financially distressed. Distressed owners sell on bargain terms or price to relieve themselves of pain; grass-is-greener sellers accept a less than market-value offer so they can quickly grab better opportunities that lie elsewhere.

Even Pros Give Bargains Sometimes   On one of several occasions where I have been a grass-is-greener seller, not only did I give my buyers a break on price but, more importantly from their perspective, I let them assume my below-market-rate mortgage and carried back an unsecured note for virtually all of their down payment. On at least a dozen occasions, I've bought from sellers who were eager to pursue better opportunities elsewhere. Each time, I negotiated a good (if not great) price and favorable financing.

If looking for distressed owners doesn't appeal to you, turn your search in the opposite direction. Sellers who want to graze in greener pastures (especially under a deadline) are frequently the easiest people to work with and the most accommodating in price and terms.

Stage-of-Life Sellers

You also can find good deals among stage-of-life sellers. These sellers are typically people whose lifestyle now conflicts with their property. They may no longer enjoy a big property or yard, collecting rent, or dealing

> **Sellers who are eager to move to their next stage of life often accept less.**

with tenant complaints. They may eagerly anticipate their move to that condo on the fourteenth green at the Bayshore Country Club. Or perhaps these sellers would rather not go through the trouble of updating and repairing their current property. Whatever their reasons, stage-of-life sellers are motivated to get on with their lives.

In addition—and this circumstance makes these sellers good prospects for a bargain price or terms—stage-of-life sellers typically have accumulated large amounts of equity in their properties. Plus, because they're older, they have accumulated savings and don't need cash. Stage-of-life sellers can be flexible. They don't need to squeeze every last penny out of their sale.

Good Prospects for OWC   Given their financial well-being, stage-of-life sellers make excellent candidates for some type of "owner will carry" (OWC) financing. Not only will OWC terms help them sell their

> **Stage-of-life sellers will often give owner financing.**

property more quickly, but an installment sale can also reduce or postpone the capital gain taxes that a cash sale might otherwise require. As another advantage, OWC financing—even when offered at below-market rates—will bring the sellers a higher return than they could earn in a savings account, certificate of deposit, or money market fund (or perhaps even stocks).

My Early Strategy   As a beginning investor, I sought out stage-of-life owners of rental houses and small apartment buildings. These people were tired of managing their properties. Yet, at the same time, they liked a monthly income and didn't want to settle for the meager interest paid by banks or to take on the risks of stocks. They also didn't want to sell their properties outright for cash and get hit with a heavy tax bill for capital gains.

Their solution: Sell on easy OWC terms to an ambitious young person who was willing to accept the work of rental properties in exchange for an opportunity to start building wealth through investment real estate. This technique still works. Because properly selected, well-managed rentals will pay for themselves, an investor who is willing to work may be able to draw on ambition and perseverance instead of a large down payment, a high credit score, and strong qualifying income.

Seller Ignorance   Some sellers underprice their properties because they don't know the recent prices at which similar properties have sold. As a seller, I have sold below market because I didn't closely follow the latest comp sales.

> **Sellers who are out of touch with the market often sell for less.**

In one case, I was living in Palo Alto, California. The rental house I decided to sell was located in Dallas, Texas. A year earlier, the house had been appraised for $110,000, which at the time of the appraisal was about right. So I decided to ask $125,000. I figured that price was high enough to account for appreciation and still leave room to negotiate.

The first weekend the house went on the market, three offers came in right at the asking price. Immediately, of course, I knew I had underpriced at less than the market would bear. What I didn't know but soon learned was that during the year I'd been away, home prices in that Dallas neighborhood had jumped 30 percent. After learning of my ignorance, I could have rejected all offers and raised my price. Or I could have put the buyers into a bidding war. But I didn't. I just decided to sell to the person with the cleanest offer (no contingencies). I was making a good profit; why get greedy?

Besides, I saw the Dallas market quickly turning from boom to bust because vast numbers of newly built condos and houses were about to come onto the market. Increasing supply and higher unemployment (due to a decline in the Texas oil-based economy) combined to foretell price declines. Sometimes market signals tell you to take the money and run.

Cranky Landlords

I love to buy from cranky landlords. These rental property owners still think they live in feudal times. These owners battle their tenants. They complain, complain, complain. Eventually, they hate the whole idea of investing in real estate. These owners see landlording as nothing but trouble. They want out.

> **Cranky landlords often become eager sellers who accept less.**

At that point, they give in to a lowball offer to get rid of their headaches.

(Whoa, you say, "Is this what I'm getting myself into? Trouble, headaches, and battles with tenants?" No, not at all. That's because in Chapter 18, you will learn the 12 secrets of successful landlording—actually I even detest the term *landlord*. That title no longer fits the modern, enlightened owner of investment properties.)

Preserve the Lender's Image and Balance Sheet

Banks, government agencies (FHA, VA), and the government-chartered mortgage companies such as Fannie Mae and Freddie Mac often become "don't wanters." When their mortgage borrowers fail to pay back their loans, these lenders end up with foreclosures (called REOs, which stands for real estate owned).

 Lenders Want to Mitigate Their Losses   Once lenders take back a property in foreclosure, they switch their thinking. They no longer focus on making money. Instead, they want to get rid of these REOs on prices or terms that will cut their losses. (Banks often name their REO departments "Loss Mitigation.")

That's where you come in. Because a pile of foreclosures hurts the lender's image with regulators and depresses its balance sheet, lenders sometimes give investors good deals to take these properties (or delinquent loans) off of their hands.

Multiple Investor Opportunities   As you will see in Chapter 10, when you learn how the total foreclosure process works in your state—the foreclosure process is governed by state law—you can play the foreclosure game with a variety of approaches. For beginning investors who put in the effort, lender foreclosures offer opportunities to snare below-market deals.

The Possibility-Impaired

Who are the possibility-impaired? This type of owner confuses his diamond in the rough with a lump of coal. These owners don't see the potential that their property offers. Why? Several reasons explain such dull vision.

◆ The sellers are out of touch with what features buyers (renters) want.
◆ The sellers lack the ability to imagine and create.
◆ The sellers have lived with the property so long that they don't critically evaluate the property's shortcomings. They simply accept them.
◆ The sellers don't know that the local zoning and building regulations actually permit a higher and more profitable use for the property.

This short list does not nearly exhaust the reasons people miss the opportunities that lie before them. As author Wayne Dyer says, "You must believe it to see it." Because the possibility-impaired don't believe their property offers great potential, they never look.

Don't Dilly-Dally with Due Diligence

Although good deals go fast, don't jump in until you see whether there's water in the pool. Not all bargain-priced properties represent good deals. You score a good deal if you can sell the property for substantially more than you have put into it. Beware of underestimating fix-up expenses. Beware of hidden defects. Beware of environmental problems (e.g., lead paint, underground oil storage tanks, asbestos, contaminated well water). Beware of pouring so much cash into improvements that you overshoot the rent level that tenants are willing and able to pay.

Temper your eagerness to buy a bargain-priced property with a thorough physical, financial, market, and legal analysis. Especially in cases of low- or nothing-down seller financing, many beginning investors grab at a "great" deal without first putting it under a magnifying glass. Act quickly when you must. But the less you know about a property, the greater your risk.

The Disclosure Revolution

Most states require sellers to complete a disclosure statement that lists and explains all *known* problems or defects that may plague a property.

But even if your state doesn't mandate seller disclosure, obtain a disclosure form (realty firms keep blank copies on hand), and ask the owners to fill it out. However, keep in mind these five trouble points:

1. Sellers do not disclose facts or conditions of which they are unaware.
2. Disclosure reveals the past. It does not guarantee the future. By completing the statement, sellers do not warrant the condition of the property.
3. Many disclosure questions require somewhat subjective answers. Are playing children a neighborhood noise problem? Is a planned street widening an adverse condition?
4. Disclosure statements may not require sellers to disclose property defects that are readily observable.
5. Pay close attention to any owner (or agent) statements that begin, "I believe," "I think," "as far as we know," and other similar hedges. Don't accept these answers as conclusive. Follow up with further inquiry or inspection.

Insist on disclosure facts—not mere opinions.

Seller disclosure statements alert you to potential problems. But even so, independently check out the property to satisfy yourself that you really know what you are buying.

Excluded Income Properties

Many seller disclosure laws apply only to one- to four-unit owner-occupied properties. If you buy an investor-owned property or an REO, the law may not require the seller to fill out a disclosure statement. If the seller does refuse, offset your additional risk by scaling down the top price you're willing to pay. Also, toughen up your prepurchase inspections.

Many states exempt investor properties from their seller disclosure statutes.

When buying income properties, verify rents and operating expenses. Ask the sellers to swear that the income and expense figures that they have reported stand true. Beware of owners who put friends, relatives, and employees into their buildings at inflated rent levels. These tenants don't really pay the rents stated (or if they do, they get kickbacks in cash or other benefits), but their signed leases sure look attractive to unsuspecting buyers.

How to Find Bargain Sellers

Want to find these potential bargain sellers. Here are five techniques:

1. Networking.
2. Newspapers and other publications.
3. Cold calls directly to owners.
4. Real estate agents.
5. Information highway.

Networking

Some time back I was leaving the country for several years and decided to sell my house with a minimum of hassle. Coincidentally, the Ph.D. student club at the university where I was teaching was looking for a faculty member to host the upcoming faculty-student party. Aha, I thought, what better way to expose my house to more than 100 people? So I volunteered. The week following the party, I received two offers and accepted one of them.

The buyers got a good price and excellent financing. I avoided the hassle of putting the property on the market and did not have to pay a real estate commission. Everyone involved was satisfied.

This personal example shows the power of networking. What's surprising is that so few buyers and sellers consciously try to discover each other through informal contacts among friends, family, relatives, coworkers, church groups, clubs, business associates, customers, parent-teacher groups, and other types of acquaintances. So don't keep your search a secret. Tell everyone you know. Describe what you're looking for. Why search alone when you can enlist hundreds of friends, relatives, and acquaintances?

> **Whether buying or selling, tell everyone you know.**

Newspapers and Other Publications

Most people browse the real estate classifieds with a highlighter, call owners or Realtors, get basic information, and, when something seems promising, set up an appointment. While this method can work reasonably well, it also can fail for two reasons: (1) if a property isn't advertised, you won't learn about it; and (2) if the ad for a property you might be interested in is not written effectively, you may pass it by without serious notice.

Run Your Own Ads　To address these drawbacks, run your own advertisement in the Wanted to Buy column. When you describe the type of property and terms that you're looking for, you invite serious sellers to contact you. When I began buying real estate, I used this technique to locate about 30 percent of the properties I bought.

As another way to use newspapers, read through the Houses for Rent, Condos for Rent, and Apartments for Rent ads. This research will not only help you gauge rent levels, often you'll see properties advertised as "lease-option" or "for rent or sale." These kinds of ads indicate a flexible seller.

Look Beyond the Classifieds　To search for potential bargain sellers in the newspaper, go beyond the classified real estate ads. Locate names of potential sellers from public notices: births, divorces, deaths, bankruptcies, foreclosures, or marriages. Each of these events can trigger the need to quickly sell real estate. If you contact owners (or their heirs) before they list with a sales agent, you stand a fair chance of buying at a bargain price. (In addition, you might subscribe to the "default" or "foreclosure" lists and newsletters published for your area.)

Cold Call Owners

To learn cold-calling, adopt the techniques of Realtors. Most successful real estate agents develop listing farms. A listing farm represents a neighborhood or other geographic area that an agent cultivates to find sellers who will list their properties for sale with that agent. Agents who cold-call might telephone property owners with names gathered from a criss-cross directory, walk the neighborhood, talk to residents, circulate flyers by mail or doorknob hangers, and take part in neighborhood or community-sponsored events. By cultivating a farm, an agent hopes to become well known in the area. An agent positions himself or herself to be first in mind when property owners contemplate a sale.

Take a lesson out of the real estate agent's playbook. Cultivate a farm in the neighborhoods or communities where you would like to buy. Circulate a flyer, for example, that reads:

> Before you list your home for sale, please call me. I am looking to buy a property in this neighborhood directly from the owners. Let's see if we can sit down together and work out an agreement that will benefit both of us.

Cultivate your farm.

When property owners learn how they can save time, effort, and money selling direct, they may be willing to offer you a favorable price or terms.

Vacant Houses and Out-of-Area Owners   Your farm area includes some properties (vacant or tenant-occupied) that are owned by people who do not live in the neighborhood. These owners may not see your flyers, nor will you see them in a criss-cross directory. To reach these sellers, ask neighbors of nearby properties or talk with the tenants who live in the property.

You can also contact the county property tax assessor's office. There you can learn where and to whom the property tax statements are mailed. It's not unusual to find that out-of-the-area property owners

Often out-of-area owners are sleeping sellers.

are actually "sleeping sellers." That is, they would like to sell, but haven't awoken to that fact. With luck and perseverance, you could become their alarm clock.

In most areas, you no longer even need to go to the tax assessor's offices to locate owners. You can find the information on the asessor's web site.

Expired (or About to Expire) Listings   Many properties listed with real estate agents do not sell during their original listing period. The listing agent will try to get the owners to relist with his or her firm. And quite likely, agents from other brokerage firms also will approach the sellers. However, here's what you can do to cut them off at the pass and perhaps arrange a bargain purchase.

> **Ask sellers to contact you after their listing has expired.**

When you notice a listed property that looks as though it may fit your requirements, do *not* call the agent. Do *not* call or stop by to talk to the owners. Instead write the owners a letter stating the price and terms that you would consider paying. Then ask the owners to contact you *after* their listing has expired. (If a seller goes behind his agent's back and arranges a sale while the property is listed, the owner is legally obligated to pay the sales commission.)

An example: Sellers have listed their property at its market value of $200,000. The listing contract sets a 6 percent sales commission. The sellers have told themselves that they will accept nothing less than $192,500, which means that after selling expenses they would receive around $180,000. You offer $175,000. Would the sellers accept your offer? Or would they relist, postpone their move, and hold out for $5,000 to $10,000 more?

It would depend on the sellers' finances, their reason for moving, and any other pressures they face. But you can see that even though your offer falls below market value, your price gives the sellers almost as much as they could expect if their agent found them a buyer. (Naturally, your letter would not commit you to the purchase. It would state the price or terms that you have in mind.)

Real Estate Agents

Do not conclude from the above technique that you should never use a real estate agent to help you find bargain-priced investment properties.

> **Real estate agents can provide valuable services.**

A top agent can assist in multiple ways. However, agents deserve to be paid for their services. If you plan to buy at a bargain price or buy on bargain terms (especially with low- or no-down-payment financing), where's the agent's fee going to come from? To pursue the best deal, forgo an agent's services and do your own legwork.

Cruise the Information Highway

Today's investors not only cruise neighborhoods, they cruise the Internet to look for properties. Thousands of web sites now list properties

Shop and compare properties on the Internet.	for sale. Property buyers (or browsers) can access the Realtor's Multiple Listing Service (MLS) through Realtor.com. For investment properties, <u>loopnet.com ranks No. 1 in listings</u>.

Also, a budding entrepreneurial industry accumulates specialized listings of everything from foreclosures to distressed properties to FSBOs. Go online, and you can locate investors looking for money—or money looking for properties.

Real estate information that in the past has been available from Realtors, public records, newspaper ads, and newsletters is now accessible on the Internet. Electronic shopping for real estate (and mortgages) has made the MLS book as obsolete as a slide rule. (For a listing of websites useful to real estate investors, see the Internet Appendix. For a quick check of techniques you can use to find owners who will sell at a bargain price, see Box 9.1.)

1. Advertise "I buy properties" in the real estate classifieds.
2. Advertise on your car or truck with a magnetic "I buy properties" sign.
3. Make your car or truck a mobile billboard. Paint it with an "I buy houses" advertising message.
4. Mail out "I buy houses" postcards to owners in your farm area.
5. Mail out "I buy houses" postcards or letters to owners who are being foreclosed.
6. Advertise your property needs to real estate agents.
7. Contact attorneys (real estate, divorce, bankruptcy, estate, tax settlement specialists).
8. Contact yard care companies that maintain properties for lenders after the owners have abandoned them.
9. Network with friends, family, acquaintances.
10. Agree to pay bird-dog fees to anyone who refers you to a great buy.
11. Approach other investors who have just bought a property at a foreclosure sale. They may be willing to quick-flip for a small profit.
12. Contact the mortgage loss mitigation (REO) departments of mortgage lenders.
13. Follow closely the foreclosure postings.   *(continued)*

Box 9.1   Quick List to Find Bargains

14. Keep your eye out for properties in disrepair, especially those that are vacant or occupied by renters.

15. Contact out-of-town owners of properties in disrepair.

16. Get to know real estate agents who specialize in distress sales, foreclosures, and REOs. These types of agents frequently run ads publicizing their specialty—or you can just notice which agents tend to run ads for distressed properties such as HUD homes.

For a more extensive discussion of these and other similar techniques, see Peter Conti and David Finkel, *Making Big Money Investing in Foreclosures* (Chicago: Dearborn, 2003), pp. 91–132.

Box 9.1 *(Continued)*

CHAPTER 10

Make Money with Foreclosures and REOs

If you've watched real estate infomercials, you might believe that it's easy to buy a foreclosed property at a courthouse auction for just pennies on the dollar—then quickly resell that property for a large and easy windfall gain. Not true.

The Stages of Foreclosure

In fact, buying foreclosures "on the courthouse steps" represents just one type of foreclosure possibility. And that widely promoted approach entails big risks and uncertain profits. Consequently, experienced and successful investors usually buy *before* or *after* a foreclosure auction— not during. As a beginner, that, too, is where you should place your efforts.

Owner's Default (the First Stage)

When property owners fail to pay their mortgage payments, their lender will encourage, coerce, or threaten them through reminder letters, telephone calls, or credit counseling. If those efforts don't produce results, the lender's lawyers take over. Talking tough, the lawyers usually

> **Lenders favor loan workouts over foreclosure.**

threaten foreclosure and warn the property owners to either pay up or face serious trouble.

Typically, lenders continue their loan workout efforts for anywhere from one to six months, or maybe longer. In contrast to the late 1980s and early 1990s, lenders today give borrowers more opportunity to reinstate or refinance their delinquent mortgages.

> **Near-record numbers of property owners need loan workouts.**

As a result, fewer properties now end up at foreclosure sales—especially compared with the tidal wave of foreclosures that flooded the market 10 to 15 years ago. Even so, lenders will get the keys to more than 100,000 properties this year. And the number of borrowers who fall behind in their payments (and are in need of a loan workout) exceeds 2 million people a year.

(Also, given the wild and crazy lending spree of 2002–2006, I expect 2008–2009 to provide a bonanza of foreclosures, lender auctions, and preforeclosure workouts.)

Filing Legal Notice

When a lender gives up on a workout, its lawyers either file a legal "notice of default" or a "lawsuit to foreclose" (depending on the state). The lender then posts notice of this suit on the Internet and in newspapers. These postings tell the property owners, any other parties who may have legal claims against the owners or their property, and the public in general that legal action is moving forward to force a sale of the property.

The Foreclosure Sale (the Second Stage)

Eventually, when the defaulting borrowers run out of time, legal defenses, or delaying maneuvers, the foreclosure sale date arrives. At this point, the court trustee auctions the property to the highest cash bidder.

On occasion, a real estate investor (a foreclosure speculator) submits the winning bid. More likely, though, the lender who has forced

Lenders often win the bid at the foreclosure sale.

the foreclosure sale bids, say, one dollar more than the amount of its unpaid claims (mortgage balance, late fees, accrued interest, attorney fees, foreclosure costs) and walks away with a sheriff 's deed to the property. From then on until the lender sells the property, that property remains on the lender's books as *real estate owned*—an REO.

Lender's Don't Want REOs (the Third Stage)

The most important thing to know concerning foreclosure should be written in headlines: LENDERS DO NOT WANT TO OWN FORECLOSED REAL ESTATE. For lenders—including such institutions as the Federal Housing Administration (FHA), the Department of Veterans Affairs (VA), Fannie Mae, and Freddie Mac—holding onto an REO that they have acquired through foreclosure rarely seems like a good idea. No matter how much potential the property offers, lenders who own REOs want to sell quickly. For you, their desire to sell quickly may mean their loss and your gain.

In sum, the three stages of the foreclosure process offer you these possibilities to gain a bargain price or bargain terms:

1. You can negotiate with the distressed property owners and, if necessary, the foreclosing lender.
2. You can bid at the foreclosure auction.
3. You can negotiate and buy directly from the lender or its insuring agency (e.g., FHA, VA, Fannie Mae, Freddie Mac) that owns the property as an REO.

Approach Owners with Empathy: Step One

No single magic system works to buy a property from owners facing foreclosure. These owners are plagued with financial troubles, personal anguish, and indecisiveness. They probably have been attacked by innumerable foreclosure sharks, speculators, bank lawyers, and recent attendees of get-rich-quick foreclosure seminars. These owners are living with public shame. For all of these reasons and more, they are not easy people to deal with.

Yet when you develop a sensitive, empathetic, problem-solving approach with people suffering foreclosure, you come up with a win-win agreement. More than likely, though, you won't be the only investor who pays them a visit. A "Here's my offer—take it or leave it" approach will antagonize owners. This approach will not distinguish you from a dozen other foreclosure buyers (sharks). Develop your offer and negotiate to preserve what little may be left of the owner's dignity and self-esteem.

Perhaps you can share personal information about setbacks you have lived through. Above all, emphasize win-win outcomes. Dire straits or not, no one wants their property stolen from them. In addition, government regulators are looking closely at preforeclosure buying practices. Many foreclosure sharks lie and deceive their victims before they eat them. Before you talk with property owners in distress, learn if any special laws apply in your area to such negotiations and purchases.

> **"Take it or leave it" rarely works in negotiations with distressed owners.**

Meet the Property Owners

You visit with the property owners to make a good buy. But also, approach the troubled owners with aid that will end their distress. When everything goes right, the owners will receive cash for some of their equity, their credit will be salvaged, and you will acquire title to the property.

Here are several approaches you can use to open negotiations with an owner in foreclosure:

> If you'll allow me to make a complete financial analysis of the property, I can be back within 24 hours with a firm offer that might solve your current dilemma.

> I would like to figure a way to give you some cash for your equity, which you will otherwise lose in a foreclosure sale. By working with me you can save your credit, leave this property financially better off, and start your life over.

May I review the loan documents on your home? Do you
have a copy of the mortgage and the loan payment record?

With an empathetic, win-win manner, you can succeed when competing against the foreclosure sharks.

Don't Fear Run-Down Properties

Do not fear cosmetic damage to a property. A run-down house gives you
more chance to profit. In fact, the more cosmetically run-down, the better. Every curable defect offers profitable opportunity.

Thoroughly check out the property. Then evaluate the selling price
that you could get after you've completed your fix-up work. If you've
worked the numbers and the total costs of pur-
chase and fix-up *exceed* your probable resale value,
don't necessarily abandon the project. Go back to
the troubled owner (or mortgage lender) and reopen negotiations. Point out that you must make a
reasonable profit. If you're still unable to arrive at a
good deal, then look elsewhere.

> **Cosmetic fixers
> offer big potential
> for profit.**

Vacant Houses

To discover a vacant house in foreclosure means to discover both a problem and an opportunity. It's a problem because you may have to do some
detective work to locate the owners. Unless the owners have purposely
tried to disappear, though, you can probably locate them in one of the
following five ways:

1. Contact nearby neighbors to learn the owners' whereabouts,
   or the names of friends or family who would know.
2. Call the owners' telephone number and see if you get a "number changed" message.
3. Ask the post office to provide the owners' forwarding
   address.
4. Find out where the owners were employed and ask coworkers.

5. Contact the school that the owners' children attended, and ask where their school records were sent. (However, with today's concerns about privacy, I've found that many school personnel will no longer give out school transfer information.)

> **Owners of abandoned properties seldom hold out for top dollar.**

Because they have abandoned the property, they probably aren't entertaining any pie-in-the-sky hopes for a sale at an inflated price. At this point, the owners may view any offer you make them as found money.

In some cases, you'll learn that the owners have split up and gone their separate ways. This situation raises another problem. Especially in hostile separations, working out an agreement with one owner in the belief that you can convince the other to go along often proves futile. To avoid this difficulty, *negotiate with all owners simultaneously*—or don't negotiate at all, unless you're just trying to sharpen your skills and won't mind failing to close the deal.

Sometimes Losing Less Is Winning

If the property goes to the foreclosure sale, the lender(s) and the property owners are likely to lose money. But think what happens when all parties agree to work with each other, rather than against each other. You create an outcome where everyone walks away better off. Maybe they receive less than they hoped for, certainly less than they were theoretically entitled to, but far more than they could expect from a bidder at a foreclosure auction.

Some Investors Profit from the Foreclosure Auction: Step Two

Although foreclosure sales typically lose money for lenders, lienholders, and property owners, savvy bidders can turn these sales into big profits. But it's not easy. Bidding blind doesn't work. You have to develop good knowledge of values, properties, and neighborhoods.

Why Foreclosures Sell for Less than Market Value

A typical foreclosed property sells for less than market value. Why? Because foreclosure auctions don't come close to meeting the criteria of a market value transaction.

As you can see from Box 10.1, foreclosure auctions seem designed to yield the *lowest possible sales price.* They take place under conditions that violate all principles of effective marketing.

Make the Puny Sales Efforts Work for You

For most would-be buyers, the potential risk, expense, and aggravation of foreclosure sales deter them from even showing up to bid. When you consider lame marketing efforts, adverse conditions of sale, and potential owner (tenant) eviction problems, is it any wonder that foreclosed properties deserve to sell at a fraction of their market value?

> **Great uncertainty produces low sales prices.**

Indeed, you might look at the foreclosure sales process and say, "Too many potential problems. No way do I want to take those risks. Besides, how could I come up with cash on short notice?" Clearly, that's the attitude of a majority of real estate

Market Value Sale	Foreclosure Auction
No seller or buyer duress	Forced sale
Buyer and seller well informed	Scarce information
60 to 120 day marketing period	Five minutes or less selling time
Financing on typical terms	Spot cash (or within 24 hours)
Owners agree to move	Owners or tenants may have to be evicted
Marketable title	No title guarantees
Warranty deed	Sheriff's (or trustee) deed
Seller disclosures	No seller disclosures
Close inspection of physical condition	No physical inspection
Yard sign	Rarely a yard sign
"Homes for sale" ads/MLS	Legal notice listing

Box 10.1　Foreclosure Sales Rely on Adverse Marketing and Sales Practices

investors. It explains why at most sales the foreclosing lender wins the bid at a price equal to (or slightly above) the accumulated balance on the borrower's outstanding debt.

Bid with Inside Knowledge

Risk looms large to block your path to foreclosure sale profits. Savvy bidding then lies in knowing as much about the property as due diligence demands.

How can you get this information? First, meet with the property owners to talk over possibilities for working out a deal before foreclosure. Even when those discussions end without agreement, you've still been able to see the property (market value, fix-up needs, improvement opportunities), evaluate the neighborhood, and understand the owner's intentions. This step puts you ahead of the game.

Second, research liens against title at the courthouse—or online. List every claim that may cloud the title. If you pursue the property, verify the quality of the title with a lawyer or title insurer. (I have usually found the workers at the courthouse helpful when I'm unfamiliar with the record-filing procedures of an area.)

Arrange Financing

After you gather information to manage the risks of buying at foreclosure, you face the problem of financing. How do you get the cash to close the sale? If you lack wealth or credit, bring in a money partner. You really can't play the foreclosure game without working cash or credit.

But maybe you can temporarily raise cash—such as a home equity loan, credit card cash advances, selling (or borrowing against) stocks, or maybe a signature loan—then bid at an auction. After the foreclosure paperwork clears, place an interim or longer-term loan against the property and pay off your short-term creditors.

> **Raise the cash to bid via partners or short-term credit.**

Experienced investors who buy foreclosures might open a line of personal credit at a bank. They draw against this credit as they need it. Or they maintain cash balances (money market funds) in amounts sufficient to cover their buying patterns.

The Foreclosure Sale: Summing Up

If you learn the foreclosure game (as it's played in your area), do homework on properties, and manage risks, you can build profits quickly. At times, you can buy foreclosures for a fraction of their market value. Your challenge is to learn which of these properties meet the test of a true bargain—and which ones carry risks or expensive problems.

The Benefits of Buying REOs: Step Three

Mortgage lenders like to make loans and collect monthly payments. They do not like to own and manage properties. As a result, they may give buyers of their REOs a bargain price, favorable terms such as low or no closing costs, below-market interest rates, or low down payments, or some combination of these benefits.

If a property needs fix-up work that the lenders prefer not to remedy, they may accept offers at deep discounts from market value. Just as important, prior to closing the sale of their REOs, lenders normally clear title problems, evict unauthorized occupants, and pay past-due property taxes and assessments. Some lenders permit buyers to write offers subject to an appraisal or professional inspection (contingency clauses).

Safer than Buying at the Foreclosure Sale

Typically, you buy an REO more safely than you could have bought the same property at its foreclosure sale. Depending on the lender's motivation, its internal policies and procedures, and the property loan-to-value ratio (LTV) at the time of the foreclosure sale, you might buy at a price lower than market value.

Why a Lower Price?

Say the market value of a property at the time of its foreclosure sale was $165,000. The lender's claims against the property totaled $160,000. To win the property away from the lender, you bid more than $160,000—a price that's too high to yield a profit.

> **It costs lenders big money to hold on to their REOs.**

However, once the lender owns the property and tallies its expected holding costs, Realtor's commission, and the risks of seeing the (probably) vacant property vandalized, it may decide to cut its losses. It may accept an offer from you within the range of $140,000 to $150,000 (especially if you offer cash, which you may raise from other source).

In desperate times REO lenders turn to mass marketing and highly advertised public auctions to unload their REOs. In stable to strong markets, they generally (but not always) play low key. No lender prefers to publicize the fact that it's throwing down-on-their-luck families out of their homes. So, absent tough times and mass advertising, you can find REOs in three different ways:

- ◆ Follow up after a foreclosure sale.
- ◆ Cold-call lender REO personnel (loss mitigation).
- ◆ Locate Realtors who typically get REO listings.

Follow Up After Foreclosure

You can learn of lender REOs by attending courthouse auctions. When a lender wins the bid for a property that catches your interest, button-

> **Open discussions with a lender immediately after the foreclosure sale.**

hole the bidder and start talking business. Schedule an appointment to see the bank officer who takes charge of the disposition of REOs. Show the lender how your bargain offer will actually save, perhaps even make the bank money, and you'll be on your way to closing a deal.

Beware of the stall. Financial institutions are run by standard operating procedures, management committees, and other precautionary rules that frequently work against sensible decisions. If you run into a bureaucratic stone wall, persevere. The reward of following through doesn't just lie in getting a good deal on a property now. More important, you will build relationships that open doors for you in the future.

Cold-Call REO (Loss Mitigation) Personnel

All mortgage lenders experience borrower defaults. No one has designed a foolproof system for predicting which loan applicants will fail to pay. It follows, then, that at one time or another all mortgage lenders must end up with REOs—even if eventually they pass them along to HUD, VA, Fannie Mae, or Freddie Mac.

Sometimes, too, lenders pick up REOs without going through foreclosure. During the last real estate downturn, lenders would open their mail to find the keys to a house, a signed deed, and a note from the distressed owners saying, "We're out of here. It's your problem now."

To find REOs that lenders have acquired through foreclosure or deed-in-lieu transfers, cold-call mortgage lenders. Ask for a list of their REOs. This technique, though, may not succeed. For various reasons, lenders may keep a tight hold on this information. Nevertheless, you won't know until you try.

> **Cold-calling lenders for REOs requires persistence.**

Until you establish relationships with REO personnel, you may find the following approach works better. Rather than ask for a complete list of REOs, narrow your focus. Tell lenders what you're specifically looking for in terms of location, size, price range, floor plan, condition, or other features. In that way, a lender can answer your request without revealing the number of REOs within its inventory.

Locate Specialty Realtors

Many mortgage lenders *avoid* selling directly to investors (though they make exceptions) for two reasons: (1) as mentioned, they don't like the unfavorable publicity, and (2) they want to promote good relations with Realtors. Because most lenders expect Realtors to refer them business, these same lenders can't then turn around and become FSBO (for sale by owner) dealers. You scratch my back and I'll scratch yours—that's what sets the rules in business.

To find REOs, cultivate relationships with Realtors who specialize in this market. (In fact, HUD, VA, Fannie Mae, and Freddie Mac almost always sell their REOs through Realtors.) In most cities, find REO specialists as you look through newspaper classified real estate ads.

Hire a Real Pro   Once you have identified several foreclosure specialists, give each one a call. Learn their backgrounds. Do they only dabble in the field of REOs and foreclosures? Or do they make this field their full-time business? When I telephoned REO specialist John Huguenard, for example, he talked with me for an hour and a half about property availability, detailed financing and purchase procedures, hot areas of town, rehab potential, estimating repair costs, portfolio lenders, strategies for buying and managing properties as well as selecting tenants, and a dozen other related topics.

> **When searching for REOs, talk with an REO specialist.**

At one point during our conversation, he asked, "I'll bet you haven't talked to other agents who know as much as I do about REOs and foreclosures, have you? I've been doing this 23 years. Last year, I sold 90 houses and rehabbed 16 others for my own account." John was right. I hadn't.

Beware of False Experts   John's the kind of real estate professional to find. Although many realty agents claim expertise in REOs and foreclosures—"Sure, I can do that for you"—only a few make it their prime activity, day in and day out, year after year. When you work with an agent who's really in the know, you won't need to do your own legwork and door knocking. Your agent will screen properties as soon as—if not before—they come onto the market. You will then be notified immediately.

Specialty agents with in-depth knowledge also stay on top of the finance plans that portfolio, government, and conventional lenders offer to homebuyers and investors. (Again, for example, John Huguenard knew of portfolio lenders doing 100 percent LTV investor loans for investor acquisition and rehab.)

Avoid the foreclosure dabblers. Work with a pro, someone who knows all the current rules, regulations, and operating procedures.

HUD, VA, Fannie, and Freddie Won't Sell Direct to Buyers   No matter what approach to acquiring REOs and foreclosures you choose to follow, talk with realty pros who make the business a career. As noted earlier, if you buy an REO from HUD, VA, Fannie Mae, or Freddie Mac, you *must* process your offer through a lender-authorized real estate agent. Only in exceptional circumstances would these organizations negotiate directly. Your REO specialist will know the ins and outs to deal with these sources.

11

More Sources of Bargains

We've not yet exhausted the possibilities for finding bargain deals. You've got at least 11 more sources of bargains.

Federal Government Auctions

Besides HUD and FHA, other agencies of the federal government sell seized and surplus real estate that include houses, apartment complexes, office buildings, ranches, and vacant and developed land. Among the most active sellers are the Internal Revenue Service (IRS), General Services Administration (GSA), and the Federal Deposit Insurance Corporation (FDIC). On occasion, you can also find properties offered by the Small Business Administration (SBA). Although space here doesn't permit detailing rules for each of these agencies, you can locate their properties and sales procedures at the following web sites:

Internal Revenue Service at www.treas.gov/auctions/irs.
General Services Administration at http://propertydisposal.gsa.
gov/propforsale.
Federal Deposit Insurance Corporation at www.fdic.gov/buying/
owned/real/index.
Small Business Administration at http://app1.sba.gov/pfsales/dsp.

Sheriff Sales

Other than foreclosures, sheriff sales or other court-ordered property sales may result because of property tax liens, lawsuit judgments, and bankruptcy creditors.

The local nature of these types of forced sales preclude details that relate to sales procedures or the possibilities for finding bargain prices. I can only say, "It all depends." Yet, to leave no stone unturned in your attempt to locate good deals, talk with real estate lawyers, courthouse officials, foreclosure speculators, and others who are in the know about these types of sales. Because such sales take place under less than ideal marketing methods, selling prices can fall below a property's market value.

Buy from Foreclosure Speculators

If you do not win the bid at a courthouse auction, negotiate with the winner.

Say a foreclosure speculator successfully bids $145,000 for a property that seems to have a market value of $195,000 if it were fixed up and marketed effectively. After the auction, you offer the speculator $170,000 (or whatever). To minimize risk, you attach several contingencies to your offer that permit you to get the property inspected, evict any holdover owners or tenants, clear up title problems, seek title insurance, and arrange financing. If the property checks out, your purchase closes and the speculator makes a quick $25,000 (more or less). You own the property at a discount without the costly surprises that turn a promising foreclosure buy into a loss.

> **Ask a speculator to flip you a property at a wholesale price.**

Probate and Estate Sales

Probate and estate sales present another source of bargains. When property owners die, their property may be sold to pay the deceased's mortgage and other debts. Even when the deceased leaves sufficient wealth in cash to satisfy claims against the estate, heirs normally prefer to sell the property.

Probate

To buy a property through probate, submit a bid through the estate's administrator (usually a lawyer) or executor. Then all bids are reviewed by the probate judge assigned to the case. Depending on local and state laws, the judge may approve a bid or reopen the bidding. Because of legal red tape, probate properties require perseverance. Judges wield discretion in deciding when and whether to accept a probate bid. You can never tell for sure where you stand.

An acquaintance tells of a probate property that came up for sale in an area of $150,000 houses. The probate administrator listed the house for sale at $115,000. A flurry of bids came in that ranged from a low of $105,000 up to a high of $118,000. Several months later the judge looked at the bids, rejected the high bid of $118,000, and solicited additional offers. Eventually, the judge approved the sale at a price of $129,850 to someone who had not even been involved in the first round of bidding.

After all was said and done, the successful buyer did achieve a bargain price. (Unlike forced sales "on the courthouse steps," in a probate sale you generally can enter and inspect the properties prior to submitting a bid.) To learn about probate in your area, talk with a probate lawyer or the clerk of the county court. Also look at local newspapers that announce upcoming probate sales.

> **Probate judges may exercise arbitrary power.**

Estate Sales

In some situations, an estate's assets need not be dragged through the probate process. You might buy directly from the heirs or the executor of the estate. In fact, some buyers of estate properties follow the obituary notices, contact heirs, and try to buy before the property is listed with a real estate agent. To succeed in this approach, employ an empathetic demeanor.

> **Contact heirs.
> You often find
> eager sellers.**

Estate sales frequently produce bargains because heirs eagerly want cash. They may need money to pay mortgage, other creditors, or estate taxes. Out-of-town heirs (especially) may not want to hold a vacant property for an extended period until a top-dollar buyer is found. Pressures of time or money lead to sales prices that fall below a property's market value.

Private Auctions

Increasingly, many sellers who want to liquidate their properties turn to private auctions. During the last economic downturn in California, banks and thrifts were pooling their REOs and jointly auctioning off dozens (sometimes hundreds) of properties at a time. New homebuilders, too, use auctions. Sometimes homebuilder auctions involve closeout sales where a builder wants to get out of a current project to devote energy to a new development. On other occasions, a homebuilder's auction represents a last desperate attempt to raise cash to head off project foreclosure or company bankruptcy.

> **Homebuilders
> (or their lenders)
> may auction off
> excess inventory.**

In Dallas, a homeowner tired of trying to sell his $1.6 million (listed price) home through a brokerage firm and was eager to move into his newly built $4.4 million home. So he hired an auctioneer. On a pleasant Saturday morning, hundreds of people showed up and within minutes of the opening bid, the house had sold for $890,000.

Prepare for an Auction

Attend a major real estate auction. You'll enjoy it. Often a band is playing, food and drinks are served, and a festive mood prevails. The auction company wants to make potential bidders feel good. But beyond this display of cheer, the auction company promotes one goal: sell every property at the highest possible price. Auctioneers earn a percentage of the day's take, plus perhaps a bonus for exceeding a certain level of sales.

Private auctions make for festive events.

To land a bargain, don't get caught up in the festive frenzy and abandon good sense (as the auction company wants you to). Instead, attend the auction armed with information. Prepare to walk out a winner—not simply a buyer. Here's how you can make that happen:

♦ *Thoroughly inspect a property.* During the weeks before most private auctions, the auction company schedules open houses at the properties to be sold. If you can't visit an open house, contact a real estate agent and ask for a personal showing. (Most auction companies cooperate with Realtors. If an agent brings a winning bidder to the auction, that agent is paid a 1 or 2 percent sales commission.) Sometimes auction properties sell cheap because they are nothing more than teardowns waiting for a bulldozer. Or they may suffer other problems. Even new properties aren't necessarily defect free. Check them out before you bid.

♦ *Appraise the property.* Even if free of defects, you can't assume value. Study sales prices of comparable properties. Don't count on list price to guide you. Just because you buy a property 25 percent below its previous listing price doesn't mean you have bought at 25 percent below the property's market value.

♦ *Set your maximum bid price.* Market value tells you what a property might sell for if fixed up and marketed by a competent and aggressive real estate agent. Market value *does not* tell you the price you should bid. Before the auction, set your maximum bid price. Ignore the auctioneer's boosters who try to cajole, excite, romance, bamboozle, or intimidate you into a higher bid.

♦ *Learn the amount of the buyer's premium.* At many auctions, you will pay a 5 or 10 percent "buyer's premium" fee in addition to your bid price.

♦ *Review the paperwork.* Before the auction begins, review the property tax statements, environmental reports, lot survey, legal description, and the purchase contract you'll be asked to sign.

♦ *What type of deed will the seller use to convey the property?* With a general warranty deed, the seller guarantees clear title subject only to certain named exceptions. Other types of deeds convey fewer title warranties. Don't accept a deed without an understanding of its limitations (liens, easements, encroachments, exceptions, missing heirs, etc.). All in all, title insurance provides your best guarantee. If a property's title is uninsurable, consult a real estate attorney to obtain an opinion of title.

◆ *Pay the deposit.* To bid, register with the auction company before the auction begins and show proof of deposit funds or cashier's checks (amount varies by auction). You then will be issued a bid card that will tell the auctioneer you are an approved bidder. Without a bid card, the auctioneer won't recognize your waving hand.

◆ *Is financing available?* Often auction companies prearrange financing on some or all of their properties. If so, find out the interest rate, terms, and qualifying standards. If not, determine how much time the auction company allows to arrange financing. Unlike most government auctions, auction companies do not expect their bidders to pay cash.

◆ *Is the sale absolute or subject to a reserve price.* Auction companies offer properties absolute or with reserve. If absolute, a property sells no matter how low the top bidder's price. With a reserve, the top bid must exceed a prearranged price or the property is pulled out of the auction. On occasion, the owner of a property may "nod" to the auctioneer and approve a bid that does not meet the reserve price.

How to Find Auctions

Auction companies advertise upcoming auctions in local and sometimes national newspapers (such as the *Wall Street Journal*). Auction companies want to attract as many bidders as possible. They want to draw large crowds so they can create a sense of excitement. If you want, auction companies will place your name on their mailing lists.

You'll find local auction companies listed in the phone book. Major auctions, though, are frequently handled by auction companies that operate nationwide. These firms include Fisher Auction Company, Hudson & Marshall, J.P. King, Kennedy-Wilson, Larry Latham, NRC Auctions, Ross Dove & Company, and Sheldon Good & Company. Large auctions are fun to attend. Try one. Plus, you'll learn the tricks of the trade as you watch the professional auctioneers and investors vie with one another.

Short Sale Bargains

You've now discovered multiple ways to find properties at a bargain price. You've learned about motivated sellers, foreclosures, REOs, auctions, probate, and estate sales. But by negotiating with a lienholder, you can *create* a bargain price. Investors call this technique a short sale.

What Is a Short Sale?

The short sale technique first gained momentum during the real estate recession that plagued California, Texas, and other parts of the country 15 to 20 years ago. Investors and lenders used the short sale to rescue *upside-down* property owners who fell behind on their mortgage payments.

> **Short sales rescue upside-down property owners.**

> **Upside-down owners owe more than their property is worth.**

To illustrate, say that during a speculative real estate boom you buy a home for $300,000. You put 5 percent down and borrow $285,000 from a lender. Three years later, you get laid off. Even worse, the market value of your property falls to $265,000. You would like to sell the house, but now the property is worth less than you owe. You're upside down.

Even if a buyer gave you a full price offer, you wouldn't net enough to pay your lender, closing expenses, a real estate commission, and accumulated deferred maintenance (repair) costs. What can you do?

Unfortunately, without a job, you can no longer make your mortgage payments. Nor is it likely that you can refinance. Your lender threatens to foreclose. Your situation looks bleak.

Lender, Too, Faces Bleak (Money-Losing) Outcome   The lender is threatening to foreclose, but it doesn't really want to. If the lender forecloses, it will surely lose money.

In your present difficult situation, you owe the lender a total of $280,000 (mortgage balance, missed payments). If the lender goes through foreclosure, it will want to collect this $280,000 plus other costs such as

◆ Attorney fees.
◆ Court costs.
◆ Lost interest.
◆ Property insurance premiums.
◆ Property tax payments.
◆ Miscellaneous costs (staff time, property upkeep, paperwork).

If these other costs total $20,000, the lender would have $300,000 sunk into this property.

How much would a foreclosure speculator bid for the property at auction? Maybe $200,000. If the lender lets this speculator take the property, the lender loses around $100,000.

Total sums owed	$300,000
Speculator bid	200,000
Lender loss	100,000

Alternatively, the lender may choose not to let the property go to a foreclosure speculator. It could shut out the speculators with a bid of $300,001. If the lender wins its bid, it then owns the property as an REO.

Does acquiring the REO solve the lender's problem? No. The lender continues to lose interest earnings on the money it has put out thus far on the property. It must still pay property taxes, premiums for property insurance, property upkeep, and repairs. To get the property sold, the lender will probably pay fix-up costs and a real estate commission.

> **REOs don't end the lender's losses.**

Lenders Lose with REOs   After these costs, will the lender eventually come out ahead with its REO? Still, the answer is no. Remember, at most, the property will bring a price of $265,000. Here's how the numbers might look.

Balance owed at foreclosure	$300,000
REO costs	15,000
Real estate commission @ 6%	15,900 (on $265k)
Total	330,900
REO sales price	265,000
Lender loss with REO	(65,900)

Even with the REO alternative, the lender loses $65,900 (and that assumes an REO sale at full market value—which is not likely). So, ask yourself if, as an investor, you could work out a way for lenders with bad loans to lose less money. Would the lender accept your solution? In many instances, the answer to that question is yes.

The Preforeclosure Workout   What if, before the lender filed foreclosure on a bad loan, you could get the lender to accept a short payoff—some amount less than the total balance the borrower owes? Quite likely you could save the lender from losing as much money as it otherwise would by going through with its foreclosure. You would help the borrowers salvage what's left of their credit record. (Late payments don't bring down a credit score nearly as much as would a foreclosure.)

What's in it for you? You acquire a property for less than its market value. Let's go back to the earlier example at the point in time when the borrowers owed $280,000—only now we'll assume that you're the investor.

How the Numbers Look   You talk with the borrowers. You learn their bleak upside-down situation. You offer them $1 for their property with the proviso that you can work out a short payoff on their loan with their lender. You succeed. Their lender agrees to accept $230,000. In exchange, the lender grants a full release of the mortgage lien it held against the property.

> **In a short sale, the lender accepts less to lose less.**

The sellers/borrowers begin a new financial life free of mortgage debt, free of mortgage payments they cannot make, and free of waking up in the middle of the night. The lender loses only $50,000, instead of the $65,900 (or more) that it would have lost by foreclosing the borrowers and eventually ending up with another REO that it does not want.

As for you, the investor, you've just become the owner of a $265,000 property for an outlay of $230,001. Everybody comes out ahead.

How to Complete a Short Sale

To complete a short sale, you typically need to negotiate well and diligently persevere. To earn your gain of $25,000 to $100,000 from this

> **Short sales yield profits for investors—but require effort.**

technique may require anywhere from several weeks to several months of back-and-forth talks and proposals. And even after this effort, you may still fail to put all of the pieces together.

But when you succeed, all of those efforts pay off. Let's look at the steps you can take to beat the odds.

Find Sellers in Financial Distress (or Otherwise Motivated to Deal)   To complete a short sale, you first need to find sellers who are financially distressed or otherwise eager to cut a deal that frees them from their property and their mortgage obligations. How can you find these motivated sellers?

You've got dozens of possibilities. Just revisit all of the techniques we've discussed so far, and especially those shown in Box 9.1. Remember, every day some people's lives change to make property ownership a burden. When you figure out a way to relieve that burden, you help the sellers and you help yourself.

Review the Sellers' Mortgage Payment Records   After you've established rapport with the sellers and set the tone for productive discussions, review their mortgage payment records and all collection letters thus far sent by their lender. Specifically, you want to learn:

- The current payoff amount on the loan including all back payments, late fees, and legal fees assessed by the lender (if any).
- Where the lender is in its collection efforts. In my experience, I've found lenders are more inclined to complete a short sale when the borrowers have missed multiple monthly payments. The borrowers are so seriously delinquent that the lender believes the property will almost certainly end up in foreclosure.
- How the full amount the borrowers owe compares with the likely selling price of their mortgaged property.
- Whether it appears that a foreclosure will lose the lender a lot of money, after adding in continued lost interest and other expenses. If so, you've located a hot prospect for a short payoff.

Review the Sellers' Total Finances   Before a lender will accept a short payoff, the borrowers must prove destitution. By destitution,

> **Lenders won't let borrowers just walk away from their mortgage.**

I don't mean that the borrowers will soon be living on food stamps in the back of their SUV. But the lender will probe to determine whether the borrowers own any valuable assets that they could sell to raise money.

The lender also will look at the borrowers' earnings history and career prospects. If the borrowers merely shirk their mortgage obligations, the lender won't likely negotiate (unless you persuade the collections staff to rethink their position).

Place the Property Under Contract When preliminary talks show that the borrowers can't pay and that the lender will lose money, get the property under contract.

Offer the sellers some token amount ($1) in exchange for a deed to their property. In addition, you agree to permanently get the lender off their backs. You save the sellers' credit and restore their peace of mind (at least as it relates to this imminent foreclosure).

Because you don't know whether the lender will accept a short payoff, include a contingency in your offer to the sellers that reads something like this:

> This agreement between [you] and [sellers] is subject to [you] obtaining full satisfaction of all claims owed to [lender] for an amount not to exceed $_____.

The maximum amount you actually commit to pay the lender will depend on the amount of profit you plan to earn and the riskiness of the property (current condition, certainty with which you can achieve your desired selling price). Do not agree to pay the sellers any money, because the lender won't approve it. Only rarely will a lender permit borrowers to put cash in their own pocket from a short sale.

> **Lenders require you to provide a seller release form.**

Obtain Permission to Negotiate with the Lender At the time the sellers accept your offer, you also ask them to authorize the lender to release the sellers' loan information to you. This form allows you to verify mortgage loan data, and it gives the lender authority to negotiate a payoff with you.

Without this written release, the lender will not share confidential loan data about its borrowers with you. Make sure the sellers understand the need for this release.

Approach the Lender   When you first approach the lender, do not—I repeat, do not—even suggest the mortgage payoff price that you have in mind. During this preliminary meeting (most probably with a staff officer in the lender's loss mitigation department), learn the lender's views about short payoffs. Learn the criteria the lender applies. Learn the lender's operating procedures.

Lenders settle their bad loans in different ways. Some hardballers won't budge. Others are glad to see you. Some (perhaps the majority) will act standoffish but can be persuaded to negotiate when you show them why your solution will work to their advantage. (Never assume that the bank personnel who staff loss mitigation departments understand why short payoffs can benefit the lender.)

> **Bank staff may not immediately open up to you.**

Prepare and Submit Your Offer   You've opened discussions with the lender and gathered information about its payoff policies. Ideally, during these talks, the lender will give you clues as to how much discount it's willing to accept. (Regardless, though, offer less than you're willing to pay.) You're now ready to prepare and submit an offer.

But wait. Don't just give the lender a number. First build your case. Submit a package of persuasive evidence. This package should include:

- *Cover letter.* Here's where you describe the evidence that you've submitted to prove why a short payoff now will benefit the lender. However, do not put precise figures in this letter. Build up the merits of the idea before you start talking numbers. Talk benefits before price.
- *Condition of the property.* Take *unflattering* photos of the property. Submit those that look the worst. Submit repair cost estimates (as high as you can reasonably justify).
- *Comparable sales.* Choose the lowest-priced, best-looking comparable sale properties. Use comp sales to support your estimate of market value for the mortgaged property. The less the lender

thinks the property will bring at foreclosure (or as an REO), the more it will accept your short-sale offer.

◆ *Owner distress pleas.* Include a hardship letter from the borrowers. This letter will explain the tough times these folks are experiencing. For support, include threatening letters the borrowers have received from the IRS, those large unpaid medical bills, the electricity cutoff notice, and the newspaper article that explains why 400 laid-off workers at the local textile plant (where both of the borrowers worked) will never be called back.

◆ *Credibility.* Provide evidence that you are ready, willing, and able to close. Prove to the lender that you will perform as promised.

◆ *Your offer.* Calculate and show the amount of losses the lender will suffer if it continues the foreclosure process. Then, reveal your payoff. This figure should show that the lender will net more if it acts now to accept your offer.

◆ *Persistence pays.* If the lender doesn't immediately respond to your offer, follow up, follow up, follow up. If the lender won't accept, then persuade the loss mitigation officer to suggest a number that might look good. Do whatever you can to keep the dialogue alive.

Come Up with the Money   To maximize the attractiveness of your offer to the lender, talk cash. Lenders prefer to cash out their bad loans. Rarely would a lender agree to a discounted payoff *and* carryback financing. (Yet, you can ask.)

How can you raise this money if you don't already have it? Return to Chapters 3–8. Given the bargain deal that you've just negotiated, you should be able to easily flip the property to another buyer (who has the cash to close), secure low- (or no-) down-payment financing from another lender, or bring in a money partner.

With a near-sure profit from the transaction, you will find the money. Nevertheless, don't wait until the last minute. Not only do you need to prove your credibility in your bid package, but when a lender accepts your offer you can't delay. Line up a *sure* source of financing *before* you submit your bid.

CHAPTER 12

Run Numbers Like a Pro

Amateurs buy property and *hope* they make money. Pros first run the numbers from a variety of perspectives. They weight possibilities and probabilities. Then they move forward only when the investment shows a strong upside with measured risks. Though savvy investors differ in their weighting of factors, nearly all review the following benchmarks.

- ◆ The construction cycle
- ◆ Per-unit measures
- ◆ Gross rent multipliers
- ◆ Capitalized value
- ◆ Cash flow returns
- ◆ Potential for creating value

After you learn these value benchmarks, you'll see that it's sometimes possible to achieve a high profit and retain a margin of safety—even if you pay above market value.

The trick, of course, is to know what you're doing and why you're doing it. Many beginning investors chase after "below-market" buys, and reject all properties priced at or above market. Instead, as a savvy, entrepreneurial investor, you'll want to run your potential buys through a variety of financial tests. When you apply a smart grading system, you can easily separate the dullards from the fast trackers.

Buying below market can give you a great bargain. But that's not the only way to score a money-making deal.

Monitor the Construction Cycle

Over the years, as construction costs go up and population increases, property nearly always increases in value. In the short run, though, current market values sometimes jump too far above construction costs.

Eyeing large profits, builders rush to construct new houses, condominiums, and apartments. They glut the market. Journalists proclaim, "Real estate's no longer a good investment." The foreclosure rate begins to climb.

The market approaches the ebb of the construction cycle. Guess what? You're now facing the perfect time to buy.

> **Over time, higher building costs pull up property values.**

How to Profit from the Construction Cycle

Here's how the construction cycle works. Typically, a city, town, or vacation area begins to boom. Jobs and wages go up. More people move in. Interest rates decline. Apartment rents and home prices climb higher. Apartment vacancies disappear. The number of homes up for sale begins to decline. Pretty soon, *existing* houses or apartments that could be constructed *new* for say, $300,000 per unit begin to command prices of, say, $400,000.

Builders Spy Opportunity

With prices of existing properties well above their construction costs, builders can quickly make a lot of money. Build at $300,000; sell at $400,000. Great! $100,000 profit. Naturally, too many builders rush in to grab a pile of profits. Because of these optimistic builder expectations, the supply of new houses or condos shoots up. What was recently a shortage becomes a surplus. Buyers who bought near the top of the cycle face disappointment (or worse) as rent levels and property prices temporarily stagnate or slide back to lower levels.

> **High builder profit margins may lead to overbuilding.**

Recovery   Over time, banks pull back their mortgage lending. Builders sharply cut their new developments. Rental vacancies begin to tighten; the number of unsold homes begins to fall. Potential renters and homebuyers again outnumber the supply of available properties. Property prices and rents stabilize and then edge up. Eventually, as shortages again loom on the horizon, vacancies fall further. Prices take off on another rapid run-up. The construction cycle turns another revolution. Prices set new record highs.

Implications for Investors

The classic major boom-bust construction cycle occurred in Texas in the mid to late 1980s. Properties that could be built new for $75,000 to $100,000 sold for as much as $125,000 to $150,000. Condominium and apartment projects multiplied like dandelions after an April rain. Back then, large real estate tax shelter benefits added fuel to the fire. In a situation similar to the dot-coms and tech stocks in the late 1990s, rapid price increases fed on themselves—until the real estate bubble burst.

Pitfalls   Could Texas *investors* have avoided getting caught in this downdraft? Absolutely. Had they kept an eye on construction costs, they could have anticipated problems. For whenever the market prices of properties push more than 10 to 15 percent ahead of their new replacement costs, the market is flashing yellow. Yet, rather than cautiously slow down, most would-be investors (and builders) speed up.

> **Large profits for builders can bring too much new supply to market.**

Savvy *investors*, though, pay attention to this warning sign. They back off from new acquisitions or buy only when they can get their price—not the inflated (and soon-to-be-deflated) market price.

The moral is to stay in touch with local builders or others who are in the know about contractor costs (building suppliers, lumber yards, real estate appraisers, building contractors, construction lenders). Also, you might consult one or more construction cost services. You can easily follow your local building costs through cost manuals (at your library) or web sites. When builder profit margins grow ever fatter, oversupply becomes a real threat.

Profit When Values Drop Below the Costs to Build New　Rents low? Vacancies climbing? Unsold houses and condos piling up in the Realtors' Multiple Listing Service? Builders going bankrupt? Lenders foreclosing? Great! That's the perfect time for investors to buy—especially when market prices end up below replacement costs. Because that means few builders will build. Builders will not knowingly pay more to build a house than they can get from its selling price.

As long as longer-term trends in an area point to a larger population, more jobs, and a desirable quality of life, prices (rents) are guaranteed to rise. More people, growing incomes, higher construction costs. You can profit from the construction cycle because decade-by-decade property prices will continue to set new peaks.

> **Depressed markets *reduce* risk.**

Have Money, Will Travel　Will local or regional shakeouts continue to occur in the future? Yes. Although investors, builders, and lenders have supposedly entered a new era of prudence, that story's been told before. It seems that each generation forgets the mistakes of the past. They must relearn the lessons taught in earlier years.

> **Stay informed about out-of-town markets.**

Stay informed. Keep tabs on various cities and real estate markets around the country. Stay alert for new speculative booms. As property prices peak and plunge, don't miss that opportunity. Adopt the motto, "Have Money (Credit), Will Travel." If the bargains don't come to you, then, as a entrepreneurial investor, go to the bargains.

Local (Regional) Recessions

Even without ruinous overbuilding, property prices can fall below replacement costs due to job declines and recession. During the early 1990s, large layoffs in the defense and aerospace industry created the housing troubles experienced in Southern California. But as with Texas, the Southern California economy had to bounce back. And when it did, we witnessed a terrific boom in property prices.

Monitor the real estate cycle. As you begin to see the peak over the horizon, step back and let the fools rush in. When others fear to tread, jump in and rescue (at a nice profit) those folks who are drowning in debt and praying for a bale out.

Construction Costs > Market Price = Bargain Hunter's Delight

Per-Unit Measures

Smart real estate investors rely on various per-unit measures to help them decide whether a property looks like a good buy. As is true for all rules of thumb, per-unit figures signal whether a property *tends* to be priced over or under some benchmark norm. Though never compelling on their own, per unit measures give you another test to apply to your potential investments.

> **To compare properties, use per-unit prices.**

Per Apartment Unit

When you look at multiunit apartment buildings, divide the asking price by the number of apartment units in the property. For example, for an eight-unit property priced at $450,000, you would calculate:

$$\text{price per unit} = \frac{\$450,000}{8}$$
$$\text{price per unit} = \$56,250$$

If you know that other similar apartment buildings have typically *sold* for $60,000 to $70,000 per unit, you may have found a bargain. This and other per-unit measures give you a quick way to compare prices when rental properties differ in the number of their units. Say you're comparing a 6-unit, a 9-unit, and an 11-unit property at the respective prices of $275,000, $435,000, and $487,500. By figuring per-unit prices, you can rank the properties from the lowest priced to the highest.

No. Units	Price	Price per Unit
11	$487,500	$44,318
6	275,000	45,833
9	435,000	48,333

Size, Quality, and Location   Ideally, compare units that closely match. If that's not possible, adjust values as properties differ in size, site features, quality, and location. Try to spot those differences that make a difference. Use a checklist to compare building features and you can rank properties according to their profit potential. (See a sample checklist at my web site, garyeldred.com.)

> **Arbitrage your investments. Buy in one market, sell in another.**

Opportunity Knocks (Arbitrage)   Price-per-unit measures help you spot "bargain" buildings. But this measure also points to opportunities in two other ways:

- *Size.* Change the size of the units from larger to smaller, or vice versa. Imagine that smaller 700- to 800-square-foot units sell and rent at substantial premiums over larger units of 1,200 to 1,400 square feet. So, if you buy a building of predominantly larger units, you could earn a big payoff when you redesign the building's space into smaller units.
- *Conversion.* You might also profit by noticing that buildings with two-bedroom rentals typically sell in the $40,000 to $50,000 per-unit range. Yet, in similar condo buildings, two-bedroom units sell in the $70,000 to $80,000 range. Or this price difference might appear in the opposite direction. Either way, buy at the lower-priced use, convert, then sell (or rent) at the higher-priced use.

Although arbitrage opportunities don't occur everyday, they do come up every now and then. Pay attention to *relative* prices. Prepare to jump when you can buy a building at a low price and then convert it to a use that sells at a higher price.

Per-Square-Foot (p.s.f.) Measures

You've probably heard buyers and sellers remark that a property sold for say, $195 per square foot. Price per square foot (p.s.f.) represents one of the most widely used methods of benchmark pricing. Investors and homebuyers alike rely on it to ballpark values. To calculate a per-square-foot figure, divide the total square footage of the unit (house, apartment, or total building) into its price:

$$p.s.f. = \frac{asking\ price}{square\ footage}$$

$$p.s.f. = \frac{\$285,000}{1,900}$$

$$p.s.f. = \$150$$

If comp properties have sold at $170 to $180 p.s.f., a price of $150 p.s.f. may represent a bargain.

> **Not all square footage counts equally.**

Naive investors can go wrong using per-square-foot figures because no fixed standards apply. All square feet are not created equal in terms of quality, design, and usability. Calculate p.s.f. figures cautiously. Unless designed with market appeal, converted garages, basements, and attics are worth far less per square foot than a property's original living areas.

Also, beware of mismatches in size. Some buildings are constructed with room counts or room sizes far out of proportion to each other, or to competing properties.

Gross Rent Multipliers (GRMs)

To value rental houses and small apartment buildings, you can also divide the property's price by its total (gross) rent collections. As shown below, this calculation gives you a gross rent multiplier.* Consider these market data:

---

*Sometimes investors express GRMs as monthly rent multipliers rather than annual. For example, measured monthly, the GRM for College Terrace equals 95.

	Sales Price		Annual Rent Collections		GRM
College Terrace	$434,500	÷	$55,000	=	7.9
Bivens Lake Apts.	526,680	÷	62,700	=	8.4
Four Palms	323,610	÷	48,300	=	6.7

GRMs vary by neighborhood. Check sales of comparable properties.

If you find an income property with a relatively high GRM, it could signal either a price too high, or rents too low. Further checking would reveal the answer. Throughout the United States and Canada, I've seen annual gross rent multipliers as low as 4.0 (such as rundown properties, unpopular neighborhoods, no-growth cities) and as high as 25 (coastal California cities). In my university town, annual gross rent multipliers typically range from a low of 8.0 (lower income housing) to 20 (single-family rental houses in professional neighborhoods or houses within a mile of campus).

High GRMs signal negative cash flow.

Generally, when annual gross rent multipliers go above 8.0, you suffer negative cash flows—unless you increase your down payment to 30 percent or more.* Because big cities and vacation towns with high housing prices often produce GRMs of 15 or higher, cash-flow investors who live in those areas should buy their rental houses and apartments elsewhere. Or, in high-priced areas, look for neighborhoods or market niches (condominiums, lower-middle income segment, outlying suburbs) that offer a more profitable balance of property prices and the rent levels.

Capitalized Value

Investors typically weigh capitalized value more heavily than GRMs. To calculate, divide a property's net operating income by the appropriate cap rate.

$$V = \frac{NOI}{R}$$

---

*Based on mortgage rates of around 7.0 percent on small rental properties.

Where   V represents the estimated market value of the property, NOI (net operating income) represents the property's rents less expenses, and R equals the market capitalization rate. To illustrate, here's how this technique would look for a six-unit apartment building:

Six-Unit Income Statement (Annual)

1. Gross annual potential rents ($725/mo. 3 12 3 6)	$52,200
2. Income from parking and storage areas	5,062
3. Vacancy and collection losses @ 7%	(4,009)
4. Effective gross income	**$53,254**
Less operating and fixed expenses	
5. Trash pick-up	1,080
6. Utilities	450
7. Licenses and permit fees	206
8. Advertising and promotion	900
9. Management fees @ 6%	3,195
10. Maintenance and repairs	3,000
11. Yard care	488
12. Miscellaneous	2,250
13. Property taxes	3,202
14. Property and liability insurance	1,267
15. Reserves for replacement	1,875
16. Total operating and fixed expenses	$17,914
Net operating income (NOI)	**$35,340**

You can easily *compute* NOI. But, you can still err. To alert you to possible NOI traps, heed these warnings (which match numerically with the entries shown on the income statement):

1. *Gross potential income.* To figure gross potential income, use the property's existing rent levels. If its current rents sit above market, use *market* rent levels. Verify all leases for rental amounts and lease terms. Do not use a rent figure based on your anticipated rent increases (if any).

2. *Additional income.* With some properties, you can charge fees for applications, parking, storage, laundry, party room,

garages, and so on. Verify all of this income. Don't count extra income that's not proven by past operating experience or reasonable market data.

3. *Vacancy and collection losses.* Use market vacancy rates, or the current owner's vacancies for the past year—whichever is *higher.* Also, when judging market vacancy rates, take your figures from the market niche in which this property currently operates. Vacancy rates may vary significantly by neighborhood, apartment size, quality, and rent level. As you compare vacancy rates by market niche, try to spot those segments that are experiencing the greatest shortages.

4. *Effective gross income.* It is from this cash that you will pay property expenses and mortgage payments. If you overestimate rent levels or underestimate vacancies, you may end up cash-short.

5. *Trash pick-up.* Verify rates and allowable quantities. Look for lower-cost alternatives.

6. *Utilities.* In addition to common area lighting, some buildings include centralized heat and air systems. Verify the amounts of these expenses with utility companies.

7. *License and permit fees.* On occasion, owners of rental properties are required to pay municipal fees of one sort or another.

8. *Lease-up expenses.* Ideally, you will generate a good supply of rental applicants from free postings, referrals, and inquiries; otherwise, you may need to advertise. Also, you'll probably need to pay for credit checks on potential tenants.

9. *Management fees.* Even if you self-manage your units, allocate some expense here for your time and effort. Don't confuse return on labor for return on investment.

10. *Maintenance and repairs.* Enter an expense to pay yourself or others. "I'll take care of that myself" shouldn't mean, "I'll work for free."

11. *Grounds maintenance.* Yard care entails mowing the lawn, trimming hedges, removing snow, cleaning up leaves, tending to the flower beds, and so on.

12. *Miscellaneous.* You will incur such odds-and-ends expenses as lease preparation, auto mileage, and long-distance telephone charges.

13. *Property taxes.* Verify amount, tax rate, and assessed value. Check accuracy. Note whether the property is subject to any special assessments (sewer, sidewalks, water reclamation).
14. *Property and liability insurance.* Verify exact coverage for property and types of losses. Increase deductibles and limits on liability.
15. *Reserves for replacement.* Eventually, you'll need to replace the roof, HVAC, appliances, carpeting, and other limited-life items. Allocate a pro rata annual amount here.
16. *Net operating income (NOI).* Subtract all expenses from effective gross income. You now have the numerator for $V = NOI/R$.

Figure a building's NOI conservatively. Don't make grand assumptions about potential rent increases. Don't understate or omit necessary

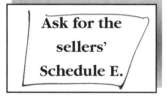

Ask for the sellers' Schedule E.

expenses. Verify, verify, verify. Allocate reasonable amounts for replacement reserves. Ask to see the sellers' Schedule E where they have reported property revenues and expenses to the IRS. (You may get resistance on this request. But listen carefully to the sellers' excuses. Are they plausible?)

Estimate Market Value

After figuring NOI, derive an accurate capitalization rate (R). Compare the NOIs (net operating incomes) of similar properties to their selling prices. Ask for this information when you talk with realty agents who regularly sell (and preferably own) small rental properties, or from other investors (a local real estate investment club, for example). Competent investment property managers should also know cap rates. After studying the market, arrange your cap rate data as follows:

Cap rates are set by local markets.

Property	Recent Sales Price	NOI	R
Hampton Apts. (8 units)	$452,900	$43,211	.0954
Woodruff Apts. (6 units)	360,000	35,900	.0997

Adams Manor (6 units)	295,000	28,440	.0964
Newport Apts. (9 units)	549,000	53,700	.0978
Ridge Terrace (8 units)	471,210	42,409	.09

If Ridge Terrace and Hampton Apartments seem most like the property that you're valuing, select cap rates of .09 and .095. Then, calculate a value range for your subject property.

$$1. \quad V = \frac{\$35,340 \text{ (NOI)}}{.09 \text{ (R)}}$$

$$V = \$392,66$$

$$2. \quad V = \frac{\$35,340 \text{ (NOI)}}{.095 \text{ (R)}}$$

$$V = \$372,000$$

You now know the value of your property most likely ranges between $370,000 and $390,000.

> **The lower the cap rate, the higher the value of a property.**

Throughout the country, cap rates for small rental properties may run from as low as 3.5 up to 8, 12, 14 percent, or higher. Generally, a *low* cap rate occurs when you're valuing highly desirable properties in good to top neighborhoods. Apartment buildings with condo conversion potential also tend to sell with low cap rates. Remember, low cap rates create a relatively high property values and high cap rates yield relatively low property values. Relatively high cap rates apply to less desirable properties in so-so neighborhoods—or properties located in areas with little (or no) perceived growth potential. Low cap rates predominate in San Francisco. Much higher cap rates can be found in Buffalo or Detroit.

Anticipate the Future, Pay for the Present

In the previous NOI example, you relied on verified income and expense figures drawn from the property's current operating history and your knowledge of competitive properties. As an entrepreneurial investor, though, you will boost the value of your properties through fix-up work and renovations, better property management, rezoning, or perhaps neighborhood revitalization. Your improvements can lift your property's net income and at the same time lower the property's cap rate. Your property's value can quickly jump by 20 percent, 30 percent, or more.

> **Sellers will ask you to pay for potential. Savvy investors pay for "as is."**

When you negotiate to buy, pay for the present, not your (or the seller's) vision of the future. Investors who anticipate great profits often pay too much. Don't let the sellers capture the value potential that you plan to create.

Mum's the Word: Don't Tell Sellers Your Plans

Beginning investors, especially, tend to reveal too much of their plans for a property. To gain a bargain price, don't turn your cards so that the sellers (or their sales agent) can see them. If you explicitly question the sellers in ways that reveal your value-creating ideas, the sellers will likely use that potential to strengthen their own negotiating position.

> **Avoid signaling your plans to a seller.**

In most cases, sellers already hold inflated ideas about all the great things you can do to enhance their property—which regrettably, they claim, they never had time (or money) to accomplish. Because such ploys are common, don't load the sellers with more ammunition to fire back at you. As much as possible, negotiate for the property as it currently is operated. Reap the upside as your bonus for entrepreneurial insights and effort.

Cash Flow Returns

To illustrate, cash flow returns bring forward that six-unit apartment building from several pages back. Assume you buy that property for $350,000 (around $60,000 per unit). You talk to a lender and tentatively arrange a mortgage for $280,000 (an 80 percent loan-to-value ratio). The lender wants an 8.0 percent interest rate with a 25-year term. You put $70,000 down. Here are the figures:

Loan amount	$350,000
Annual mortgage payments @ 8.0%; 25 years	25,932
Net operating income (NOI)	35,340
Less mortgage payments	25,932
BTCF (before tax cash flow)	9,408

$$\text{Cash flow return} = \frac{\text{BTCF}}{\text{Down Payment}}$$

$$= \frac{\$9,408}{\$70,000}$$

$$= 13.44\%$$

Not bad. But say your required return (hurdle rate) equals 15 percent. How might you boost your cash flow returns? Get the lender to extend the loan term to 30 years. If successful, your payments (assuming no change in interest rate) would drop to $24,652 a year; your annual pretax cash flow would increase to $10,688 (35,340 minus 24,652):

$$\text{Cash flow return} = \frac{\$10,688}{\$70,000}$$

$$= 15.3\%$$

If you prefer not to extend the loan term to 30 years, push the lender down to a 7.625 percent interest rate. Your mortgage payments (25 years) would total $25,102 per year. Your cash flow would equal $10,237 (35,340–25,102):

$$\text{Cash flow return} = \frac{\$10,237}{\$70,000}$$

$$= \$14.28\%$$

That lower interest rate won't quite do it. But as an enterprising investor, you've other options:

- Try for an even lower interest rate (7.5 percent would work).
- Ask the seller to take back an interest-only balloon note for five years at 7.0 percent in the amount of, say, $20,000.
- Negotiate a lower price for the property.
- Switch from a 25-year, fixed-rate mortgage to a 7.0 percent 5/20 adjustable-rate mortgage. This tactic would work especially well if you plan to sell (or exchange) the property within five years.

◆ Look for reasonable and certain ways to boost the property's net income. Increase rent collections, raise occupancy. Cut expenses.

◆ Agree to pay the seller a higher price in exchange for owner financing on terms more favorable (lower interest rate, lower down payment) than a bank would offer.

> **You find a property. But you negotiate and structure a good deal.**

Any or all of these techniques *could* work. Experiment with the numbers and negotiate some mutually agreeable solution. As an investor in real estate, the "market" will never provide you a return. You earn your return based upon the price, terms of financing, property improvements, and market strategy that you put together. [Note: Many investors today use computer software programs to run their financial sensitivity analyses. To see a good example, visit www.erealinvestor.com.]

Create Your Own Appreciation

You never need to passively accept market rent increases or property appreciation rates of just 3 percent, 5 percent, or even 7 percent a year. Use your entrepreneurial skills to study the market, improve the property,

> **Create your own appreciation.**

develop a competitive edge for your target market, and locate communities and neighborhoods that are poised to beat the market. Any or all of these efforts will quickly shoot up your net worth.

I love to buy properties that score well on all of the value benchmarks that you've just learned. But even more—I love to buy properties that include large doses of hidden value, value that I can bring to life through market-researched, profit-yielding improvements. In fact, in sellers' markets (when too many buyers are chasing too few properties), it's often easier to discover hidden value begging to be realized than it is to find properties to buy at below-market prices. Naturally, when possible, do both. Buy at a bargain price *and* add value.

CHAPTER 13

Greatly Increase the Value of Your Investment Property

Want to immediately jump your net worth by $25,000, $100,000, $250,000, or more? Then put to work this simple method for figuring out the value of a property:

$$\text{Value} = \frac{\text{Net Operating Income (NOI)}}{\text{Capitalization Rate (R)}}$$

To refresh your memory, let's go through another example. Assume that you find a ten-unit apartment building located in Columbus, Ohio. This property brings in net income (NOI) of $48,000 a year. Based on talks with local real estate agents, appraisers, and other investors, you figure this property "as is" should sell with a cap rate of 9 percent (.09). You can calculate the "as is" value of these six units at $533,333.

$$\frac{48,000 \text{ (NOI)}}{.09 \text{ (R)}} = \$533,333 \text{ (V)}$$

If you could boost that property's NOI to $60,000 a year, you would push its value up 25 percent. You would gain another $133,000 in equity.

$$\frac{60,000 \text{ (new NOI)}}{.09 \text{ (R)}} = \$666,666 \text{ (V)}$$

Even better, if you can reduce the riskiness of the property, you justify a lower cap rate than .09, say, 8 percent (.08). With a higher NOI and a lower cap rate, the value of that property skyrockets from the original $533,333 up to $750,000—an immediate gain in value of $212,000.

Are such large increases in value possible within a period of 6 to 18 months? Absolutely! Why? Because many owners of small investment properties still think of themselves as landlords (with the accent on "lord") and their residents merely as renters who don't deserve customer care. But just the opposite is true. Today (and in the future) market conditions require savvy investors to treat their tenants as valued customers—not serfs.

Search for Competitive Advantage

Most small investors mismanage their properties because they do not intelligently survey and inspect competing properties. Without this market knowledge, they can't strategically customize their properties to make them stand out from other rentals. In other words, these owner-investors fail to monitor their competitors, and they fail to carefully adapt their market and management strategies to wow their customers (tenants, buyers).

> **Boost your property values. Outperform your competitors.**

Your Properties Should Stand Above the Competition

Develop a profit-generating mindset. Never think of yourself as a landlord. Never define what you do as "owning rental properties." Instead, provide your customers with a product (housing) that stands out and stands above your competitors. If you adopt this modern attitude, your profits (and the value of your properties) will climb above average for two reasons:

> **Never think of yourself as a landlord.**

1. *Better resident relations.* The residents of your properties will reward you with lower turnover, fewer problems, and higher rents.
2. *Alert to opportunities.* With a customer-oriented, constant-improvement attitude, you systematically come up with ideas to add value to your property operations.

A Strategy of Your Own

Good management and marketing depend on good knowledge of competing properties and resident (tenant) preferences. You want to create a *specific* strategy that will yield *you* the highest profits. You can read a dozen books on landlording and most give you a list of do's and don'ts that range from applications to waterbeds. Although books suggest ideas, never accept their advice as the final word.

What works today may not work tomorrow. What works in Peoria may not go over in Paducah. What works in a tight rental market may prove less effective in a high-vacancy market. What works best with HUD Section 8 tenants may actually turn away those upscale young professionals who live in your more expensive buildings. Should you accept pets, smokers, or college students? It all depends.

> **Adapt your property to your local market.**

Offer your selected target market of renters (or buyers) the value proposition that they will prefer—yet, at the same time, a value proposition that fattens your bottom line (NOI). In practice, you create that profit-maximizing value proposition by understanding your competitors. Then execute a competitive edge.

Here's the $100,000 question: What can you actually do to boost your property's investment value? Here are some ideas.

First, Verify Actual Rent Collections, Not Merely Rental Rates

Before you buy, verify. Many new investors accept an owner's rent figures and then subtract a so-called standard 5 percent vacancy factor. In truth, many property owners do not *collect* 95 percent of their scheduled rents—even when they achieve 95 percent occupancy. To verify rents, verify the lease rates the tenants have agreed to pay. Second, estimate realistic vacancy and collection losses. Your profits, and the building's value, rest upon bankable funds, not leaky leases. If you overpay for a property because you overestimate the property's current rent collections, you must increase value with a strong headwind.

Talk with Tenants

Before you buy an investment property, talk with tenants who live in the building. This practice serves four purposes.

◆ Identify problems in the building.
◆ Identify problems with tenants.
◆ Verify lease application data.
◆ Generate ideas for improvement.

Problems in the Building

"Not enough parking."
"Too much noise."
"The bills for heat and air are outrageous—$277 last month."
"These walls are paper thin."
"This place lacks security. We've had three break-ins during the past six months."
"The closets in this apartment are too small, and there's no place for long-term storage."
"No place to park or store my boat—or even my bicycle."
"Cockroaches, ugh. This place is crawling with cockroaches."

> **Ask tenants, "What don't you like?"**

To really learn about a building, talk with the tenants. Gain valuable insights by asking tenants, "Tell me, what don't you like around here?" On occasion, the tenants will speak well of the building (or its owner). But more often they complain. Will you hear glowing praise? Not likely. Tenants know that too many good comments might spur a rent increase.

Problems with Tenants

Bad tenants can ruin a good building. If some tenants create hassles for others, learn about it before you offer to buy the property. Problems within a building *and* problems with disruptive tenants can stir up vacancies, turnover, and rent collections. Solve these problems, and you create value.

Verify Lease and Application Data

Leases and tenant application data do not always portray the true facts about a property's tenants. Some sellers show investors phantom leases with false data. Aside from fraud, talks with tenants may reveal rent concessions that aren't recorded in the written file that the sellers gave you to review. You may find that some tenants sublet their units. Or maybe they let additional friends and family move in with them.

> **Closely review the rent roll.**

Before you buy, put together a rent roll that's accurate. Otherwise, both your NOI and cap rate (risk rate) figures may err.

Generate Ideas for Improvement

When you value a building, divide the problems you find into two piles: (1) economically unsolvable and (2) opportunity-laden. As talks with tenants reveal the strengths and weaknesses of the as-is property, you value the property as it stands today. But at the same time, you constantly roll ideas through your mind. How might you profitably improve the property tomorrow? Through the eyes of a critical buyer, you find faults and profit-draining negatives. Through the alert eyes of an entrepreneurial investor, you visualize ways to turn a lump of coal into a diamond.

> **Critique the property, but look for opportunities to create value.**

Set Your Rents with Market Savvy

Many owners of rental properties merely guesstimate rental rates for their units. As a result, they underprice; they overprice. They don't make rent-enhancing improvements. They fail to adequately segment their tenants. They spend for ineffective advertising. They devote little time and money to target marketing. If they experience high vacancies, they blame a soft market. If they experience low vacancies, they pride themselves on their skill as a landlord.

All in all, these mistakes (and many others) flow from the same source. Property owners don't realize the profits they miss when they set their rents according to whim or arbitrary judgment—rather than market reality.

> **Mispricing rents costs you dearly.**

Think of missed opportunities like this. You own a 12-unit building. You underprice each unit by $25 a month. The cap rate is .09 (9 percent). How much does this underpricing error cost you?

$$\text{Lost income} \quad = \$25 \times 12\,\text{units} \times 12\,\text{months}$$
$$= \$3,600\,\text{per year}$$
$$\text{Lost building value} = \frac{\$3,600}{.09}$$
$$= \$40,000$$

You've lost $40,000 of value just by underpricing $25 per month! Move that rent shortfall up to $50 or $100 a month, and you lose $100,000 to $200,000. Make no mistake: Underpricing can cost you a pile of money. Overpricing, too, can also cost you plenty. Charge too much, your vacancies, turnovers, advertising costs, conversion rates (meaning that you must show the property 15 to 20 times before you find a willing tenant), malicious tenant damage, and bad debts shoot up. To set rent rates, inspect competing properties. Acquire personal knowledge of competing properties, features, amenities, and pricing. Then, adopt a price strategy that maximizes net income (NOI) and property value.

Your Apartment Checklist

If rental houses and apartments were like cans of Campbell's tomato soup or bottles of Coca-Cola, you could expect every unit to rent for the same price. You could discover an actual "market" rent level. But houses and apartment buildings differ in dozens of ways that their potential tenants find appealing or unappealing. Tour properties. What do you see? How do properties differ with respect to these features?

- ❑ Views
- ❑ Energy usage/efficiency
- ❑ Square footage
- ❑ Natural light
- ❑ Ceiling height
- ❑ Quiet/noisiness
- ❑ Parking
- ❑ Room count
- ❑ Appliances (quality, quantity)
- ❑ Landscaping
- ❑ Quality of finishes
- ❑ Heat/air conditioning
- ❑ Decks/patios/balconies
- ❑ Cleanliness
- ❑ Carpeting/floor coverings
- ❑ Electrical outlets
- ❑ Emotional appeal
- ❑ Color schemes/aesthetics
- ❑ Living area floor plan
- ❑ Closet space
- ❑ Storage space
- ❑ Kitchen functionality
- ❑ Kitchen pizzazz
- ❑ Entryway convenience
- ❑ Tenant demographics
- ❑ Tenant lifestyles, attitudes
- ❑ Lighting
- ❑ Security
- ❑ Laundry facilities
- ❑ Fireplace
- ❑ Physical condition
- ❑ Window coverings
- ❑ Types/style of windows
- ❑ Image/reputation
- ❑ Furniture

And this checklist doesn't even mention other tenant concerns such as the amount of the security deposit (total move-in cash), the terms of the lease, the quality of the management, and last but far from least, location. When you omit such differences, you can't intelligently say that your two- bedroom, two-bath units should rent for $675 a month. First, you want to compare and contrast your units feature by feature to a broad sample of competing properties.

> **Profit-maximizing investors pay attention to each feature of their properties.**

With quality competitive information about property features and rent levels, you sharpen your ability both to evaluate a property and to spot opportunities to increase its value.

Give the Interior a Martha Stewart Makeover

As you walk into the unit, are you met with a bland neutrality? Do you see faded paint, scuff marks, outdated color schemes, cheap hollow-core doors, nail holes in the walls, worn carpeting, torn linoleum, old-fashioned light fixtures, cracked wall switch plates, or stained toilets, bathtubs, and sinks? If you answer yes to any or all of these questions, great! You've found the easiest path to creating value.

Pay Special Attention to Kitchens and Baths

To really wow your potential tenants, bring in Martha Stewart to redo the kitchens and bathrooms. Flip through the pages of kitchen and bath magazines. Look for that right combination of materials and colors that will create a light, bright, cheerful, and inviting look. Eliminate those harvest-gold appliances, the chipped and stained sinks, and that cracked glass in the shower door.

As you inspect these key rooms, focus on each of the following features *for at least 30 seconds*:

- ❏ Floors
- ❏ Ceilings
- ❏ Sinks
- ❏ Toilet bowl
- ❏ Windows and window sills
- ❏ Electrical outlet plates
- ❏ Lighting
- ❏ Faucets
- ❏ Walls
- ❏ Cabinets
- ❏ Cabinet and drawer handles
- ❏ Appliances
- ❏ Counter tops

When you focus for 30 seconds on each feature, you notice how features clash or coordinate to give rooms their overall feel. Throughout the apartment or house, details count. But they especially count in the kitchens and bathrooms. The right pizzazz in the kitchens and bathrooms transform a ho-hum unit into a showplace.

> **Focus sharpens your ability to see what others miss.**

How much will transformation cost? If you spent $25,000 to remodel your own kitchen, you may think pizzazz in a rental unit would run you into the poorhouse. Not true. An outlay of between $2,000 and $5,000 can transform plain Jane into Paris Hilton. Replacing sinks, hardware, toilet bowls, and toilet seats requires relatively little money. As to cabinetry, even a lower-cost refinish (not a full replacement) can work wonders.

Cleanliness Generates Profits

Want to attract tenants who will care for your properties? Thoroughly clean the units as if a drill sergeant were about to perform a white-glove inspection. Do not think "rental property." Think "home."

> **Clean units attract clean tenants.**

Clean everywhere. Remove the dirt, dust, cobwebs, and dead bugs from all corners, baseboards, light fixtures, and shelving. Pull out kitchen drawers. Dump the bread crumbs and other accumulated debris. Make sure windows and mirrors sparkle and shine. Look for grime in the shower and shower door tracks. Scrape the rust out of the medicine cabinets and repaint where necessary. Eliminate odors. Each unit should look and smell fresh and clean.

Natural Light and Views

If units seem dark, brighten them up. In addition to color schemes, add windows or skylights. If you're lucky, you might find one of those older buildings with 10-foot ceilings—now reduced to 8 feet via suspended acoustical tile. For a reason unknown to me (energy conservation?), dropped ceilings became popular in the 1960s and 1970s. Today, they're ugly and outdated. Rip them out. Your rooms will seem larger and brighter. Also, in rooms with high ceilings, install clerestory windows to bring in more light.

> **Create a view with landscaping.**

For first-floor rooms, enhance views with landscaping or fencing. To create views for upper-story units, think long term. Plant trees. When financially feasible, create a view by moving a window. Ugly views turn off tenants. Pleasant views provide selling points. Give tenants better views than dumpsters, parking lots, high-traffic streets, and the rooftops of other buildings.

Special Touches

For aesthetic touches, try chair railings, wallpaper borders, upgraded door handles, paneled doors, and wood stains (instead of paint).

> **Create gee whiz features.**

Upgrades in light fixtures, too, help add pizzazz. Newer types of lighting are gaining popularity for both form and function.

Get ideas for special touches from decorating and remodeling magazines. Visit model homes and newer upscale apartment, townhouse, and condominium developments. Don't go too far with special touches, or you will cut into your profitability. Still, a few gee whiz features will help rental prospects differentiate and remember your units.

Safety, Security, and Convenience

Often safety and convenience go together as with the number and capacity of electrical outlets. Older buildings, especially, lack enough outlets and amperage to safely handle all of the modern household's plug-in appliances, computers, printers, fax machines, and audio/video home entertainment centers. Many tenants don't notice functional obsolescence until they move into a unit. Then they "solve" the problem with adapter plugs and roaming extension cords. If a unit lacks electrical capacity, plan an upgrade.

Other Issues of Safety and Security

Other safety issues include smoke alarms, carbon monoxide detectors, fire escape routes, door locks, first-floor windows, and first-floor sliding glass doors. Environmental health hazards may exist because of lead paint, asbestos, or formaldehyde—any of which may be found in building materials used in construction (or remodeling) prior to 1978. Insist that sellers disclose these hazards. If a building is suspect, don't buy it without advice of an environmental expert.

> **Ask an expert to assess risks for an environmentally suspect property.**

Costly remedial improvements in these areas seldom pay off with higher rents. To profitably deal with environmental issues, negotiate a large discount in your purchase price. As to security against break-ins, make sure all windows and doors lock securely and cannot be jimmied with a credit card (as in the TV shows), or even a screwdriver. Deadbolt locks are best. Entry-door peepholes give tenants a sense of security.

In a criminal-infested world, tenants need to feel safe in their homes. If doors, door locks, and windows seem flimsy, many tenants won't rent a unit—regardless of its oohs and aahs.

Stairs, Carpets, and Bathrooms

Pay attention to steps or stair railings that pose a threat. Frayed carpets, bathtubs that lack no-slip bottoms, and no handrails provoke falls. Remedy every safety or security hazard within the property. Even when a repair doesn't add to your rent collections, it protects your tenants. It reduces the chance that a tenant will sue you for negligence.

> **Unsafe properties invite lawsuits.**

Rightsize the Rooms

Have you ever walked into a house and found some rooms too large and others too small? It seems today that in many houses builders construct a huge great room along with a huge master bedroom and bath, and then finish off the house with three or four dinky bedrooms. The house lacks a sense of proportion (which evidently is what some buyers like).

Create a Sense of Proportion

What sense of proportion should a house or an apartment unit display? The answer varies by tenant segment, price range, and timing (because over the years tenant preferences change). As people and property change, opportunities arise for you to notice possibilities for improvement. Buy an out-of-style building, then rearrange the internal floor plan to better appeal to the intended market segment of renters or buyers.

Postwar Units Are Modernized

I once bought an older eight-unit apartment building. It had been built in 1949 to house the veterans of World War II and their fast-growing families. The units were arranged in a 3BR/1BTH style (common to that period) with one moderate-sized bedroom for the parents and two small bedrooms for those recently born early boomers. In the 1990s (when I bought the property), most tenants looked at the units and said, "Ugh, no way could we live here."

Because the owner had trouble keeping the units rented, I got a bargain price. To create value, I split up one of the small bedrooms. I used half of that space to enlarge the other small bedroom, and half to add a second bathroom. I then rented the building to tenants looking to share their rentals with a roommate. Rent collections jumped by $175 per unit per month—a profitable return on my investment.

Create More Storage

Self-storage (miniwarehouses) now represent one of the fastest growing types of properties in the United States. We've all become pack rats. "Throw it away? Why I might need that sometime."

Talk with tenants. Talk with homeowners. Many will tell you the same thing. "I like my home, but we lack space for storage." If you want to add appeal to your rental houses and apartment units, add storage space. To do so, think about storage in three ways:

◆ Bring dead space to life.
◆ Increase the capacity of existing space.
◆ Create new storage space in basements or attics. Install storage sheds.

Bring Dead Space to Life

Let me illustrate with an example that seems trivial but mildly amuses prospective tenants. Look in the cabinet under your kitchen sink. You will see a small gap between the front panel of the cabinet above the door and the sink. In other words, dead space. How might you use that space? Install a small pull-down compartment to stow away soap, sponge, and scrubbing pads. No more sink clutter. Whenever I show this little innovation to other people, I always get an approving response.

Okay, it's trivial. But it illustrates the point. All houses and apartments include dead spaces (large and small) that you can bring to life.

- Under stairs and stairwells.
- Bay windows with storage built under the window seat and under the outside of the window.
- Garden windows.
- On the tops of kitchen cabinets.
- Dead-end cabinets.
- Walls suitable for shelving.
- Recessed storage between studs (as with an in-wall medicine chest).
- Kitchen hanging bars for pots and pans.

These ideas sample possibilities. If you go through any house or apartment and ask, "Where are the dead spaces that I can bring to life for purposes of storage?" you will find them.

Increase the Capacity of Existing Storage Space

My favorite examples to illustrate how to achieve more with less come from the California Closet Company (CCC). As ideas from this innovative firm have proven, you can double (or triple) your storage capacity without adding even one square inch of new space. Simply reorganize and redesign the raw space that already exists. Although founded as a closet company, CCC now redesigns garages, offices, workshops, and kitchens. Put these reorganizing principles to work and you wow your prospective tenants. You give your rentals a sought-after benefit.

> **Let the California Closet Company guide your ideas to add space for storage.**

Design space to serve multiple purposes. You can multipurpose through use of a Murphy bed that folds up against a wall. A Murphy bed adds usable floor space and opens up the possibility of shelving alongside the bed. Either use the wall cavity or create a new, larger cavity by building out a new wall even with the Murphy bed.

Check Noise Levels

No one likes noise. Before you invest, test the units for soundproofing. Will noise from a television or stereo carry throughout the house or apartment? When you inspect properties, bring along a portable radio. Test various rooms. Turn up the volume. Do the walls provide enough soundproofing? Families and roommate tenants want privacy and quiet. If your rental property fails to offer quiet, your units will lose appeal.

Check for Neighborhood Noise

Will your tenants hear neighbors or neighborhood noise from inside their units? People pay for quiet. They discount heavily for noise.

No doubt, you'll typically hear more noise in neighborhoods filled with apartment buildings. But single-family neighborhoods can suffer from loud stereos, barking dogs, and unmuffled car engines. Does the drum corps of the nearby high school practice outside three hours a day? When possible, visit a property during periods of high traffic or peak noise. Don't assume that a neighborhood offers peace and quiet. Verify.

> **Check noise levels at various times.**

Ask for Written Disclosures

Seek written disclosures from the seller of a property. Talk with tenants and neighbors. Find out whether anyone has tried to enforce quiet by complaining to city government, a homeowners association, or by filing a nuisance suit. If you invest in the property, could you effectively invoke city noise ordinances against these noisy tenants (or homeowners) who live nearby? Can you add features

> **Seek disclosures about noise.**

to the property (soundproof windows, fencing, heavy doors, more wall insulation, or tall, thick hedges) to reduce noise? Suppress noise; create value.

Overall Livability

Never think rental property. Think home. As you design appeal into a property, imagine how the units will live for your intended target market of residents.

- ◆ Do the units offer enough square footage?
- ◆ Are the units spotlessly clean, fresh, and bright? Do they smell clean and fresh?
- ◆ Do the room counts and room sizes represent the most profitable use of space?
- ◆ Do the aesthetics of the units excite with emotional appeal?
- ◆ Does the unit bring in enough natural light?
- ◆ What views will the tenants see from inside the units looking out?
- ◆ Do the units offer generous amounts of closets and storage space?
- ◆ Are the units quiet?
- ◆ Will tenants feel safe and secure within the units?
- ◆ Do the kitchens and baths offer eye-pleasing pizzazz?

Experience proves that *homes* rent faster and enjoy lower vacancies than mere rental houses and apartments. Give your tenants something special. You earn higher profits. You accelerate the appreciation of your properties.

14

Twenty-One More Ways to Push Up the Value of Your Properties

You're now well on your way to build wealth. Your great livable units sparkle with pizzazz and emotional appeal. These units will keep your building full of residents who gladly pay premium prices.

Yet, before sharp interiors woo your prospective tenants, you must entice them to keep their appointments to inspect the units that you offer. Toward this end, you design curb appeal.

Create Strikingly Attractive Curb Appeal

> **Position your property with a well-kept outstanding exterior.**

You can write an award-winning ad that makes your phone ring. But your Madison Avenue talents will fall flat when great tenants pull up in front of the building and immediately begin to ask themselves, "What are we doing here? This place is nothing like I imagined. Do you think we should go in?"

"Nah, why waste our time? This place is a dump. We shouldn't even think about living here."

Your Building Publicizes Your Quality

More than likely, hundreds (maybe thousands) of people pass by your property each week. What do they notice about the property? Will it appear as that run-down rental of the neighborhood, a nondescript Sad Sack? Or does it cause passersby to remark, "Isn't that building kept up well? Those flower gardens and brick walkways seem to reach out and invite us to come inside."

To generate more income, artfully design an enticing exterior. Create award-winning publicity with knockout curb appeal. An attractive, well-kept exterior appeals to a better class of tenants, increases tenant satisfaction, and reduces turnover. To entice prospects through curb appeal, make these improvements:

1. *Clean up the grounds.* When you first take over a property, clean up the grounds, parking area, and walkways. Pick up trash, accumulated leaves, and fallen tree branches. Build a fence to block that view of the dumpsters. Tell tenants to remove their inoperable cars from the parking lots, parking spaces, or driveways. If abandoned cars are parked on the street, ask the city government to post them and tow them.

2. *Yard care and landscaping.* Tenants and homebuyers alike love a manicured lawn, flower-lined walkways, mulched shrubs, and flower gardens. With landscaping, you turn an ordinary building into a showcase property. With landscaping you create privacy, manufacture a gorgeous view looking out from the inside of the units, or eliminate an ugly view. Especially if you plan to hold for three to five years (or longer), put in those small plants, shrubs, flower gardens, and hedges now. When you sell, those mature plantings will easily earn you a return of at least $10 for each $1 the landscaping cost.

3. *Sidewalks, walkways, and parking areas.* Replace or repair major cracks and buckling that appear in sidewalks and parking areas. Remove grass or weeds growing through the cracks. Edge the areas where the yard abuts concrete or asphalt. Neatness pays. Overgrown grass and weeds stain the curb appeal of a property—precisely because these types of blemishes send signals that the property is a rental (and uncared for).

4. *Fences, lampposts, and mailboxes.* To achieve good looks, privacy, and security, install quality fencing. A rusted, rotted, or tumbledown fence blemishes a property; likewise, rusty

lampposts with broken glass light fixtures. For a decorative touch, add a white picket fence or a low stone fence in the front of a building. If the building houses a cluster of mailboxes, keep the mail area neat and assure that the mailbox lobby or porch area presents a good first impression.

5. *The exterior of the building.* Turn your attention to the exterior of the building. The building must signal to prospective tenants that you care for your property. Paint where necessary or desirable. Repair wood rot. Clean roof and gutters. Imagine ways to enhance the building's appearance with shutters, flower boxes, a dramatic front door and entryway, and new (or additional) windows. Can you add contrasting color for trim or accent the building design with architectural details? How well does (or could) the property's exterior distinguish it from other comparably priced rental properties?

> **Clean up the mailbox area and keep it clean.**

How to Achieve Dazzling Curb Appeal

Unless you're creatively gifted, you may not spontaneously generate *great* ideas for improving a property. Creative design doesn't come easily to me. I rank high among the artistically challenged. So here's how I compensate for my dull artistic vision.

> **To generate ideas, snap photos of role-model properties.**

I carry a camera in the glove box of my car. Often when I see a building or yard that displays eye-catching features, I snap a picture. Over time, I've put together a collection of photos. When I'm trying to figure out how to give a property strikingly attractive curb appeal, I pull out these photos and select model properties to compare feature to feature with my investment property. Viewing better and worse brings forth a rush of value-creating ideas.

You don't even have to rely on your own snapshots. Dozens of "house and home" types of books and magazines fill the shelves of grocers and bookstores. Buy these publications. Their articles and photos definitely enlighten creative thinking and aesthetic sensibilities.

Look closely for ways to generate extra income.

Collect More than Rent

Review the income statements of rental buildings. You will sometimes come across a line-item entry called "other income." These amounts may include money earned from laundry machines, parking, storage lockers, or various services and amenities.

1. *Laundry.* Ideally, your rental units will each include hookups for a washer and dryer. But if they don't, look for space somewhere else on the property where you can install coin-operated (actually electronic card-operated) washers and dryers. Without on-premises laundry facilities, your building will suffer a serious competitive disadvantage. Today, most tenants have been raised in homes with washers and dryers. These tenants do not want to wash their clothes at a laundromat.

2. *Parking.* If parking spots are scarce in the neighborhood where you own properties, consider an extra charge for parking (or perhaps an extra charge for a second car). Do not arbitrarily give one parking space per unit. Some tenants may not have cars. Others may be willing to park on the street. Price scarce parking separately from the units. Those tenants who want it most will pay more.

3. *Build storage lockers.* Back to the idea of adding storage space. You create value any time you can squeeze some profitable use out of every nook and cranny within the building, and within every square foot of the site. One such profitable use is storage lockers. Does the property include an attic, basement, or crawl space where you could carve out room for more storage? You can easily rent such lockers for $10 to $20 per month (or more). Generally, you can achieve payback in less than four years. If no existing space within the building serves this purpose, install prefabricated storage sheds.

4. *Add other amenities or services.* Whenever you take over a property, think through a list of services or amenities that you could provide (preferably at a price) that would increase your revenue *and* strengthen your competitive edge. Consider services such as cleaning, day care, or transportation. In terms of amenities, would your tenants appreciate (and pay for) a

swimming pool, tennis courts, racquetball (or squash) courts, a fitness center, or a study room? As apartment syndicator, Craig Hall, advises, "Keep an open and searching mind. Seek out things you can do to attract and satisfy the best tenants for each specific investment." Amen!

Convert a Garage, Attic, or Basement

As you shop for properties, look for those with an attic, garage, or basement that you can convert to *quality* living space. I emphasize the word *quality* because beginning investors often convert as cheaply as possible. As a result, their finished spaces not only look cheap, they may lack natural light, the ceilings may hang too low, or the newly created floor plans and traffic patterns may seem weird, convoluted, or garbled.

> **Add quality space, not space that looks weird.**

In contrast, savvy improvers who design and finish conversions to wow tenants or buyers can make serious money for their efforts. To earn good profits, your space conversion should achieve the following objectives:

◆ Fit the needs of the target market.
◆ Please the senses.
◆ Integrate the new with the overall plan and design of the existing property.

Target Market Needs

> **Use research to answer the question, "What features would tenants pay most for?"**

When you remodel for personal use, it's okay to convert a basement into a rec room that mimics the look of your favorite bar. For *profitable* remodeling, please your target market. What type of highly valued space can you offer that competing properties lack? A dynamite home office, a study, a playroom for the kids, a workout area, a library, an entertainment center, a seductive master bedroom and bath? Think visually. What can you imagine?

Aesthetics: Please the Senses

Basement conversions often fail because they lack windows and emit that damp, musty odor so common to below-ground living areas. To overcome these problems, use window wells and carve-outs to bring in natural light. To eliminate the musty smell and dampness, use high-quality sealants and fresh air ventilation. Follow the same general ideas for attic and garage conversions. These finished areas should look, live, feel, and smell as good as the rest of the house. Create light, height, warmth, and color. Do not tack up cheap paneling, hang acoustical tile ceilings, or lay down a roll of indoor-outdoor carpeting. Romance the space. Think pizzazz!

> **Can you make a basement seem homey?**

Integrate the Conversion into the House

When you evaluate houses for conversion potential, don't just add living space as an independent area. Work to expand the total integrated living area of the house. The best conversions flow smoothly to and from the original living areas. Think access and flow. How well can you blend the conversion into a natural traffic pattern?

Avoid signaling to your prospects, "Now entering a converted garage (basement or attic)." Or "Watch your head. The ceiling's a little low in here." Look for properties that are designed with potential for an integrated addition. A well-planned conversion can easily add three dollars of value for every dollar invested.

> **Well-designed conversions do not announce themselves as conversions.**

> **Accessory apartments pay large returns.**

Create an Accessory Apartment

Variously called in-law suites, basement suites, garage apartments, mortgage helpers, or accessory apartments, these separate living units can easily pay back their cost many times over. Depending on the city and neighborhood, accessory apartments rent for $250 to $750 per month. Unless you build from scratch, you can typically create desirable space for as little as $5,000 and certainly no more than $15,000.

As return on investment, $10,000 to $15,000 in renovation costs might yield rental income of $4,000 to $6,000 per year. You'll rarely find as much return for so little risk.

Create a Special Purpose Use

Renovate toward some special purpose use and generate a premium resale price or rental rate. Most fixer-upper investors go generic. In return, they receive a generic profit. When you renovate toward specific needs of a bullseye segment of seniors, the disabled, children, home businesses, college students, or other target of tenants (buyers), you favorably differentiate your product.

To discover a profitable niche, talk with people at social service agencies, hospitals, and local colleges. Imagine the special needs of single parents, multigenerational households, hobbyists, roommates, group homes, and shelters. Stay alert to markets where demand runs strong and supply falls short. Whereas most investors know how to fix up a property, entrepreneurs search for a special niche of customers. They tailor the features of the property to perfectly fit that target market.

> **Tailor unique features of a property to niche segment of buyers (tenants).**

Change the Use of a Property

> **To maximize value, convert to a more profitable use.**

Apartments revitalized as condominiums . . . gas stations now operating as retail outlets . . . old homes converted to office space . . . what was once farm acreage now a shopping center. These properties are examples of adaptive use of both land and buildings brought about by a city's growth and change.

Conversions provide boundless opportunities for the creative investor. Converting an old house located in the downtown area can earn good profits. Office space sometimes rents at twice the rental rate of housing. The opposite also can occur. Recently, in London, housing prices have climbed so high that all types of retail, warehouse, and offices are being converted to apartments. Likewise in the Wall Street area of New York City.

Condominium Conversion

To plan a condo conversion, study the local area. Learn the sales prices of comparable condo units. When you can buy a similar apartment building at a low enough price, renovate and sell the converted units as condos to earn a profit.

Here's how to calculate the potential profits of converting rental units into individually owned condominiums for a 16-unit apartment building:

Acquisition price	$480,000
Rehab at $7,500 per unit	120,000
Attorney fees (condo document preparation, government permitting process, sales contract preparation, closing document review)	40,000
Marketing costs (advertising, sales commissions)	45,000
Mortgage interest (12-month renovation and sellout)	50,000
Incidentals (architect, interior design, landscaping, government permits)	35,000
Total costs	$770,000
Cost per unit	$48,125

> **Condo conversions offer an opportunity for quick profits.**

You paid $480,000 ($30,000 per unit) to acquire this 16-unit rental property. After costs of conversion, your investment increased to $770,000 ($48,125 per unit). But these figures haven't yet considered profits. If you want to net $10,000 per unit, sell the units at a price approaching $60,000 each (twice your purchase price).

To decide whether such a project is feasible, research rental properties, condo prices, and conversion laws. Do some scratch-pad feasibility calculations. If preliminary estimates look promising, talk with an investor, contractor, attorney, or real estate consultant experienced in the conversion process. With the knowledge gained from these talks (and follow-up research), decide whether this investment approach offers enough profit potential to offset risks such as cost overruns, slow sales, and bureaucratic delays.

During the early 2000s, condo conversions yielded extraordinary profits. Today, that potential has disappeared in most markets. But this possibility runs in cycles. Stay informed about relative prices. Your day will come.

Convert Apartments or Houses to Office Space

Sometimes it's profitable to convert apartments or houses to office space. To mull over this possibility, answer these questions:

1. Is the property in a commercial zone? If not, can you get the property rezoned?
2. What is the current vacancy rate for office space in the area of the subject property? If too much space is already available, can you identify an underserved niche?
3. Do you have adequate parking for office space? The city may require one parking space for every 250 to 500 square feet of rentable office space.
4. How much will it cost to convert? Could you borrow the money to finance such a conversion? And, finally, will the profit potential outweigh the cost, legal hassles, time, and effort necessary to complete the project?

Study the property and the market. Figure the finances of the conversion. Verify government rules. If you can convert at a reasonable cost and earn a good profit, take a chance. You'll gain valuable experience.

(Don't forget, for more complex investments, partner with someone who is experienced. Place the promising property under option or purchase contract with contingencies. Then line up your partner and proceed.)

Cut Operating Expenses

As a rule of thumb, each $1,000 you slice from your property's operating expenses can add $10,000 (or more) to the value of a building. With gains like that, meticulously track expenses. Continuously reduce or eliminate those that do not provide a commensurate benefit. Here are some ideas.

Energy Audits

Nearly all utility companies will help you discover ways to reduce your gas or electric bills. Some will even audit and inspect your property. Others will provide booklets or brochures and, perhaps, a customer service department to answer specialized questions. You can also find dozens of articles and books at your local library that discuss energy conservation.

Energy-audit a building before you buy it. Judge beforehand the amounts you can save.

Maintenance and Repair Costs

Savvy investors need to reduce or eliminate money-wasting property maintenance and repair expenses. Focus on these five issues:

1. *Low-maintenance houses and apartment buildings.* When shopping to buy, favor those properties that are constructed with materials, HVAC, and fixtures that require low maintenance. Nothing beats a property that's built to last with minimal care. Ditto for yards, shrubs, and landscaping.
2. *Tenant selection.* Just as there are both low- and high-maintenance houses and apartment buildings, so too are there low-maintenance and high-maintenance tenants. Avoid the latter and select the former. Personally, I steer clear of chronic complainers and people who show no house sense.
3. *Repair clauses.* To further promote tenant responsibility, a growing number of property owners shift the first $50 or $100

of every repair cost onto their tenants' shoulders. Also, I favor high security deposits.

4. *Handyman on call.* Ease the drain on your time and pocketbook; employ a trustworthy and competent handyman (or persons) to take care of your property maintenance and repairs.

5. *Preventive maintenance.* You inspect and maintain your car. Do likewise with your investment properties. Anticipate and alleviate when the cost is relatively small. Ask maintenance experts how to replace high-maintenance components with low-maintenance components.

Property Taxes

"If you think that your property taxes are too high," writes tax consultant Harry Koenig, "you're probably right! Research shows that nearly half of all properties may be assessed illegally or excessively." While Koenig probably overstates the situation, millions of property owners do pay more in property taxes than they need to. With planning, you can shave dollars off your tax bill.

1. *Check the accuracy of your assessed valuation.* Usually tax assessors base their tax calculations on a property's market value. Look closely at the assessor's value estimate on your tax bill. Can you find comp sales that support a *lower* value for your property? If so, you may have grounds to request a tax reduction.

2. *Compare your purchase price to the assessor's estimate of market value.* Apart from providing comp sales, if you show the assessor that you recently paid $690,000 for a property that the assessor appraised at $740,000, you make a good case for lower taxes.

3. *Look for unequal treatment.* Under the law, assessors must tax properties in a neighborhood in a fair and uniform manner. Ask for lower taxes. Show that the assessor has assigned lower values to similar nearby properties.

4. *Learn tax assessment laws before you improve or rehabilitate a property.* The property tax laws of every state list the types of property improvements that are taxed and the

applicable millage rates. Once you discover the detailed nature of these laws, develop your property improvement strategy to add value without adding taxes.

Gentrification and Other Value Plays

In large and midsized cities across the United States and Canada, gentrification has pushed property prices through the roof in neighborhoods like Kerrisdale (Vancouver), Buckhead (Atlanta), South of Market (San Francisco), Chicago North Side, Chicago West Side, College Park (Orlando), "M Street" (Dallas), and Coconut Grove (Miami). Most of these neighborhoods have become name brands.

> **You can find the next Buckhead or College Park.**

In earlier years, though, most of these neighborhoods were modest, even lower-priced neighborhoods. Several areas such as Chicago Near North and San Francisco South of Market included industrial and commercial properties.

In each instance, the in-close accessibility of these neighborhoods overwhelmed their negatives. Prior to gaining cachet, these neighborhoods still gave residents an easy walk, drive, or commute to major job districts. And their prices looked dirt cheap when compared with conveniently situated premier neighborhoods.

Many gentrified name brand neighborhoods no longer yield good rental value. That's not to say that these areas won't continue to appreciate. But as a rule, their high prices mean that your rent collections probably won't cover your mortgage payments plus property expenses (with an 80 percent LTV).

The Good News

Now, the good news. All across the country, other emerging neighborhoods are poised for turnaround, revitalization, and rapid appreciation. Become a neighborhood entrepreneur and you can score the same large gains that those early investors earned in College Park, Near North, and Thorton Park.

Revitalize the Neighborhood

You've probably heard it said: "Buy in the best neighborhood you can afford. You can change anything about a property except its location." At first glance, this advice seems plausible. But rethink what the term "neighborhood" actually refers to:

- Convenience
- Aesthetics
- People: attitudes, lifestyles
- Legal restrictions
- Schools
- Taxes/services
- Microclimate (weather)
- Safety and security
- Image/reputation
- Affordability

Even *Money* magazine agrees. In an article on homebuying, *Money* advised its readers, "With interest rates sinking, it's a great time to shop for your dream house. . . . You'll need to seek out the neighborhoods where property values are rising faster than your community average." Surprising to many investors, though, is the fact that the neighborhoods where prices are positioned to rise fastest may not be the most prestigious or well-established neighborhoods. Often, the largest price increases can be expected in areas that are poised for turnaround or renewed popularity.

> The "best" neighborhoods don't always appreciate the fastest.

> Find neighborhoods that will gentrify within the next decade.

Entrepreneurs Improve Thorton Park (and Make a Killing)

"Florida's new urban entrepreneurs have the vision to see a bustling district of sushi bars, loft apartments and boutiques on a glass-strewn lot or rat-infested warehouse," writes Cynthia Barnett in the August 2001 issue of *Florida Trend*.

Phil Rampy is proud to have been one of those early entrepreneurs. Twelve years ago, Rampy bought a property in the then-shunned Thorton Park neighborhood near trash-strewn Lake Eola (or as they used to call it, Lake Erie-ola). Today, Thorton Park has climbed up the status ladder to rank among "the trendiest addresses" in Orlando. That $60,000 bungalow that Rampy renovated is now valued at more than $250,000. Although Thorton Park still sits on this Earth in the same place it did 10 years ago, nearly everything else about this neighborhood (location) has changed.

Many Neighborhoods Show Potential

When you compare neighborhoods, imagine potential. List all of a neighborhood's good points. How could you and other property owners join together to highlight and improve these features? List the neighborhood's weak points. How can you and others eliminate negative influences? Who can you enlist to promote your cause? Can you mobilize mortgage lenders, other investors, homeowners, Realtors, not-for-profit housing groups, church leaders, builders, contractors, preservationists, police, local employers, retail businesses, school teachers, principals, community redevelopment agencies, elected officials, civic groups, and perhaps students, professors, and administrators of a nearby college or university? People can make a difference.

> **Learn what people say about different neighborhoods.**

Become a Neighborhood Entrepreneur

You don't have to live in a big-trouble, inner-city location to become an urban entrepreneur. You can do it anywhere. No neighborhood is perfect. I suspect that even Beverly Hills and Scarsdale could stand improvement in at least a few ways.

> **Values jump with neighborhood improvements.**

Because neighborhood quality drives up property values and rent levels, search for ideas to initiate (or join in) to make a neighborhood a better place to live. When you simultaneously improve your property *and* its neighborhood, you more than double your profit potential. Would any of the following suggestions work for areas that you're considering?

> **Attract new retailers, coffee houses, and restaurants.**

Add to Neighborhood Convenience Recruit new stores, cafes, and galleries. Would a stoplight, wider road, or new highway interchange improve accessibility? Where are the to and fro traffic logjams? How can they be alleviated? Is the neighborhood served as well as it could be by buses and commuter trains? How about social service transportation? Could you get the vans that pick up seniors or the disabled to place this neighborhood on their route? What about the traveling bus for the library? Does it stop in the neighborhood?

Improve Appearances Put together a civic pride organization. Organize a cleanup and fix-up campaign. Plant trees, shrubs, and flowers in yards and in public areas. Lobby the city to tear down or eliminate eyesore buildings, graffiti, or trashy areas. Reduce on-street parking. Get abandoned vehicles towed. Enforce environmental regulations against property owners and businesses that pollute (noise, smoke, odors).

> **Fix-up becomes contagious.**

Zoning and Building Regulations Are property owners in the neighborhood splitting up single-family houses and converting them into apartments? Do residents run businesses out of their homes and garages? Are high-rise or midrise buildings planned that will diminish livability? Are commercial properties encroaching on the area? Then lobby for tighter zoning and building regulations. Or, do areas within the neighborhood and those nearby make more intense use of properties desirable? Yes? Then lobby the city to rezone the area to apartments or commercial.

> **Enlist the help of the code enforcers. Change the zoning.**

Eliminate Neighborhood Nuisances Do one or more properties or households in the neighborhood make a nuisance of themselves? Junk cars in the driveway, barking dogs, loud vehicle exhaust systems, constant yelling and shouting, out-of-control yards littered with debris—you and other

> **Rules eliminate nuisances when responsible neighbors complain.**

property owners can force them to clean up their act or suffer severe and continuing legal penalties.

Pore over local ordinances and HOA rules, and deed restrictions. Sift through the regulations for zoning, aesthetics, occupancy, use, parking, noise, disturbing the peace, health, safety, loitering, drug dealing or possession, extortion, and assault. You will find some regulatory rules under which you can file a legal complaint.

If after receiving a citation the nuisance neighbors continue to offend common decency, a judge can issue an order to cease and desist (or something similar). Further violations then bring the scalawags a citation for contempt of court. They've now angered the judge. Each day the breach persists could rack up multiple fines, and possibly jail time. In some cases the government will even remedy the problem—cut the weeds, haul off a junk car—and then bill the offenders.

Upgrade the Schools   Foretelling a trend, the *Wall Street Journal* (August 23, 2001, p. A-1) reported that throughout the United States "parents and property owners have become increasingly aggressive about trying to improve their public schools." When you think that in many areas parents spend $3,000 to $10,000 a year to send their kids to private schools, why not rechannel those monies and support into the neighborhood schools?

> **Improve school performance and watch property values set new highs.**

Safety and Security   Bolster safety within the neighborhood (especially for children and seniors). Slow down or reroute traffic. If you can persuade the city to lay down speed bumps, you achieve both objectives. Speed bumps not only force motorists to let up on the gas pedal, they tell drivers who want to speed that they're wise to travel a different street.

Reduce posted speed limits and seek intense enforcement. In Berkeley, California, neighborhoods lobbied the city to erect traffic barriers at residential intersections. This effort converted many formerly through streets into cul-de-sacs.

Lobby the Politicians   Property owners pay taxes. Now insist that you get what you pay for. As the Berkeley experience shows, when

> **Insist on the government services for which you and other property owners pay taxes.**

> **Give your neighborhood or community a new name.**

property owners and neighborhood residents join together to form a political force, they can push the city politicos to alleviate traffic problems, clean the streets, enforce ordinances, upgrade the schools, beef up police patrols, create parks, and provide other services that neighborhoods should expect.

Add Luster to Your Image Friends of mine used to live in Miami, Florida, but now they live in the up-scale Village of Pinecrest, Florida. Did they move? No. They and their neighbors persuaded the post office to give them a new address so they could distinguish themselves from that diverse agglomeration known as Miami. As part of their efforts to create an improved neighborhood, some residents of Sepulveda, California, have formed a new community and renamed it North Hill. In Maryland, Gaithersburg changed its name to North Potomac to capitalize on the prestige of its nearby neighbor. Residents of North Hollywood got the official name for part of their community changed to Valley Village. "With the name change," says Realtor Jerry Burns, "residents take more pride in their neighborhood."

Talk Up the Neighborhood Most people learn about neighborhoods through word of mouth and articles they read. As all good publicists know, you can influence these methods of "getting the word out." Talk up the neighborhood to opinion leaders. Comment to friends, coworkers, relatives, and acquaintances about the great improvements of the community.

Convince a reporter to play up the neighborhood's potential for turnaround, quality of life, convenience, or affordability. Let everyone know that the area deserves a better reputation. When you revitalize a neighborhood, you can double or triple the value of your properties within just six to eight years.

PART FOUR

Onward and Upward to Build Wealth

15

Win What You Want through Negotiation

Sometimes you *find* great deals in real estate. But more often, you *create* your great deals through negotiation.

> **Negotiate to create great deals.**

When you buy, sell, arrange financing, obtain bids from contractors, or write a lease, your skills as a negotiator influence what you get and what you give up. As Herb Cohen, the negotiating trainer, says, "You can get anything you want in life, but you must do more than ask. You must negotiate."

Now you will see how to win what you want through negotiation.

How to Define Win-Win

You've heard of the negotiating style called win-win. But do you really know what that negotiating style implies? Most people don't—even though they think they do.

Myth Versus Reality

In the fairy-tale world of win-win, you and the other party to the negotiation sit down together, openly share information about each other, explore options and possibilities, express concerns, focus on goals, and then come up with a solution that satisfies both of you. In the land of Oz negotiations may proceed this smoothly, but not in the real world of real estate.

"Why not?"

> **Real-world negotiators go for *almost* as much as they can get.**

Because in the real world, we all want the best deal we can cut. I want to pay less. You want me to pay more. I want possession within 30 days; you do not want to give up the property for 90 days. I want you to finance the deal with 10 percent down. You insist on 30 percent. I want to pay you 6 percent interest. You say no deal unless I pay 8 percent. The list of potential deal points for discussion goes on and on.

Forget "What's Fair"

At least 9 out of every 10 times, the people with whom you negotiate will try to pull more chips into their own pile and leave you with less. Likewise (unless you're sporting a halo), you want the larger pile. Maybe this sounds crass, but that's the way most investors play the negotiating game. Forget "what's fair" as the deciding arbiter.

To succeed as a wealth-building real estate investor, cast aside your illusions. To get what you want, you must go well beyond the idealized view of win-win.

The Real Meaning of Win-Win

Yes, win-win does foster cooperation. It does promote mutual problem solving. And it does require you to think up more deal points to make the pie bigger.

But face facts. No matter what negotiating style you choose, you will run bluffs, drag red herrings across the other party's path, create subtle ways to extract information, and protest that you cannot pay more even though you know full well that you are willing and able to do so.

You Win; the Other Party *Feels* Like a Winner   In the real world version of win-win, you avoid the hostile, "rip your face off" negotiating style so common with New York lawyers and Hollywood moguls. You do not try to disrespect, belittle, denigrate, or put down the other party. You do not press the other party against a wall, pick his pockets of everything you can find, and then let him loose just to watch him fall to the floor.

> **People want to *feel* like they've won the negotiation.**

You choose to avoid this win-lose style of negotiating not because you're a nice guy or gal (although you may be) but because you can get more of what you want by adopting a softer, more conciliating manner. As Zig Zigler says, "You can get anything you want in life, *as long as* you help the other fellow get what he wants."

What is it that people want most from a negotiation? They want to *feel* like a winner. They want to *feel* like they cut the best deal they could.

Who Feels Most Like a Winner?   Imagine that you negotiate with a seller. You go back and forth on price. Finally, the seller gives in to give you almost everything you ask for. You're pleased as punch.

Then, after closing, you learn that the seller was really pressed for cash. Had he not bluffed you into believing that he would go no lower, he would have sold for $50,000 less than you agreed to pay.

Now, how do you feel? How would most people feel? Right. Their sense of victory just melted away.

I have negotiated hundreds of agreements, and I can assure you that most people value their feelings as much as the objective deal points. Exceptions occur. But more often than not, you win the most deal points when you encourage the other party to *feel* like he or she is winning the negotiations.

Experience Rules   I know of no serious real estate investor who enters a negotiation to strike a "fair" agreement in any objective sense. Investors enter negotiations to extract (almost) as much from the other party as possible. These investors differ primarily in the way they try to win these deal points.

- *Win-lose style.* The egocentric dealmaker wants to win while forcing the other party to admit defeat. These investors want the other party to know that they've been outmaneuvered, out-smarted, and overpowered.

◆ *Win-win style.* The investor who puts this style to work remains content to know that he persuaded (not forced) the other par-ty to push chips in his direction. But this negotiator never lets on that he got the best of the deal. He allows the other side to win that prize. That ploy stands as the real-world meaning of win-win.

> **Win-win does not imply an objectively fair agreement.**

Which negotiating style works best? Each method attracts advocates. Personally, I favor win-win. Not because it's the nice-guy, "how to win friends and influence people" approach. Rather, ex-perience tells me it's the best approach to win what I want. Try it. I think you will agree.

Now let's see what methods, tactics, and gam-bits you can draw on to win more deal points.

Know Thyself

To get what you want from negotiations, know what you want. As you envision it, does this potential deal match your wealth-building goals? Does it fit within your frame of time, money, and talents? If completed, will this deal move you closer to where you want to go?

Many beginning investors jump to buy a property because in some way it seems like a good deal. But before you rush into something be-cause it seems to look good, figure out whether the deal will be good for *you*. Evaluate the deal in terms of your longer-term personal and financial goals. Ask, "Regardless of the bargain price (or terms), is this a property I want to own?"

Know the Property and Neighborhood

Before you talk with sellers (or the sellers' agent), learn about the prop-erty. Here's some information to discover.

◆ How is the property zoned? Are more profitable uses possible?

◆ How large is the lot? What are its dimensions and boundaries?

◆ When did the property last sell? At what price?

◆ Is there a mortgage on the property? What's the (likely) amount of the outstanding balance? What interest rate?

◆ What school districts apply to the property?

◆ What employers are located nearby?

◆ What are the neighborhood demographics? Who's moving in? Who's moving out?

◆ What percent of neighborhood residents rent versus own?

◆ What range of rents and property prices apply to the neighborhood?

> **Each question you ask the sellers may tip off your intentions.**

You may wonder why you should go to all of this trouble. Why work to discover this property and neighborhood information on your own when you could easily ask the sellers (or their real estate agent)? But here's the downside to that approach. You might alert the sellers to some piece of information that they could use to strengthen their own negotiating position. You might tip your hand about hidden value you see in the area or the property.

Know the Sellers

Have the sellers accepted or declined any offers on the property? If so, what were the terms and price? (Sometimes agents will disclose this information. Sometimes you can learn it from a lender, an appraiser, the sellers' neighbors, or even the sellers themselves.) If a previous deal fell through, find out why. Will their past experiences help or hinder the sellers' negotiating positions with you?

Do the Sellers Face Pressure?

Nearly all real estate books advise you to find "motivated" sellers. Who are these wonderful folks who will gladly give you a good deal?

Generally, they're sellers who face severe pressures of time, money, or family situation (divorce, death, job move, retirement).

Know the sellers' personal or financial circumstances, and you learn the deal points that they value most. You also discover issues the sellers will resolve in your favor (bargain price, owner financing, lease option, "subject to" purchase).

Get the Sellers to Like You

People give better deals to people they like. Build rapport with the sellers. Read Dale Carnegie's *How to Win Friends and Influence People* (New York: Pocket Books, 1936). Don't insult, argue, contradict, or directly challenge anything the sellers say. Hedge differing views with statements such as "Have you considered," "It seems to me," "In my experience," "Oh, it was my understanding that," and "What if I were to . . ."

> **Sellers give better deals to buyers they like.**

When sellers like you, they help you get what you want. If they dislike you, they favor other buyers—even though other buyers propose what objectively appears to be a less attractive offer. Never come at sellers from sharp angles. Appear willing to accommodate.

Tact, Not Ultimatums

When you negotiate with sellers in distress, never use the cliché, "Take it or leave it." Apart from proving you to be a tactless amateur, such ploys seldom work. Even property owners under duress would sooner lose money than lose their ego and self-esteem. Most sellers quickly reject out-of-the-blue, lowball offers that spill forth untethered by reason, empathy, and understanding. To work best with a troubled owner, work together, not against. With these types of sellers (as well as nearly all others, too), mutual problem solving outperforms one-upmanship. Don't conquer, conciliate.

> **Don't conquer, conciliate.**

Negotiate an Agreement, Not Just Price

In contrast to buying stocks where transactions take place according to a set price and essentially fixed terms, in real estate almost anything (not everything) is negotiable. If the sellers seem inflexible on price, look for other value-added concessions. Or if it is they who require a quick close or sure sale, oblige their demands in trade for requests of your own.

For purposes of bragging rights, some sellers insist on a "high" price. Okay, give them what they want. Then take back more as favorable financing, seller-paid closing costs, possession date, warranties, inspections, repairs, personal property, title insurance, or other terms and conditions of value. You can negotiate a winning agreement without directly negotiating a bargain price. As a win-win negotiator, remain alert to white-chip issues and concerns that you can trade off to win blue chip issues that you prize most.

> **Trade your white chips for the seller's blue chips.**

Establish Favorable Benchmarks

Sellers often entertain strange ideas about why their property warrants a particular price. If you encounter such a situation, probe further. Seek information. Ask the sellers (or their agent) how they arrived at such a value. Frequently, you will find their benchmark either inaccurate or irrelevant. For example:

1. *Add-in costs.* "We paid $25,000 for that kitchen remodel," the sellers might say.
2. *The Joneses' house.* "The Joneses down the street just got $845,000 for their house, and it's 600 square feet smaller than ours."
3. *The appraisal.* "$185,000 is a great price for this property. Look, here's an appraisal. The appraiser says it's worth $205,000."
4. *Their past purchase price.* "We paid $425,000 a year and a half ago. At $445,000 you're getting a steal. Properties in this neighborhood are going up 10 to 15 percent a year."

> **Avoid direct argument; change the benchmarks to those that favor your interests.**

To negotiate successfully with owners who use these and other familiar benchmarks, subtly undermine their accuracy or relevance, but not with direct "put-you-on-the-spot" challenges. Rather, tactfully phrase your investigative questioning. Lead the sellers to doubt the applicability of their benchmark "facts." Then supply your own more appropriate (and more favorable) benchmarks.

When you can get the sellers to recognize and accept your benchmarks, you effectively move them toward your price (or other terms and conditions). When you try to pull down the seller's price while they hold tightly to their benchmarks, you'll usually find it tough to break their grip. (For various legitimate benchmarks of value, see Chapter 12.)

Tit for Tat

Never concede without asking for a return concession. "If I can meet your need on point X, would you accept Y?" To concede without a return request invites continued "nibbling." In addition, agreement without request gives the seller second thoughts. "Why is Mr. Buyer jumping at this? Am I selling too low?" Do the sellers a favor. For each concession you give up, let go reluctantly, and ask the sellers for something in return.

Get Seller Concessions Early

Eager to entice your interest, many sellers will concede deal points before you formally open negotiations. During casual discussions, test the water. "Have you thought about carrying back financing? You're asking $415,000,

> **Guide the sellers into making early concessions.**

but what price would you be happy with? Which of the appliances are you willing to leave? At that price, you're paying closing costs, right?"

By *casually* asking such questions, you lower the floor on which later negotiations will stand. Once negotiations begin, sellers play their cards closer to the table.

Come Ready to Buy

Know the sellers. Know the property. Know the neighborhood. Know the market. Know values. Know your finances. Know what you're looking for. Then, when you see it, move, move, move. The "well-let-me-think-it-over" investor won't score nearly as many great buys as that investor who comes into the game ready to play. You can't expect good buys to remain unrecognized for long. During the past year, I've looked at around a dozen properties that I considered good-to-great buys. Nearly all of them sold within six to eight weeks (or less) of hitting the market. Several sold the first week their FOR SALE listings were posted.

Ask for More than You Expect

Tempt the sellers to sweeten the deal before you write your offer. But at some point, you submit a written purchase contract. When you do, ask for more than you expect to eventually settle for.

Your Goal Is to Make Money (and Provide Homes for People)

You are doing deals to make money. Remain calm, cool, and emotionally detached from an investment property. With an investment, the numbers either work to give you a great buy, or they don't. When they don't, negotiate further—or look elsewhere.

> **Go for more than you expect to get.**

When you negotiate to buy a *home* that truly suits your personal needs like no other, I would caution you to avoid a lowball offer because—unless presented tactfully—that offer could backfire. It could offend the sellers. In response, the sellers might reject you as a buyer or accept another offer. You could end up severely disappointed. You missed the home of your dreams.

Not so with an investment property. With an investment property, alternatives always exist. With investment properties, you negotiate for financial reward, not for any one property per se.

The Benefits of Asking for More than You Want or Expect

How would you feel if you offered $200,000 and the sellers quickly said, "We'll take it. When do you want to close?" Undoubtedly, you would regret your offer. You tell yourself, "That was a dumb move. I bet the sellers would have accepted a lot less."

Likewise, the sellers will begin to question the wisdom of their decision. They begin to think, "If this buyer was willing to open with an offer of $200,000, he surely would go up to $210,000, maybe even $225,000. We acted too hastily. We should have countered."

When you ask for a better deal than you could possibly expect, you promote your goals in several ways.

- ◆ It gives you room to negotiate.
- ◆ It reduces seller expectations.
- ◆ It permits you to concede and helps the sellers feel like they have won.

And last, but far from least,

- ◆ The sellers may surprise you. They might fulfill your wish list with only minor changes.

In that pleasant situation, you want to assure the sellers that they got nearly all that you were willing to give. Had they not accepted, you would have bought that fourplex you were looking at. "In fact," you tell the sellers, "I now wish I had tried to make that other deal. I think those sellers were willing to carry back financing at 6 percent interest with just 10 percent down."

Establish Credibility

No one wants to negotiate with a flake. To entice the sellers, let them know that they can count on you to do what you say. Emphasize your strong points:

◆ Character
◆ Credit
◆ Capacity (cash and/or income)
◆ Consistency

If your record plays too weakly in any area, emphasize compensating factors.

What evidence bolsters your ability to close a deal and perform as promised? To the extent these documents would help your case, set up a file for seller review (when necessary) any or all of the following items:

◆ FICO score and credit reports.
◆ Past payment records on other real estate (rent or mortgage).
◆ Experience with contractors, rehabs, renovations.
◆ Bank statements to prove you have more than enough cash to close plus substantial reserves.
◆ A letter of intent from your partners or a copy of your partnership agreement.
◆ Testimonials and references from others who have worked with you.
◆ Prior real estate ownership or management experience.

Before you sell your offer to the property owners, sell yourself as a credible, trustworthy investor.

Never Offer to Split the Difference

Facing a perceived negotiating stalemate, you may be tempted to blurt out, "Okay, let's just split the difference." Resist this impulse.

> **Get the sellers to offer to "split the difference."**

You want the *sellers* to propose this solution. Because once they've put this offer out, they've essentially announced that they will accept this new lower price.

Now you counter the sellers' "split the difference" offer. "I don't know," you say. "I really can't go any higher than the $590,000 figure that my calculations require. Your new price of $610,000 won't give me the return I must have. But here's what might work. If you can carry back $50,000 at 7.0 percent instead of 7.75, I think I can squeeze out my minimum return at a price of $595,000."

The Mental Commitment

Now, you're within $15,000 and 0.75 percent of agreement. The sellers have mentally moved their position from $630,000 to $610,000. It's almost certain that your deal will close at a price less than $610,000 and at an interest rate of less than 7.75 percent.

You win the deal points. The sellers—provided you have protested long and loud enough—feel they won the negotiation. They managed to extract from you your absolute best offer—or so they believe. Then when you congratulate and compliment them on their tough bargaining skills, you put the icing on their cake.

The Price Dilemma

Avoid a split-the-difference solution for one more reason. It focuses negotiations on price. Rather than let price alone create a deadlock or impasse, search through your bundle of deal points. Look for high-value, low-value tradeoffs. What might you or the sellers need or want besides money?

> **Hold other options in view. You strengthen your walk-away willpower.**

List Your BATNAs

In negotiating lingo, BATNA stands for your best alternative to a negotiated agreement. To negotiate a winning agreement, maintain walk-away willpower. When you negotiate, explicitly list your other potential choices. Say to yourself, "If I can't get the deal I'm looking for here, what other deals can I pursue?"

Do not negotiate to buy a property, per se. Negotiate to earn a good profit.

Negotiate for Yourself

Writing in *Real Estate Today*, a national trade magazine for Realtors, sales agent Sal Greer tells of an offer he received on one of his listings. Sal says that after receiving the purchase offer from a *buyer's agent*, this agent told Sal, "This is their [first] offer, but I know my buyers will go up to $350,000."

"Of course," Sal adds, "I told my sellers that information, and we were pleased with the outcome of the transaction."

The lesson for you is plain. Never let your agent negotiate for you. Withhold information from the agent you do not want the other side to learn. Do not let on to an agent that you will pay a price higher than your first offer. Use an agent as a fact finder and conduit. But guard your emotions, confidences, and intentions.

First-time investors mistakenly rely too heavily on agents to actually come up with the terms of their offer and carry out their negotiations. These investors will ask agents, "What price do you think I should offer? What's the most you think I should pay? Will the sellers pay closing costs or carry-back financing?" The buyers then follow whatever the agent recommends.

> **Never abandon control of negotiations to your agent (or your attorney).**

Such buyers abdicate their negotiating responsibilities. If you follow their example and shift decision making to an agent, you run the following risks.

You May Be Working with a Subagent

You may be working with the sellers' listing agent or a subagent. Often "your" agent's legal duty is to the seller. In favoring the sellers' interests, the agent may persuade you to boost the price or terms of your offer. Or the agent may disclose your confidences to the sellers.

> **Agents may violate the confidences of you or the sellers.**

As a practical matter, many sellers' agents don't strictly follow the letter of the law. Even though technically they represent the sellers, in their heart and efforts they may feel more loyalty to you. I know subagents who work hard for their investors—even to the detriment of their sellers.

Nevertheless, because you don't know for sure how an agent will use the information you share, limit your disclosures. Likewise, when it comes to price and terms, rely on an agent for facts about the sellers, sales prices of comparable properties, neighborhood statistics, and general market conditions. Listen to the agent's price recommendations and accept the benefits of his or her knowledge and experience. But don't delegate decision making. You may be led into giving up more than you need to.

Agents get paid only when you close on the deal. They do not get paid according to the number of deal points that they successfully negotiate on your (or the sellers') behalf. They want to earn a commission, not get you (or the sellers) the best deal possible.

Be Cautious of Buyers' Agents

Increasingly, brokerage firms promote buyers' agency. Because sellers are represented by their listing agents, buyers presumably need someone to look out for their interests. Marilyn Wilson, a Bellingham, Washington, real estate broker, says, "Buyers should think of their agents as attorneys. Would you want to have one attorney representing both parties in a divorce settlement?"

> **Buyer's agents, too, face conflicts of interest.**

Superficially, the idea sounds reasonable. But if you employ a buyers' agent, guard your disclosures and negotiating strategy. First, like the buyers' agent Sal Greer referred to earlier, *your* agent may disclose confidences—either intentionally or unintentionally.

Second, we're subject to subtle influences. A buyers' agent may talk you into offering a higher price or less favorable terms because it will make his or her job easier. Under which scenario do you think an agent will work the hardest: when you offer $385,000 but you told the agent that you will go up to

$410,000; or when you offer $385,000 and say, "If they don't accept this offer, there's four or five other properties I'd like to make appointments to see"?

Watch What You Say

I will repeat. Whether you work with a sellers' agent, a buyers' agent, a dual agent, or a facilitator, watch what you say. Don't tell an agent everything and then turn the negotiations over to her with the simple instructions, "Do the best job you can," or "Why don't you try $235,000 and if that doesn't fly, we can go up to $250,000."

> **All types of agents compromise their principals (and principles).**

In fact, whether you employ a lawyer, insurance agent, mortgage broker, financial planner, real estate agent, or other professional relationship, conflict of interest lurks nearby. Walk a fine line. Release enough information to promote the results you want, but not so much that you invite an advisor to sacrifice your interests to the interests of someone else (not least of all, the advisor).

Leave Something on the Table

Negotiating expert Bob Woolf says, "There isn't any contract I have negotiated where I didn't feel I could have gone for more money or an additional benefit." Why leave money on the table? Because skilled negotiators know, "The deal's not over 'til it's over." If you push too hard, you create resentment and hostility in the other party. Even if they've signed a contract, they'll start thinking of ways they can get out of it. Even worse, if you stumble on the way to closing, they won't help you up. They'll just kick dirt in your face.

> **Push the sellers' limits, and later they may shove you back.**

Especially in the purchase of real estate—where egos run strong—you gain when you leave something on the table. The purchase agreement forms stage one of your negotiations. Later, on the way through due diligence and closing, you might encounter problems that pertain to property inspection and repairs, appraised value, terms/ costs of financing, possession date, closing date, site boundaries, zoning, building permits, or other issues.

Without a reservoir of goodwill, trust, and cooperation, unpleasant setbacks on the way to closing can throw your agreement into contentious dispute.

When you leave something on the table, sellers feel more inclined to save the agreement and pitch in to help solve the unexpected snags and detours.

CHAPTER 16

Write Your Purchase Offer

When you offer to buy a property, quite likely you'll be handed a so-called standard purchase agreement to fill out and sign. But wait. Before you rely on that form, read each clause closely. Many traps lie within those so-called standard contracts.

No Single Contract Form

In fact, no all-purpose "standard" contract has ever been printed. Just as important, the form used in your area may not fully serve you or the sellers' interests. Although space doesn't permit us to discuss every contract clause that you might see, we will address many of those that you should pay special attention to.

> **Review a blank contract form before you need it.**

Before you write an offer on a property, ask a real estate agent to provide a blank copy of the form contract(s) that the agent typically relies on to complete a purchase agreement. Then read each clause. Compare it to the discussions in this chapter. Ask the agent (or legal counsel) to clarify terms or clauses that you could not easily explain to a 13-year-old.

Draft Clauses with Understanding

Although "standard" purchase contracts do not exist, most property agreements cover common issues. Nevertheless, responsibilities and remedies differ. Even with relatively straightforward clauses, pitfalls lurk. Assume nothing. Understand before you sign.

Names of the Parties

Your agreement must name all parties to the transaction. Especially name all owners (sellers) and make sure all are available to sign your offer as soon as you reach agreement. Be wary of negotiating with a seller whose spouse or partners do not actively join in the negotiations. If later one refuses to sign, you have no deal.

> **Don't fall for the good guy-bad guy gambit.**

Some sellers claim that their co-owners will go along with whatever they say. Then, after you commit, the seller comes back and says, "Gee, I'm terribly sorry. My partner refuses to sign. He thinks I'm giving the property away. He wants another $25,000. I told him I can't renege and change the terms. But he insists. So I tell you what, if you can agree to pay another $10,000, I'll go back to my partner and do my best to convince him to go along. I'm really sorry, but sometimes my partner gets obstinate and there's little I can do to reason with him."

This ploy remains one of the oldest tricks in the book. But it often works. Sellers (and buyers) continue to use it. Just don't be surprised when you have it pulled on you—if you negotiate with someone who lacks the legal authority to carry out the agreement. (Or some sellers say, "Gee, I'm sorry. I know I agreed to these terms, but my lawyer says 'no way.'")

Site Description

Identify the property that you're buying by street address and legal description. As a safeguard, walk the boundaries of the property as you follow the lines on a survey or a plot plan. When you walk the boundaries, note any encroachments. Does a neighbors' building encroach the property line? Is there a crooked driveway, a misplaced fence, or overhanging tree limbs that could create a problem? Do buildings violate zoning setback rules?

> **Walk and confirm the boundaries of the site.**

Make sure the lot size you think you're buying actually measures up to the size you're getting. Especially where a property site borders a vacant site, woods, field, or creek, don't assume the lot lines run where they seem to run. Sometimes, too, what appears to be the subject site actually belongs to a neighboring property. Visually verify where the surveyed boundaries lie.

Building Description

Your real estate agreement may identify only the lot, not the building. That's because legally real estate (the surface of the Earth) automatically includes all structures permanently attached to the delineated land—plus air rights and subsurface rights.

If the seller represents that the buildings are of a specific size or are built of certain materials, or of a certain historic date or design, write those features (whatever they are) into the property description. In Berkeley, California, buyers sued the sellers of a gracious old home because the sellers had (mistakenly) told the buyers that the home had been designed by Julia Morgan, a famous San Francisco Bay Area architect of the early 1900s.

> **If you think you're buying a Julia Morgan design, write it into your purchase offer.**

The buyers claimed that they had not just agreed to buy a house on a specific site. They had offered to buy a *Julia Morgan* house. Lacking the Julia Morgan prestige, the buyers believed they were entitled to damages. (The court agreed and awarded damages to the buyers.)

If you think you're buying a prewar brownstone, or maybe the house where Elvis Presley was raised, write it into your agreement. Let the sellers know exactly what you expect to receive in all critical details. Verify that the building fits the description that you think you're buying. Should your expectations (the seller's representations) prove incorrect, you may be able to rescind the agreement, negotiate a better deal, or sue for damages.

Personal Property

Although legally real estate incorporates land and buildings, it does not include any personal property the sellers promise to leave for you. (Generally, the term personal property refers to items that are not "permanently" attached to a building or the land.) Say the sellers of a fourplex provide window air conditioners, miniblinds, gas ranges, refrigerators, and ceiling fans. In your written offer to buy that property, expressly list these additional items.

Some Courts Extend the Definition of Real Property Although it's true that some courts extend the concept of real estate to include personal property that is "adapted for use" with a specific building, don't depend on litigation to force the sellers to convey the personal property that you believed included in the sale. Leave no doubt—write it out. Go through every room of the property. List items that form a part of your agreement.

Who Owns What? Sellers or Tenants? Listing personal property serves another purpose. It requires the sellers to clearly point out which personal property they own and what property belongs to their tenants. Investors who do not obtain an accurate list of the seller's personal property may later find themselves in dispute with tenants when the tenants claim, "That refrigerator is ours. That junk icebox the landlord provided was carted off to the dump two years ago. We bought this refrigerator from Heather's parents."

> Ask the tenants to verify the list of owners' items.

Play it safe. Ask the tenants to okay any list of personal property that you and the sellers prepare. After you close, you do not want to learn that the furniture and appliances you thought you bought are actually claimed by your tenants.

Price and Financing

When you prepare your offer, write the precise purchase price and terms of financing. List the amounts payable, how payable, when payable, and the applicable interest rate(s). Make it easy for a disinterested third party to interpret your intended meaning. Leave nothing to decide at a later date. "Seller agrees to carry back $20,000 on mutually agreeable terms" leaves ambiguity.

When you arrange new financing, or even if you assume the seller's mortgage, this same advice holds: Don't leave the amount and terms open to question. If you need a 95 percent LTV at 6.0 percent interest, write those exact terms into your financing contingency.

Earnest Money Deposit

Contrary to popular belief, the validity of your purchase offer does not depend on the amount of your earnest money deposit, or for that matter, whether you place a deposit. Earnest money is nothing more than a good-faith showing that you intend to complete your purchase. More than anything else, choose your deposit amount as part of your negotiation strategy.

> **Earnest money signals your intent and credibility.**

Size of the Deposit   Large deposits signal to the sellers that you are in the game and ready to play. Some investors use large deposits to mitigate the shock of a lowball offer. A large amount of earnest money tells the sellers, "You can count on me to buy your property. This large deposit proves that I mean what I say. Wouldn't you rather go for a sure thing now rather than hope for a better offer that may never arrive—or if it arrives, never closes."

A small deposit may signal that you're financially weak, or that you're trying to tie up the property cheaply while you mull over other options. Smart sellers refuse offers that don't seem to commit you to buying their property.

Learn Local Custom   To some degree, whether the sellers perceive your deposit large or small, serious or trifling, depends on local custom.

Gauge the impression you will make with your deposit by the deposit amounts local sellers and realty agents think reasonable for the property you are buying.

A deposit that seems low weakens your credibility. A high deposit strengthens your credibility. You might employ a low deposit strategy and then rely on other factors to support your credibility (current ownership of multiple properties, strong FICO score, high net worth, person of integrity). But this tactic may fail. As a rule, few things speak louder than ready cash.

Quality of Title

Arcane legalities affect the issue of title quality. To get good title, you need either a real estate attorney or, better, a title insurer. Your purchase agreement will state the title guarantees and exceptions that govern your transaction. Know your risks before you sign. Exercise caution when you buy a property through foreclosure, tax sale, sheriff's auction, probate, or some other type of sale where the previous owner of the property does not sign a general warranty deed.

> **Rely on legal counsel and/or title insurance for opinions of title quality.**

Property Condition

Evaluate property condition in two ways. First, ask the sellers to complete a property disclosure statement that lists every conceivable problem or defect that now or ever has affected the property and the neighborhood.

Second, while you can learn from seller disclosures, you can't learn everything. Generally, sellers disclose only what they know (not necessarily what they suspect). As protection, include an inspection contingency in your offer. Then, check out the property with one or more property pros who can assess the condition of the plumbing, heating and air conditioning, electrical system, roofing, and foundation.

Write an inspection contingency to limit necessary repair costs (e.g., $2,500). Ideally, the sellers should pay these costs. But if you've negotiated a bargain price, you might accept responsibility. If repair costs go over the stated amount, your contingency clause should permit you to withdraw your offer and take back your deposit.

Preclosing Property Damage (Casualty Clause)

Require the sellers to deliver their property to you on the date of closing (or the date of possession) in the same condition as it stood on the date the sellers accepted your offer. If the property suffers damage (fire, earthquake, vandalism, hurricane, flood) after the purchase contract has been signed, but prior to closing, the sellers must repair the property at their expense. Alternatively, in the event of damages above $XXX, you or the sellers can pull out of the agreement, and you get your deposit back.

Closing (Settlement) Costs

Real estate transactions run up thousands of dollars in closing costs. You or the sellers might pay for title insurance, an appraisal, mortgage points, buy-down fees, application fees, lender-mandated repairs, lawyers' fees, mortgage assumption fees, recording fees, transfer taxes, document stamps, survey, property inspections, escrow fees, real estate brokerage fees, and other expenses. These costs add up to a fair-sized chunk of money. Who pays each of these costs—you or the sellers? Local custom frequently dictates, but negotiation overrides custom. If the sellers won't drop their price as low as you'd like, ask them to pay more of the settlement costs.

> **Some cash-short investors trade off a higher price for seller-paid closing costs.**

Closing and Possession Dates

Set dates for settlement and possession. When you or the sellers place great importance on either a quick (or delayed) closing date, that date can play a role in your negotiations. Because of their need for ready cash, the sellers might trade a lower price for an early closing date. Or for tax reasons, the sellers may prefer to delay settlement until they've begun a new tax year or perhaps until they locate a replacement property to complete a §1031 tax-free exchange.

Likewise for the date of possession. The sellers might want a fast closing but to keep possession of the property (especially if it's their home) for some period that extends beyond the settlement date. Maybe their new house isn't yet completed. Maybe they want to postpone moving until their children finish the school term. Reasons vary, but a smart negotiator feels out sellers on their preferred closing and possession dates. Use this information to shape your offer. If you meet the sellers' needs on this issue, they may meet your requests on price or terms.

Leases

When you buy a rental property, the law requires you to honor the valid leases and promises that the sellers have entered into with the tenants. Especially investigate these issues:

- *Rent levels.* How much do the tenants pay in rents? Are any tenants in arrears? Have any tenants prepaid? How long have the current rent levels been in effect?
- *Concessions.* Did the tenants receive any concessions for signing their leases such as one month's free rent, a new 18-speed bicycle, or any other incentives that lower the effective amount of rents the tenants are paying?
- *Utilities.* Do the leases require the tenants to pay all of their own utilities? If not, what utilities do the owners pay?
- *Yard care, snow removal, other services.* Who provides yard care, snow removal, or other necessary services such as small repairs within the rental units? Who pays for garbage and trash pickup? Do the leases obligate the sellers to provide laundry facilities, off-street parking, a club house, exercise room, child-care center, commuter transportation, or other services or facilities?
- *Furniture and appliances.* Determine whether leases obligate you to provide tenants with furniture or appliances. If so, which

ones, what quality, and who is responsible for maintenance, repairs, and replacement?

♦ *Duration.* What term remains for each of the leases? Do the tenants enjoy the option to renew? If renewed, does the lease (or rent control laws) limit the amount of rent increase that you can impose?

♦ *Security deposits.* How much money has the owner collected from the tenants in security deposits? Have any tenants prepaid their last month's rent? Did the seller file an inspection sheet that shows the condition of each of the units at the time the tenants moved in? Have the tenants signed those inspection sheets?

♦ *Tenant confirmation.* Ask the tenants to confirm the terms of the lease as the sellers have represented them. Verify that the sellers (or the property manager) have not entered into any side agreements with tenants that would modify or override the terms of the lease. Learn whether the sellers orally promised tenants special services, rent relief, or other dispensations.

Warning: Even though you own the property, the tenants were there first. For the term of their leases (and renewal options, if any), their leasehold rights limit your rights of ownership.

Contingency Clauses

Hedge your purchase offers with a financing contingency and a property inspection contingency. If you can't finance on the terms you want, or if the condition of the property doesn't meet your standards (as written into your purchase offer), call the deal off. The sellers must return your earnest money to you.

> **"No strings attached" offers persuade sellers to accept a lower price.**

Even though you *can* condition your offer on anything you want, that doesn't mean the sellers will accept it. They may tell you, "No way are we going to take our property off the market for several months while you try to put together a syndication deal. Come back and talk to us after you've raised the money." The more you hedge your offer with deal-threatening contingencies, the less likely the sellers will sign it.

On the other hand, a clean no-strings-attached offer may gain the sellers' approval even when your price or terms fall short of their hopes and expectations. Sellers dislike weak offers that swamp them with doubts.

Assignment and Inspection

In many states, buyers may freely assign their real estate purchase contracts. However, assume nothing. Talk this issue over with a lawyer. As a buyer who (at least on some occasions) may want to flip a contract, verify whether the sellers cannot legally object. As a safeguard, insert an assignment clause into your offer similar to the following:

> Buyers may assign this Contract and all rights and obligations hereunder to any other person, corporation, or trustee.

The sellers may oppose such broad language and try to negotiate language such as:

> Buyer may assign this Contract only with the written approval of the sellers. Consent by the sellers shall not be arbitrarily withheld.

The sellers may want to approve your assignees just to satisfy themselves that the assignees possess the money and credit to complete the purchase. The sellers also may want you to remain liable for damages (or specific performance) should your assignees default. Obviously, you would like to avoid (or limit) this liability. If you assign the purchase agreement, you want out of the deal permanently.

When you obtain the right of assignment, insert a clause that gives you access to the property. Your potential assignees must be able to inspect and evaluate the property. Otherwise, only speculators would show any interest in buying the contract from you.

Record in the Public Records

If you write a lease option, lease purchase, contract-for-deed, or some type of purchase offer that delays closing of title for, say, more than six months, record the signed contract in the public records. This record serves notice to the world that you hold rights in that property.

Without such notice, the sellers may place mortgages or other liens against the property that could jeopardize your legal interests. Without a public record, the sellers' judgment creditors, or perhaps the Internal Revenue Service, might stake a priority claim to the property.

Discuss these issues with competent legal counsel. Do not make payments to the sellers only to find sometime later that they cannot deliver clear title to you.

Systems and Appliances

Whether your closing takes place within 30 days or 3 years, specifically list who is responsible in the interim for maintenance, repair, or replacement of any malfunctioning systems (heating, air conditioning, electrical, waste disposal, well water) or appliances. Set procedures to resolve the "repair or replace" dilemma.

> **Sellers should guarantee the condition of all appliances and HVAC systems.**

For example, if the air conditioning goes out, the sellers may want to repair it at a cost of $450 in lieu of a total system replacement that would cost $6,200. Yet, if the repairs will only keep the HVAC clanking and clunking for, at best, 6 to 12 months, insist on replacement.

Environmental Hazards

Today, with both heightened costs for environmental cleanups and extensive regulatory controls, your contract needs to address environmental hazards that affect the property. Lead paint, asbestos, mold, urethane, formaldehyde, underground heating oil tanks, radon, and who knows what other dangers the Environmental Protection Agency may discover, can cost property owners thousands in remedial or replacement expenses.

> **Make the seller responsible for environmental risks.**

Your purchase offer might read as follows:

Sellers warrant that the property complies with all current federal, state, and local environmental laws, rules, and regulations. Sellers agree to indemnify buyers for all required cleanup costs that shall be necessary to remedy environmental hazards (known or unknown) that existed during the sellers' period of ownership.

This language only suggests, but it covers two main points: (1) Is the property free of hazards? and (2) If hazards are discovered, who is going to pay for cleanup? Under federal (and many state) laws, as owner of a property, you may have to pay for its environmental cleanup—even when you are innocent of creating the hazard. Be wary of this possibility. Shift this potential liability to the sellers—unless a price discount pays you to assume the risk.

Summing Up

Your offer to buy (or lease) real estate will include many important terms that control the relationship between you and the sellers (tenants). Read these terms and conditions before you sign your offer. Then with counsel, add, rewrite, amend, or strike out terms and conditions as warranted.

Once you and the sellers sign, you're both bound to the extent of the law. Draft your offer so that you understand the agreement—including what recourses, legal remedies, damages, and costs apply if you or the other party pulls out of the deal without a contractually (or lawfully) justified reason.

CHAPTER 17

Craft Your Lease to Increase Profits

Most owners of small investment properties draft leases to control tenant behavior. Although never foolproof, a written lease does help protect your interests—more so than an oral agreement. But a lease serves another purpose. It helps you gain competitive advantage over other property owners.

Achieve Competitive Advantage

Before you draft a lease, review the leases of other property owners. Look for ways to differentiate your rental agreement that would encourage tenants (your target market) to choose your property over competing properties. To gain competitive advantage, you might

- ◆ Lower your upfront cash move-in requirements.
- ◆ Offer a repair guarantee.
- ◆ Shorten (or lengthen) your lease term.
- ◆ Guarantee a lease renewal without an increase in rent.
- ◆ Place tenant security and rent deposits in an investment of the tenant's choice. Accumulate earnings for the tenant's benefit.

Or you might develop a tight lease and position your property as rentals that cater to more discriminating and responsible tenants. You could include severe lease restrictions on noise and nuisances common to other rentals. Then, promote your property as "the quiet place to live." Adapt leases to fit your target market. You increase rental revenues, achieve a higher rate of occupancy, and lower operating expenses.

Craft Your Rental Agreement

Creatively adapt (or omit) specific clauses to better appeal to your tenants. Properly crafted, your lease protects legally and attracts topflight tenants.

Names and Signatures

Most property owners require a lease to name all residents who live in the unit—including children, if any. All adult residents should sign the lease. As a rule, do not permit tenants to freely bring in additional tenants or to substitute new cotenants for those moving out. Require all new tenants to satisfy the qualification process.

Joint and Several Liability

When you rent to cotenants (even if husband and wife—divorces do happen), include a "joint and several liability" clause. This clause makes all tenants individually and collectively responsible for all owed rents and tenant damages.

> **Make each tenant responsible for all rents and damages.**

Without this clause, individual cotenants often claim that they're liable only for "their share of the rent." Or, maybe you'll hear, "I didn't burn that hole in the carpet. Jones did. Collect from him." Most of the time, Jones has already moved out and disappeared. Joint and several liability gives you the legal right to collect payment from the other cotenants who have the money.

Guests

To avoid notice to you, some tenants won't formally add new *cotenants* to the lease. When you show up and wonder who these new people are, you'll be told, "They're *guests*." "Joe's just staying here for a couple of weeks until he's called back to work at Ford." Two months later, Joe's still there and now his girlfriend, Jill, also has taken up "guest" status.

> **Be wary of guests who become undocumented tenants.**

Whether you might deal with these kinds of tenants depends on the type of people your property attracts as well as your tenant-screening standards. As a precaution, place a "guest clause" in your lease that limits the number and length of time guests can stay.

Term of Lease

Many landlords reflexively set the term of their leases at one year. In some markets, this tendency creates too few properties available for shorter (or longer) terms. Because short-term (especially seasonal) tenancies bring in higher rents, boost your income by appealing to this potentially underserved market. Another possibility: To reduce turnover and vacancy, give tenants a discount if they sign up for a lease term of, say, two or three years.

Property Description

Precisely describe the property rights you give to tenants. For example, do they receive the right to use the garage, parking spaces, attic, basement, or outdoor storage shed? Or should you rent those areas at an additional price? Can you convert any of these spaces to a higher, better, and more profitable use?

Inventory and Describe Personal Property

If you provide personal property (washer, dryer, refrigerator, stove, microwave, blinds, drapes, curtains, furniture), inventory and describe (with photographs or serial numbers if possible) each separate item and include the list as a lease addendum. Unbelievable as it may sound, I know of vacating tenants who have taken their landlord's almost-new appliances and left in their place appliances that ranked just above junk.

Rental Amounts

Some owners set rent levels low to reduce turnover, vacancy losses, and tenant complaints. (Complaints fall because tenants don't want to give reason to raise their bargain rent.) Also, slightly below-market rents give a larger pool of applicants from which to select topflight tenants. Nevertheless, lower rents may not be necessary. With scarce, desirable features, your units will attract quality tenants even with rents that sit at the top of the market.

Late Fees and Discounts

To encourage tenants to pay rent early, some owners offer an "early payment discount." Others levy late fees if the tenant's check comes in, say, three to five days past its due date. In recent years, more owners have adopted the carrot approach over the stick approach. These owners claim that discounts create better tenant relations, work more effectively, and are easier to enforce.

> **Rent only to people who pay on time, every time.**

Regardless of which method you choose, never, never, *never* allow tenants to get behind in their rent. Begin an eviction as soon as your lease and local ordinances permit. Tenants who won't pay today rarely pay tomorrow.

Multiple Late Payments

What about the tenant who regularly pays on the eighth or ninth every month—even though the rent falls due on the first? As long as the late fee is included, some owners tolerate this behavior. I will not. I insist that rents are paid on time, every time.

To enforce the on time, every time requirement, I either work out a new payment date with the tenants that better matches their cash flows or I enforce the multiple late payment clause. This clause sets forth a "three strikes and you're out rule." When tenants won't pay on time, kick them out and keep their security deposit (if local law permits). Ditto for repeated bad checks.

Tenant "Improvements"

"If we buy the paint, is it okay for us to paint the living room?" As an owner of rental properties, you will receive requests like this from tenants. Or you may end up with tenants who don't ask. They redecorate first and wait for you to ask questions later—like, "How could you paint the living room deep purple?" or "What happened to the oak tree that was in the back yard?" To stop tenants from diminishing the value of your property with their weird improvements, require them to obtain your written permission before they paint, wallpaper, redecorate, renovate, repanel, remove, or in any other way modify your property.

> **No tenant improvements without permission.**

Owner Access

Under the laws of most states, you may not enter your tenants' home (except for emergencies) without their permission. If you want access to make inspections and repairs, take care of damages (like an overflowing toilet), show the unit to prospective tenants (or buyers), or for any other reason, include a reasonable and nonintrusive owner access clause in your leases.

Quiet Enjoyment

Do you want to guarantee your tenants that they will not suffer from noise and disturbances created by other tenants? Then tightly restrict their neighbor-disturbing partying, fighting, arguing, and loud lovemaking. Allow them to play their television, radio, and stereo only at low volumes. Place a clause in your lease such as:

> Residents agree not to create, broadcast, or otherwise cause sounds or disturbances to emanate from themselves, their automobiles, their guests, or their residences into the residences of others. All residents agree to respect and promote the quiet enjoyment of the building by all other residents.

Beware of buying buildings with those notorious paper-thin walls. Unless you solve this problem, your tenants will constantly complain.

Noxious Odors

Noise and noxious odors drive away good tenants.

As with noise and disturbances, noxious odors wafting throughout a building can stir up tenant complaints. Noxious odors include smoking, cooking (especially some types of ethnic foods), and heavy users of perfumes. If any of these (or other odors) seem likely to present a problem, then include a lease clause that limits or excludes the source of these odors.

Tenant Insurance

Your property owners' insurance policy will not cover the personal property of tenants. Require them to buy a tenants' insurance policy. Many investors have learned

Require tenants to buy insurance to cover their own possessions.

through experience that when uninsured tenants suffer damage to their property (through fire or other peril), they sue the owner for negligence. Even if the building burns after a lightning strike, the tenants (or their lawyers) will claim that you should have installed a better lightning rod.

Sublet and Assignment

When tenants plan to be away from their home for an extended period (summer in Europe), they may want to *sublet* their unit. When tenants plan to relocate permanently (job change, bought a house), they may want to *assign* their lease to someone else. To address this issue, adopt one of these positions:

1. No right to sublet or assign.
2. Right to sublet or assign with owner's written permission. Original tenants and new tenants both assume liability for rent payments and damages.
3. Right to sublet or assign with owner's written permission. Original tenants released from any liability for future rent payments or damages. Owner must look exclusively to new tenants for financial performance.
4. Unlimited right to sublet or assign. Original tenants remain liable.

Without a lease restriction, some courts rule that tenants may freely assign or sublet their units. Avoid that outcome. Protect yourself; write a restrictive sublet and assignment clause into your lease.

Pets

Many property owners prohibit pets. In my experience, responsible tenants care for their pets in a responsible manner. Irresponsible people treat their pets irresponsibly. If you select responsible people, you usually can eliminate your pet problems without excluding all pets. Accept responsible people with well-behaved pets; you boost profits. Often, you can charge a pet premium that requires higher rents and a higher security deposit.

> **Develop your rules about pets to meet the needs of tenants and the pets.**

If you do accept pets, draft a pet rules addendum and attach it to your lease. Please consider the needs of the pet. I have seen pet rules that require large dogs to be kept permanently tethered in the back yard on an eight-foot chain.

Other inhumane rules require that a dog must be permanently kept in a basement or on a back porch. If you feel so little for the lives of animals, totally exclude them from your rental properties. Moreover, any pet owner who accepts such cruel restrictions does not qualify (in my opinion) as a responsible person or a responsible pet owner.

Security Deposits

Collect a security deposit from all tenants and cover these issues in your lease:

1. Amount of the deposit
2. When payable
3. Rate of interest, if any
4. Under what conditions tenants will forfeit all or part of their deposit
5. When the deposit will be refunded if tenants satisfy all terms of the lease

Amount and When Payable   In terms of amount, I favor high security deposits plus first and last month's rent—*always* payable in advance. (This lesson I learned the hard way.) You undoubtedly will get prospects who want to pay their deposit piecemeal over one to three months. Yield to this request, and you invite trouble. (Ditto for postdated checks.)

Interest   Some local and state laws require owners to pay some minimum rate of interest to their tenants. If such a law applies in your area, make sure your tenants know they'll receive interest. In fact, I recommend paying interest to tenants even if the law doesn't require it. Today, many tenants get upset if you insist on a deposit (especially a large one), yet refuse to pass along its earnings to them.

Forfeiture   When they sign their lease, inform the tenants that their security deposit does not limit their liability for rent or damages. Explain the level of care (cleanliness, damages) they must meet to get their full security deposit returned to them. Explain how you will calculate any amounts that you subtract from their deposits (or under what

Return deposits promptly.

conditions you will collect additional money from them). Security deposits have become a large source of dispute between owners and tenants. Explain your deposit policies (and always comply with the landlord/tenant law).

Deposit Return   As a courtesy to tenants, return deposits (with interest) as soon as you know the correct amount. The best time is at the end of the final walkthrough. You pay. The tenants accept. You shake hands with them and wish them well in their new home.

Yard Care

When you rent out a house or duplex, require the tenants to care for the yard. But don't just say, "tenants are responsible for yard care." I once made this mistake with otherwise excellent tenants. To these tenants, "yard care" meant cutting the grass. To me it meant watering the lawn when needed, tending the flowers and shrubs, and trimming the hedges to maintain them at their existing height of four feet.

Because the house was located in Florida and I was living in the San Francisco Bay Area, my visits to the property were not frequent. When after two years I did return, the hedges had grown wildly to a height of seven or eight feet, many flowers and shrubs were dead, and the lawn had scattered brown spots.

If you require your tenants to care for the yard, spell out the care and condition you want them to maintain.

Parking Areas, Number and Type of Vehicles

Don't let tenant vehicles create parking problems.

Some tenants believe that if they can't find parking in a driveway or on the street, it's okay to park in the front yard. Or they may persist in blocking their neighbors' driveways. Or they leave unsightly junk (inoperable) cars to accumulate around the property. RVs, boats, and trailers also can create aesthetic and parking problems.

To head off trouble, place a parking clause in your leases. List the number and types of permitted vehicles. Then designate the *only* places where they may be parked properly. You also may want to restrict the backyard (or frontyard) mechanic who disassembles his car and leaves the parts scattered about for days, weeks, or even months.

Repairs

Increasingly, owners of rental properties shift some costs of repair to their tenants. Stopped-up toilets and broken garbage disposals rarely occur without tenant abuse. As a minimum, charge your tenants, say, a $50 repair fee for each time a repair becomes necessary. Some owners impose full responsibility for certain types of repairs—unless the service provider establishes that the tenants were not to blame. Your repair policy should encourage tenants to care for the property as well as reduce your out-of-pocket costs for unscheduled maintenance and replacement.

Appliances   Some owners tell their tenants that they may use the appliances currently in the property, but that the owner will not pay for repairs or replacement if the appliances fail to work properly. If the tenants don't agree to accept the appliances on those terms, the owner then removes them and the tenants provide and maintain their own appliances.

> At best, your repair policy encourages care and reduces costs.

Which Approach Is Best?   As with all lease clauses, no one approach works best in all situations. It depends on the types of tenants and properties you're dealing with. Undoubtedly, some people will show little care for your property. Yet at the same time, they expect you to jump into action whenever their abuse or neglect creates a problem. These are the people at whom you want to aim your tenant repair clauses. (Of course, ideally you want to avoid these kinds of tenants.)

Neat and Clean

Whether you rent houses or apartments, set standards of neatness and cleanliness. Proper disposal of trash and garbage are bare minimums.

Roaches do not like to live in clean apartments and houses.

When tenant neglect invites roaches, ants, or fleas into the property, the tenant should pay the exterminator—not you.

Other do's and don'ts may address unwashed dishes; disposal of used motor oil, broken furniture, or appliances; bicycle storage; materials awaiting pickup for recycling; and vehicles that drip motor oil or transmission fluid.

Rules and Regulations

Especially for apartment buildings—or for rental units in co-ops or condominium projects—prepare a list of rules and regulations that tenants must follow. Incorporate these rules (usually by addendum). Note within your lease that you (or the homeowners' association) reserve the right to reasonably amend or modify the listed rules.

Wear and Tear

So-called standard leases state that tenants are responsible for all damages *except* normal wear and tear. I would not use such a clause. It invites tenant neglect and abuse. Many tenants believe that soiled carpets, cracked plaster, broken screens, and other damages reflect nothing more than normal wear and tear.

I disagree. If a tenant properly cares for a property, it will not suffer any noticeable wear and tear during a tenancy of one year or less. For such short-term periods of residence, tenants should leave the property in the same condition in which they accepted it. Eliminate the wear and tear clause. Save yourself money and argument.

Avoid a wear and tear clause.

Lawful Use of Premises

As good business practice and as a good-neighbor policy, require tenants to abide by all applicable laws, ordinances, and regulations. This clause may help you to remedy undesirable behavior that you didn't think to put in your lease. Especially enforce a zero-tolerance rule against illegal drugs or other offenses that can bring trouble with the police (or even asset forfeiture).

Notice

To reduce rent loss during unit turnover, require tenants to give you advance notice of the exact date they plan to move. Publicize the unit's upcoming availability. Ideally, you'll find a new tenant who will move in within a day or two after the previous tenants have moved out.

Most owners require 30 days' *written* notice. But if you operate in a weak or seasonal rental market, ask for 45 or 60 days' notice. Or if you expect immediate demand for your rental property, reduce your advance notice to, say, 15 days. Tie your written notice requirement to the length of time necessary to locate a new, qualified tenant. (Note, too, any statuatory notice that governs—absent an applicable lease clause.)

Nonwaivers

> **Don't let exceptions become the rule.**

As a matter of courtesy or practicality, you may, on occasion, permit tenants to temporarily breach a lease clause or house rule. To prevent tenants from stretching this courtesy beyond your intent, include a nonwaiver clause. Make clear that your kindness today in no way waives your right to enforce the letter of the lease tomorrow.

Breach of Lease (or House Rules)

In a breach-of-lease clause, you reinforce your right to terminate the lease of tenants who breach *any* lease requirement or house rule. Without this clause, tenants may sometimes believe that if you accept the rent, you waive your enforcement of other tenant violations. Together, the nonwaiver and breach-of-lease clauses impress on tenants their obligation to comply 100 percent—or suffer the consequences of eviction.

No Representations (Full Agreement)

On occasion tenants try to get out of their lease obligations by claiming you misled them with false promises. They could claim that to entice them to sign their lease you promised to completely paint and recarpet their unit. You know the tenants are lying, but a judge may not. To the judge, it's your word against theirs.

> **Don't permit your tenant to accuse you of making false promises.**

To prevent this charade, include a clause stating that the lease and its addendums covers the full extent of the rental agreement. This clause could also state that the tenants have not relied on any oral or written representations or promises that are not explicitly written into the lease.

Arbitration or Mediation

In many cities, the legal process is too slow, expensive, complex, and cumbersome to effect timely and affordable justice. As a result, some property owners write an arbitration (or mediation) clause in their leases. This clause steers unresolved owner-tenant disputes away from the courthouse and into a more informal hearing.

Before you adopt such a clause for your leases, investigate how well arbitration (mediation) works in your area. Learn whether your local courts show bias for or against property owners. Arbitration and mediation tend to work best for investors faced with courts that generally side with tenants. (Unfortunately, some protenant judges—at the urging of lawyers who fear a loss of business—refuse to enforce lease arbitration clauses.)

Attorney Fees (Who Pays?)

"Standard" preprinted leases often include an attorney fees clause that strongly favors property owners. In cases where you prevail in court, this clause requires losing tenants to pay your "reasonable" attorney and court costs. In contrast, when your tenants prevail, the clause (through its silence) leaves attorney fees and costs on the shoulders of each party who incurred them.

> **Some judges won't enforce a landlord's one-sided attorney fees clause.**

Courts that honor the principle that "judges shall not rewrite lawful contracts" generally enforce this one-sided attorney fees clause. These courts reason that any tenant who wanted to modify or eliminate this clause was free to negotiate the point prior to signing the lease.

So-called activist judges may use this clause to declare you liable for a winning tenant's attorney fees and costs. These judges hold that "what's good for the goose is good for the gander." These judges often lean toward the left-wing mindset of "powerful greedy landlords" versus "powerless victimized tenants." They see it as their duty to upset this supposed imbalance of power by placing their thumb on the scales of justice to favor tenants.

So, do not place any attorney fees clause in your leases until you explore its practical and legal implications in your locale. I prefer an "each party shall bear his own legal fees and costs" clause. I do not want to run the risk of both an adverse court ruling (often unjust or ignorant) along with a multithousand-dollar lawyer's bill run up by some so-called tenants' rights group.

Written Notice to Remedy

A written notice to remedy requires an owner (or tenant) to give written notice prior to taking legal action to enforce a lease provision that the tenant (or owner) is currently breaching. From your perspective, written notice can help you in two ways: (1) When you evict a tenant for cause, previous written notices lay a paper trail that supports your case; and (2) if to defend an eviction (or suit for rent) a tenant falsely claims, "We didn't have any heat for most of January," you can force the tenants to prove that they sent you written notice of this problem. Because their claim lacks truth, their defense fails.

Landlording: Pros and Cons

From the preceding collection of lease clauses, you might say, "Forget it! Landlording involves too many potential headaches and risks."

> **Anticipate and prevent problems.**

But imagine reading a list of laws, regulations, accidents, breakdowns, repairs, lawsuits, hassles, and expenses that you face when driving a car. If you focused only on the risks of driving, you might park your car in a garage and leave it there permanently.

When I point out potential sources of trouble, I don't mean to scare you away from owning income properties; rather, I want to present areas of concern. It is the naive and unknowing investors who experience landlording difficulties.

Think of these concerns as issues to prepare for and guard against, not as probabilities certain to upset your life. They won't—unless you let them. Indeed, to own a smooth, trouble-free investment, just follow the 12 secrets of successful landlording.

CHAPTER 18

The 12 Secrets of Successful Landlording

You've heard the frightening stories about managing rental properties. According to popular lore—mostly propagated by people who have never owned properties—residential rentals require you to answer 2:00 A.M. phone calls from irate tenants, fix leaky plumbing on Saturday mornings, and chase after deadbeats.

You may have seen the movie *Pacific Heights* (see Box 18.1). In that rental-property horror film, Michael Keaton plays a demented tenant who viciously torments his landlords (a naive newlywed couple played by Melanie Griffith and Matthew Modine). In the end, the couple triumphs, but Keaton's character puts them through so much grief that they begin to question their own sanity.

The Good News

Neither popular lore nor *Pacific Heights* paints an accurate picture of landlording—which I redefine as providing homes for good people. Think of any activity from jogging to taking a vacation flight. At times, bad things happen. But the benefits far outweigh the risks. The same stands true for owning investment properties.

Yet even if the frightful stories did reflect rental property experience, the great wealth-building power of properties would more than compensate for the aggravation.

1. They failed to obtain a prepurchase property inspection.
2. They failed to reasonably anticipate repair and renovation expenses.
3. They stretched so far to buy that they exhausted their cash and credit.
4. They believed their tenant's fish story.
5. They permitted their tenant to bring in an unapproved "guest."
6. They failed to get the cash before their tenant moved into their rental unit.
7. They did not understand or follow San Francisco's onerous tenants' rights laws.
8. They relied on the legal system to promote justice.
9. They failed to immediately consult a lawyer when their legal situation went awry.
10. They tried (illegal) self-help tactics to coerce the tenant to vacate the building.

The good news: Did these beginning investors do anything right? Absolutely—they bought real estate. Had they continued to own that Pacific Heights property, they could sell it today for a price $2 million higher than what they paid for it in 1991 (when the movie was filmed).

Box 18.1 The *Pacific Heights* Investors Violate the Rules of Successful Landlording

> **A management system gives you wealth without worry.**

Fortunately, owning rentals need not cause hassles and headaches. To gain the benefits of property ownership without work and worry, you can either hire a property manager or develop a first-class system of self-management.

Hired Management versus Self-Management

You may think the task of property management includes cleaning the rental unit, advertising vacancies, showing vacancies to prospects, collecting rents, handling yard work, making repairs, and numerous other chores.

Although it's true that someone needs to run the routine rental operations effectively, that someone does not need to be you.

Employ a Caretaker or Property Management Company

Delegate to a caretaker or a property management company whatever duties you choose to avoid. As a true *manager* you supervise the work of others, not do everything yourself. As the leadership consultant, Phil Van Hooser, says, "A good manager is not someone who can do the work of 10 people. It's someone who can get 10 people to work."

> **A good manager manages.**

The best owner-manager knows what needs to be done and then directs the performance of others. When delegating everyday activities, I prefer to work with caretakers.

What Is a Caretaker?   A property caretaker looks after as many details of a rental property's operations as you wish to delegate. My caretakers have done everything from renting apartments to supervising tradespeople to dealing with routine maintenance.

Though caretakers look after details, I design market strategy, major improvements, and policies and procedures. In other words, I *manage* properties, but rarely get involved in the day-to-day issues.

Over the years, I have found two types of caretakers work best:

- *A qualified tenant.* A well-qualified tenant who knows basic property maintenance and can deal effectively with people makes a good caretaker. Generally, I provide my caretakers free (or partial) rent plus an hourly fee for special jobs (repairs, improvements) that fall outside their normal scope of their responsibilities. (No set rules apply here because I vary the responsibilities according to the competencies and time commitment of each specific caretaker that I have hired.)
- *A jack-of-all-trades.* Another type of caretaker that I prefer is the retired or semiretired jack-of-all-trades. In my experience, older people tend to show a work ethic and sense of personal responsibility. They also tend to know more about how to remedy specific repair problems.

Again, the scope of our work agreement determines the amount of base pay. On average, I've found that $15 to $25 an hour will attract a skilled person to the job. Depending on wage levels in your area, you may pay more or less. Often, individuals find the caretaker job attractive because they control (within reason) their own work schedule.

(I might add that I never advertise for help wanted. To find good candidates, I depend on referrals and informal job discussions, not formal applications for employment.)

Property Management Companies   To passively own your investments, you might hire a property management company. Typically, these companies manage hundreds of rental units for dozens of property owners. These firms offer four benefits:

◆ They talk with hundreds of tenants each month and (if they choose to) can develop excellent knowledge of the rental property market.
◆ Because of their broad experience, they may have developed well-tested policies and procedures that cover everything from repairs to tenant selection to rent collection to fair housing compliance.
◆ They may know when one of their investor-clients plans to sell a property and can give you heads-up notice.
◆ By managing all rental activities, your management company minimizes the time and effort you devote to your properties.

For some passive investors, property management firms offer a needed and desired service. However, these services impose two severe drawbacks:

◆ No company that manages hundreds of rental units for multiple owners will design an optimal rental strategy for your property. Management firms develop policies and procedures to advance their own revenues and economies of scale. They won't try to maximize the profits earned by your rental units.
◆ Property management firms not only charge a monthly fee (6 to 10 percent of all rent collections), but may also assess extra fees for tasks such as renting a vacant apartment (one-half month's rent, for example), carrying out an eviction, and contracting for repairs or improvements. In total, these costs can turn a property with positive cash flow into an alligator that chews up cash.

Investors who rely on property management firms seldom come close to maximizing their profits. They can, though, take life easy.

Self-Management

My advice to the beginning investor: Self-manage your properties. As you build a portfolio of rentals, you can gradually withdraw from day-to-day activities. Self-management offers these advantages:

- ◆ *You save money.* You eliminate the costs that would otherwise go to a management company, and by self-contracting repair work (or by doing it yourself) you spend less.
- ◆ *Vacant units rent faster.* Whenever I see a long-term vacancy, 80 percent of the time that property is being "professionally" managed. Management firms seldom work diligently to fill vacancies. They're content to put up a sign, maybe run an ad, and wait for rental prospects to show up. (As you will soon see, you can do much better than that.)
- ◆ *Learn firsthand how to manage a property.* This knowledge will serve you well even if at some point you choose to delegate some or all of this work. Although I do not now get involved in the day-to-day work of property operations, the knowledge and experience I gained from the early do-it-myself years still pay off. If you've never done it yourself, how will you know enough to design (or critique) the rental policies and procedures of your property manager?
- ◆ *Learn about the market.* When you personally talk with prospective renters, look at competing properties, and monitor vacancies and rent levels, you build a valuable base of market information. With that market knowledge, you choose the most profitable target market of tenants and adapt your property, features, amenities, leases, and rental rates to display a competitive advantage.

For beginning investors, the benefits of self-management stand so far above the alternatives that even Robert Griswald, author of *Property Management for Dummies* (and owner of a large property management firm), advises,

> If you have the right traits for managing property, and if you have the time and live in the vicinity of your property(ies), definitely do it yourself (New York: John Wiley & Sons, 2002, p. 14).

No matter which management choices you adopt, learn and practice the 12 secrets of successful landlording (see Box 18.2).

1. Before You Buy, Verify, Verify, Verify
2. Prepare the Property for Rental
3. Craft a Winning Value Proposition
4. Attract Topflight Tenants
5. Create a Flawless Move-In
6. Retain Topflight Residents
7. When the Market Supports It, Raise Rents
8. Anticipate and Prepare for Special Problems
9. Maintain the Property
10. Process Move-Outs Smoothly
11. Persistently Find Ways to Increase Your Cash Flow
12. Keep Trading Up

Box 18.2   The 12 Secrets of Successful Landlording

Before You Buy, Verify, Verify, Verify

Good management begins before you close on your first investment. Understand the nature of the beast you are buying. You want no voracious alligators that will chew up your available cash and credit within the first few months of ownership.

Your prepurchase due diligence should include:

Property Inspection

Obtain a professional report on the condition of the property as well as reliable cost estimates for repairs and improvements.

People Inspection

Talk with the property owner's current (and past, if possible) tenants, managers, neighbors, contractors, repair people, and suppliers. Search for inside information that might signal potential problems (e.g., neighborhood noise or crime, tenant dissatisfaction, persistent trouble with plumbing, wiring, or roof leaks).

List Personal Property

Many property sales include some appliances, window coverings, storage sheds, and other personal property. List these items. Verify the list with current tenants.

Tenant Rent Roll and Files

Obtain the names, telephone numbers, application files, and leases for all residents of the property. Also, try for the names, new addresses, and phone numbers of past tenants. Conversations with a few past tenants can prove insightful.

Verify Security Deposits and Paid Rents

At closing, the seller should provide security deposits and pro rata rent payments for the remainder of the month. (Sometimes credits on the closing statement.) Insist on an accurate accounting. Verify the amounts with tenants. Remember, you are the person who will return security deposits when the tenants move out. Also, verify whether the seller has collected "last month" rent as part of a tenant's move-in cash payment. If so, obtain a credit at closing.

Licenses, Permits, Zoning, Building Regulations, Occupancy Codes

Multiple laws apply to rental properties. Find out whether the property complies with these laws (or, if not, what changes will bring it into compliance).

Copies of Warranties and Service Contracts

If repairs or replacements of roof, water heaters, appliances, HVAC, or other components of the property are guaranteed in some way, get copies of the warranties or service agreements (e.g., pest control, damage repair). Notify the service providers and pay transfer fees.

Arrange for Insurance Coverage

In some areas of the country, property insurance rates have shot up and some coverages have become difficult to obtain (e.g., mold, hurricane, earthquake). Before you commit to buy, review rates and coverages in detail with an insurance pro (not an office clerk). Coverages and premiums for new owners often differ (unfavorably) from those that are available to the property's current owner.

Prepare the Property for Rental

If tenants occupy the property you buy, you must honor existing rental agreements until these agreements end. Nevertheless, to deal with vacancies (and perhaps a market repositioning of the property), prepare in the following ways:

Choose a Segment of Tenants

Generic properties attract average tenants who pay so-called market rents. Uniquely differentiated properties attract topflight tenants and yield more profits (that result from some combination of higher rents, lower operating expenses, lower turnover, and quicker rent up). Survey the market and decide the segment of tenants (Section 8, college students, seniors, families, young professionals, empty nesters, other) you wish to appeal to.

You are free to develop a market strategy, but you can't turn away any member of a protected class for reasons related to any protected characteristics such as race, religion, ethnicity, children, and so forth.

Clean and Paint

No matter which market segment you appeal to, clean, paint, and sharpen the appearance of the property. The interior and exterior of the property should appear well kept and attractive. Never show a unit that fails the white glove test. Unless you enjoy a tight rental market, dirty units attract those tenants to whom no sane owner would want to rent.

> **Apply the white-glove test.**

Everything Must Work

Verify that the appliances, electrical outlets, and HVAC operate. Check that all windows and doors open and close easily. Repair or replace broken locks, doors, windows, and screens. Remedy any condition of the property that signals disrepair.

Craft a Winning Value Proposition

When tenants compare your rental unit to the units offered by other property owners, they want the best total value proposition. For example, your tenants might prefer any of the following:

Owner Demeanor

Do you (or your rental agent) come across as a pleasant person? To achieve this demeanor, play down the authoritarian do's and don'ts. Play up your please the customer attitude.

Pets, Furniture, Appliances

Can you better attract your target market if you accept pets or provide units with furnishings, furniture, window blinds, or appliances?

Hot-Button Features

What desirable features can you provide that other properties lack? Views, storage, parking, study area, open floor plan, roommate-friendly floor plan, soundproof walls, great kitchens and bathrooms? Learn your tenants' hot buttons. Then offer those benefits that will wow your prospects.

Lease Terms and Conditions

Craft your lease to suit tenant preferences (while still offering you legal protection against defaults). What lease period seems best—weekly, month-to-month, annual, longer? How will you handle repairs?

Security Deposits

Many cash-strapped tenants prefer low deposits. Can you figure a way to reduce security deposits without increasing your risks (cosignor, lien against tenant's car, phased payment, automatic transfer of funds)? On the other hand, some tenants will pay a high security deposit in exchange for a top-quality property and perhaps a favorably priced unit.

Rental Rate

Learn the features, lease terms, and rent levels of competing properties. Learn tenant likes and dislikes. Then design and price your units to give your target market their best value—yet still provide you a good profit.

Attract Topflight Tenants

Superior management requires you to perform two tasks. First, market the property effectively, and second, finely screen your rental applicants.

Get the Word Out

Many owners do little but hang out a FOR RENT sign and run a classified ad. Savvy owners think of inexpensive ways to quickly and directly reach their target prospects. Techniques might include craigslist.org, networking, referrals from current or past tenants, info flyers, brochures, bird dogs, employer bulletin boards, newsletters, or a college housing office.

> **Reduce ad costs through referrals and word of mouth.**

Discover where the tenants you would like to attract currently live, work, shop, play, worship, or go to school. Once you learn how to reach desirable tenants, get the word out about your great rental units.

What to Say

Use your sales message to do more than list basic features. Include a benefit headline followed by the hot-button features that will pique the attention, desire, and action of your target market (see Box 18.3).

Don't Show the Property, Sell It

Your prospective tenants may not intuitively recognize the advantages your property offers. Just as with your printed sales message, conversations with tenants should emphasize features and benefits. Explain why your units (and your lease) offer prospects their best value.

Thoroughly Screen All Tenants

Before any tenant moves into one of your units, verify that person's credit score, credit record, rental history, current and past employment, current and past residences, and personal photo identification. To get credit information, ask the prospective tenants to run their three reports at myfico.com and provide copies to you, or you can subscribe to this service as provided by a local credit bureau. Obtain other necessary tenant data from the rental application form you use.

Property manager and author, Robert Griswald, tells about one of the lessons he learned about marketing rentals:

I once had a rental property located near a major university. The property had several vacancies in the 2-bedroom/1-bath units. Because I was wary of renting to large numbers of undergraduate students, my marketing plan was to attract university faculty or graduate students who I thought would have a roommate and be perfect for the 2-bedroom unit. Although many prospective tenants looked at the units, our actual rentals were very slow and our 2-bedroom vacancies remained unacceptable. Clearly, I was trying to define and force the rental market and prospective renters to adapt to my perception of their needs.

When it became obvious that my rental efforts were not having much success, I began to carefully review the comments of prospective tenants and actually listen to their needs. What I found was that there was a strong market for faculty and graduate students, but that they preferred to live alone. The WIFM (what's in it for me) from the perspective of the targeted faculty and graduate students was the desire for a quiet place to work or study without roommates. With this new perspective on the needs of our prospective tenants, I quickly realized that I could market these very same 2-bedroom/1-bath units to this new target market.

Armed with this knowledge, I revised my marketing efforts and changed my advertising in the college newspaper to read, "1 bedroom plus den." This change led to an increased interest in the property as well as a greater occupancy percentage. Just by changing the way the units were advertised, I found that I was able to reach my original target market of faculty and graduate students who wanted to live off campus.

Remember: Look at your rental property from the perspective of the most likely tenants. Then create and promote the features that will impress these prospective customers.

Reprinted with permission from Robert Griswald, *Property Management for Dummies* (New York: John Wiley & Sons, 2001), p. 70.

Box 18.3 Write Your Ad to Promote the Benefits and Features Your Prospects Want

Payment of Rent and Security Deposit

Allow enough time for your tenants' rent and security deposit checks to clear before they move in. If you can't get the checks cleared prior to move-in, decide whether you should ask them to pay with a cashier's check drawn on a local bank.

Never Accept Fish Stories

As a property owner, you will hear your share of fish stories as to why the prospect says he cannot comply with your request for background information and verified payment of funds. Nine times out of ten, you want that fish to get away. (Review Box 18.1. In the *Pacific Heights* movie, Michael Keaton's character always concocted some fish story as to why he could not—or did not—comply with the landlord's request for references or payment.)

> **Let your fishy tenants get away.**

Do not let your sympathy (or an urgent need for money) motivate you to accept a tenant who offers excuses that beg forbearance. If you do, those initial excuses won't be the last ones you hear from that tenant.

Learn and Comply with All Fair Housing Laws

As an owner of rental properties, your advertising and tenant selection process is governed by federal, state, and local law. Learn these rules and regulations. Visit your community's fair housing agency. Talk with the staff and pick up their brochures. Learn how the Americans with Disabilities Act (ADA) might govern your rental policies and property features (companion animal, parking, entryway access, etc.).

Maintain a Waiting List

Strategically manage your properties and you will never want for tenants. Your advertising or word-of-mouth referrals will turn up more willing prospects than you can accommodate at any one time. Keep these potential tenants on your radar screen. Create a waiting list. With an active waiting list, your vacancies will fall to nearly zero.

Set Up a Flawless Move-In Policy

Use move-in policies and procedures to satisfy these goals:

◆ Establish cordial relations that smooth the tension that frequently characterizes a landlord-tenant relationship.
◆ Make sure you and your tenants see eye to eye on all rules that govern tenant conduct, property upkeep, and unit occupancy (e.g., parking, guests, alterations, cleanliness, tenant insurance, pets, names and number of residents).
◆ Prepare the property in make-ready condition.

Cordial Relations

Your property make-ready should confirm the cleanliness of the rental unit as well as the good repair of all appliances, plumbing, electrical, and HVAC. Assure that the

> **Provide your new tenants a welcome home gift.**

tenants enjoy their move-in week without need of complaint. As a special touch, give your new tenants a welcome basket of flowers, fruits, beverages, and snacks. If the tenants are new to the neighborhood, provide them a map and a list of nearby shops, stores, schools, services, and restaurants.

Rules and Regulations

Never just hand a list of house rules to your tenants. Explain each item. Explain why the rule is important and how it contributes to tenant welfare, property appearance, or upkeep. Ask the tenant to sign a copy of the rules and put it in your files with the lease, rental application, and background reports.

Remind the tenant in a friendly way that the rental agreement incorporates the rules. A breach of the rules means a breach of the lease and triggers whatever remedies your lease provides.

Verify Move-in Condition

At the time tenants move into the property, walk through with them. If you have performed your make-ready, you should find no broken windows, soiled carpets, or dirty appliances. If you find damages that remain unrepaired, note them on your move-in checklist. Once the tenants are satisfied that they have discovered (and you have listed) every flaw, ask the tenants to sign the list to certify the move-in condition of the property.

> **On move-in day, capture a video record of the unit's condition.**

You might videotape the unit on move-in day. If a dispute arises later, a picture may be worth a thousand dollars.

Retain Topflight Residents

You've filled your rental units with good tenants. What can you do to retain them as long as possible? Fortunately, that task's pretty easy.

Keep Tenants Informed

Don't let tenants come home to find a backhoe noisily digging up the parking lot or a pest control man spraying in their apartment. Notify tenants and explain when anything out of the ordinary is about to happen on or within the property. Tenants don't like it when you thoughtlessly and unexpectedly disrupt their lives or invade their privacy.

Plan Preventive Maintenance

Emergency repairs cost you big dollars and upset residents. No tenant likes a furnace that won't throw out heat, a roof that leaks, or a sink that won't quickly drain. Eliminate these problems. Execute a program

Anticipate and prevent repair problems.

of preventive maintenance. Don't wait for things to go wrong and then react. Anticipate what can go wrong and prevent (or at least minimize the probabilities).

Expect the Unexpected

Even the best preventive maintenance programs won't prevent every appliance malfunction or HVAC breakdown. Set up a procedure for dealing with these problems before they occur.

Arrange with trustworthy service providers. Give their telephone numbers to your tenants and instruct when and under what conditions they should call for service.

For ordinary, nonemergency repairs, give your tenants a a voice mail number. Ask your tenants to call and state their problem. Then acknowledge their request within 24 hours. If warranted, repair within 72 hours (less is better). Nonresponsive landlords generate tenant complaints. Make repairs courteously and quickly and your tenants will sing your praises to their friends (and your future residents).

Enforce House Rules Strictly and Fairly

Topflight residents want you to enforce house rules consistently and without favor (or prejudice) among all tenants. Don't let those bad apples spoil the barrel. Whether the rules pertain to parking, noise, unauthorized residents (long-term "guests"), or mishandling of trash and garbage, cite violators.

When you let bad things happen, your good residents will move out, and you will only be able to replace them with lower-quality residents. Draft rules for the benefit of all. Then enforce them against everyone.

Strong Market? Raise Rents

Since we've talked about rent collections and late fees in Chapter 17, I won't repeat that discussion. Still, there's the topic of how to handle rent increases.

When you raise rents, you risk losing good tenants. Nevertheless, low rents depress cash flows and diminish the value of your property. When you know the market will support higher rents (i.e., when you know topflight tenants will to pay more than you currently charge), raise the rents.

Verify Market Support

Remember, I said initiate a rent increase *if* the market supports it. Some owners try to increase their rents even when the rental market softens and numerous large-scale complexes offer move-in concessions such as two months' free rent or an all-expense-paid trip to Hawaii. In a market of many competitors, foolhardy attempts to raise rents extend vacancies, encourage unit turnover, and stir up tenant complaints.

Soften the Blow with Communication

When the market (or your improvements) support rent increases, justify the increases with evidence. Give tenants your survey of competing properties. Let them know you've placed 16 names on your waiting list. Show how your property taxes, insurance, and maintenance expenses climbed 12 percent this past year.

When possible, phase in rent increases frequently and gradually. A 10 percent increase at one time will chase out more tenants than, say, a 4 percent increase levied each 6 months over a period of 18 months.

Do Something in Return

You dampen tenant grumbling and nonrenewals when you do something in return for that rent increase. Should you plant more flowers and shrubs, add covered parking, install new carpets or appliances, put in ceiling fans, or upgrade the security system? Don't wipe out the money gained from the rent increase. But you create better tenant relations if you enhance the desirability of the property in a way the tenants appreciate.

Prepare for Special Problems

On occasion, even the best selected residents face difficulty. Divorce, accident, ill health, unemployment, and bankruptcy pose problems that tenants may run up against. If such a setback affects your tenants' ability to pay their rent, what do you do?

Express Understanding and Forbearance? Be Careful

In my early years as an investor, I was a soft touch for sob stories— real and fictional. Several times, with previously good-paying tenants, I offered forbearance. In every case, the tenants eventually moved out and never paid the rent money they owed.

Experience advises to collect the rent every time, on time. Otherwise, request (or legally compel) the tenants to move. If tenants need financial assistance, refer them to a charity or social services agency. Forbearance seldom pays off with a win-win solution.

(This same advice holds for tenants who persistently break the rules. If the rule is wrong, change it. If it serves a valid purpose, enforce it. Forbearance forecasts regret.)

Negotiate a Voluntary Move-Out

When your problem tenant pleads or threatens, but doesn't move out, you negotiate a voluntary settlement rather than get involved with the costly, frustrating, and often ineffective court system.

To entice tenants to leave, forgive some of the monies they owe you. In some instances (although I never have done this), owners will even agree to pay the tenant to move. In some circumstances, it's better to get rid of tenants and accept a small loss than to drag out a bitter conflict and possibly lose thousands in rent collections and attorney fees.

If You Evict, Follow the Law

States and cities set procedures that property owners must follow to terminate a lease and evict a tenant. This procedure normally covers (1) lawful reasons, (2) written notice, (3) time to cure or remedy the breach,

> **Never use illegal self-help tactics to evict a tenant.**

(4) the time period before a hearing (or trial), (5) allowable tenant defenses, and (6) the number of days the tenants have to vacate after the judge orders them out.

Learn the legal procedure for your area. Then follow it precisely. Failure to dot your i's and cross your t's can get your case thrown out. You then must go back and restart the process. Never threaten or assault a tenant, change door locks, turn off the tenant's water, heat, or electricity, or confiscate a tenant's personal property. Follow lawful procedure. Illegal self-help risks civil liability lawsuits and criminal charges.

Maintain the Property

To attract and retain topflight tenants, deter complaints, and enhance the value of your property, maintain your grounds and buildings. In addition to preventive and corrective maintenance and repairs, schedule three other types of maintenance programs:

- ◆ *Custodial maintenance.* Assign someone the tasks of yard care, picking up litter, and washing windows. Keep your property neat and clean.
- ◆ *Cosmetic maintenance.* Periodically inspect the grounds, common areas, and rental units to freshen up their cosmetic appearance. Don't ignore peeling paint, carpet stains, countertop burns, and other signs of disrepair. Without consistent care, a property will soon appear rundown.
- ◆ *Safety and security.* Spot problems of safety or security. Repair broken stairs, lighting, locks, window latches, or doors. Verify that all smoke alarms work. Ask tenants to call immediately should they discover threats to safety or security.

Process Move-Outs Smoothly

Alas, all good things end. At some point, your tenants move on. When that time comes, your move-out process includes the following steps.

Require Written Notice

Require your tenants to give formal, written notice (typically 30 days, more or less) of their specific move-out date. This notice gives you time to get the word out to topflight prospects that the area's best landlord (you!) will soon have a unit available for some lucky person. Early notice also gives time to line up and schedule contractors or tradespeople to make improvements and repairs to the unit.

Schedule a Final Walkthrough

Do not under any circumstances postpone your damage inspection of the unit until after the tenant has moved away. Always schedule a final walkthrough of the unit on the same day your tenants are loading their moving van. Compare the unit's condition to your move-in checklist, photos, or video.

> **Settle damage claims the day the tenants move out.**

At that time, settle damage claims that you think the tenant should pay. If you've treated the tenants fairly throughout the time they've lived in your building, you usually can settle up without controversy.

Owners who run into move-out problems generally make one or more of these errors:

◆ They fail to maintain the property and try to stick the tenant with costs that were properly the obligation of the owner.
◆ They do not monitor the condition of the unit throughout the tenancy, and then during the final walk-through, allege all kinds of expensive damages.
◆ They charge tenants far more for cleaning or repairs than the owners pay to correct the problem(s).

With infrequent exception, I have found that when I treat tenants with respect and consideration throughout their tenancy, when I document their damages, and when I don't try to overcharge them, they readily honor their responsibility to cover the reasonable costs of cleaning or repair.

Persistently Seek Ways to Increase Your Cash Flow

Do you know the word *kaizen*? Tony Robbins popularized this Japanese term that means "continuous improvement." Persistently search for ways to improve. Few of us ever perform at the top of our game. Much of the time we get lazy. We turn off our creative impulses. We fail to see obvious opportunities. We achieve much less than we're capable of achieving.

More Income, Higher Value

Remember, every $1,000 you add to your net operating income (NOI) boosts the value of your property by at least $10,000 to $12,000. Every $1,000 you eliminate from your operating expenses boosts the value of your property by $10,000 to $12,000.

$$V = \frac{\text{NOI (Rent collections less expenses)}}{\text{R (Cap Rate)}}$$

Reread Chapters 13 and 14 at least once every several months. Review your possibilities for improved cash flows. Even if you operate your properties today at peak performance, markets change.

> **Stay up to date with changes (opportunities) in the market.**

Over any six-month period, your competition can change. Your tenant segment may change their preferences. You may discover new, more profitable tenant segments to serve. Successful investors persistently adapt and refine their market strategies and management policies.

Periodically Refinance Your Properties

Because (in the early years of property ownership) mortgage interest costs eat up more of your rent collections than any other expense, stay in touch with several savvy mortgage brokers. Tell them about the costs and terms of your current financing. Tell them how long you plan to own the property.

Then ask these loan reps to notify you when a refinance might make you money. Slice your mortgage payments by, say, $500 a month and you add $6,000 a year to your cash flows. Additionally, as you build equity in your properties, consider a cash-out (tax-free) refinance to raise money to acquire more properties.

Keep Trading Up

In the real estate classic, *How I Turned $1,000 into a Million in Real Estate in My Spare Time* (New York: Simon and Schuster, 1958), William Nickerson tells how he first bought a $10,000 duplex. After creating value with that property, Nickerson then traded up to a $40,000 property. He repeated his process of creating value and next traded up to a $150,000 multiunit apartment complex. After just 16 years, through the continuous process of creating value and trading up, Nickerson owned millions of dollars in properties.

Although today's prices dwarf those of Nickerson's day, the technique of creating value and trading up still works. I've used it. Most of the professional investors I know have used it. Likewise, you can use it.

Create value, trade up, offers the safest and surest path to building wealth. Start now. Experience proves that within 8 to 15 years (or less) you, too, will enjoy a multimillion-dollar net worth. I wish you good luck and good fortune. Call me and let me know how you're doing at (352) 336-1366, or post a question at my web site at geldred.com.

Throughout this book, I have referred you to a variety of web sites that complement or expand upon the topics covered. For your convenience, I have listed below these and other web sites by category.

City and Neighborhood Data

www.census.gov
http://stats.bls.gov
http://usacitylink.com
www.virtualrelocation.com
www.ojp.usdoj.gov/bjs/www.crime.org

Comp Sales

www.dataquick.com
www.latimes.com

Credit Information

www.econsumer.equifax.com
www.experian.com
www.transunion.com
www.creditscoring.com
www.creditaccuracy.com
www.myfico.com

www.ocpa.gov.uk/
www.qspace.com
www.ftc.gov
www.creditinfocenter.com
www.fairisaac.com
http://credit.about.com/

Financial Calculators and Spreadsheets

www.erealinvestor.com
www.loan-wolf.com
www.mtgprofessor.com
www.mortgagewizard.com
www.hsh.com

Foreclosures and Repos

www.brucebates.com
www.bankhomes.net
www.4close.com
www.all-foreclosure.com
www.homesteps.com
www.hud.gov
www.va.gov
www.bankreo.com
www.treas.gov
www.premierereo.com
www.fanniemae.com
www.bankofamerica.com
www.foreclosureworld.net
www.realtytrac.com

Home Improvement

www.hometime.com
www.michaelholigan.com
www.askbuild.com
www.hardware.com
www.bhglive.com
www.housenet.com (redirects to http://www.move.com/)

www.doityourself.com
www.askthebuilder.com
www.goreal.com
www.improvenet.com
www.livinghome.com

Home Inspection

www.ashi.com
www.creia.com

Homes for Sale

www.realtor.com
www.homeseekers.com
www.cyberhomes.com
www.homes.com
www.bamboo.com
www.ipix.com
www.owners.com
www.buyowner.com
www.fsbo.com
www.homegain.com
www.open-house-online.com
www.byowner.com
www.zillow.com
www.fsboguide.com
www.ired.com (International Real Estate Digest)
www.mfdhousing.com (Mobile Home Central—Manufactured
Housing Modular Homes)

Insurance Information

www.cpcu.com
www.statefarm.com

Law Information

www.lectlaw.com
www.lexis.com

www.lawstar.net
www.nolo.com

Mortgage Applications

www.interest.com
www.mortgage101.com
www.mortgagequotes.com
http://mortgage.quicken.com (directs to http://www.quicken-loans.com/)
www.fhatoday.com
www.loanweb.com
www.mortgageauction.com
www.clnet.com
www.eloan.com

Mortgage Information

www.loan-wolf.com
www.mtgprofessor.com
www.hsh.com
www.homefair.com (house moving relocation calculators/Real Estate Mortgage Loans, Van Lines, Apartments)

Mortgage Providers (Underwriters)

www.fanniemae.com
www.homesteps.com
www.va.gov
www.hud.gov
www.loanworks.com

Real Estate Information

www.inman.com/bruss
www.ired.com
www.ourfamilyplace.com
www.realtor.com
www.johntreed.com
www.arello.org

School Data

www.2001beyond.com
www.schoolmatch.com
www.schoolreport.com

With hundreds of thousands of web sites related to real estate and mortgages, the above list only samples some of the most popular sites. Nevertheless, if you've got the time and the will to sort through the data overload that the Web now offers, you can certainly make a more informed investing and borrowing decision.

Still, beware. Many sites do not provide accurate data, nor does the data necessarily relate to your specific need. For example, neighborhood data and school data are plagued with inconsistencies, omissions, errors, and ill-defined measures. Don't accept Web-based data as the last word. Check and verify all information. The web does not reduce your need to walk and talk the neighborhood; visit schools, shops, parks other facilities; physically view comparable sales; and drive areas you might like to search out "For Sale" signs.

On a final note, I will admit that real estate investing can seem challenging at times. But persevere. You'll never regret owning. In the meantime, should you have questions about your investing, give me a call at 352-336-1366 or e-mail me at b-prof@hotmail.com. If you e-mail me, though, please include your address and phone number. I will respond one way or another. (However, because I frequently travel abroad, I may not be able to answer your inquiries right away.)

Once again, I wish you the best and know that you can profit from the successes (and mistakes) of the thousands of people who in some way have contributed to the contents of this book. Good luck and good fortune.

INDEX

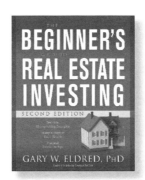

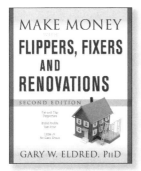

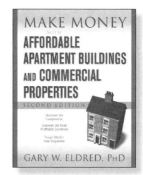